The Vattimo Dictionary

The Vattimo Dictionary

Edited by Simonetta Moro

EDINBURGH
University Press

Edinburgh University Press is one of the leading university presses in the UK. We publish academic books and journals in our selected subject areas across the humanities and social sciences, combining cutting-edge scholarship with high editorial and production values to produce academic works of lasting importance. For more information visit our website: edinburghuniversitypress.com

© editorial matter and organisation Simonetta Moro, 2023, 2024
© the chapters their several authors, 2023, 2024

Cover image: Giulio Paolini, L'arte e lo spazio – Quattro illustrazioni per…, 1983 Hardcover book, mold and plaster fragments, 31 × 25,5 × 36 cm
Courtesy Studio la Città, Verona
Photo credits: Michele Alberto Sereni
Copyright: © Giulio Paolini
Cover design: www.hayesdesign.co.uk

Edinburgh University Press Ltd
13 Infirmary Street
Edinburgh EH1 1LT

First published in hardback by Edinburgh University Press 2023

Typeset in 11/13pt Ehrhardt
by Cheshire Typesetting Ltd, Cuddington, Cheshire

A CIP record for this book is available from the British Library

ISBN 978 1 4744 8908 9 (hardback)
ISBN 978 1 4744 8909 6 (paperback)
ISBN 978 1 4744 8911 9 (webready PDF)
ISBN 978 1 4744 8910 2 (epub)

The right of Simonetta Moro to be identified as the editor of this work has been asserted in accordance with the Copyright, Designs and Patents Act 1988, and the Copyright and Related Rights Regulations 2003 (SI No. 2498).

Contents

Acknowledgements vi
List of Abbreviations for Main Works by Gianni Vattimo in English vii

Introduction 1
Simonetta Moro

Entries A–Z 21

Bibliography 209
Notes on Contributors 228
Index 242

Acknowledgements

A philosophical dictionary of this kind is a choral enterprise, and could not exist without the contributions of the many scholars who participated in it. I would like to thank each of the fifty-two contributors who made this work possible, and made it better by often suggesting changes and additions to the entries.

I would also like to thank my editor, Carol Macdonald, and the editorial staff at Edinburgh University Press for their generous assistance and support throughout. In addition, I would like to thank Dr Zane Derven and Dr Derek Pollard for their careful editorial work.

I am particularly grateful to Santiago Zabala, ICREA Research Professor at Pompeu Fabra University (Barcelona, Spain), who facilitated access to bibliographical and other source materials at the UPF Center for Gianni Vattimo's Philosophy and Archives. It is my hope that this dictionary will inspire other scholars and students of Vattimo's thought to visit his archives and make further contributions to the interpretation and dissemination of his work.

Finally, a special thanks goes to Professor George Smith, founder and president of the Institute for Doctoral Studies in the Visual Arts, for his unwavering encouragement, precise feedback and commitment to the advancement of hermeneutics as a shared philosophical project.

List of Abbreviations for Main Works by Gianni Vattimo in English

Dates in parentheses refer to the first Italian edition – see Bibliography

AC   *After Christianity*, trans. Luca D'Isanto. New York: Columbia University Press, 2002 (2002a).

ACT   *Art's Claim to Truth*, ed. Santiago Zabala, trans. Luca D'Isanto. New York: Columbia University Press, 2008.

AD   *The Adventure of Difference: Philosophy after Nietzsche and Heidegger*, trans. Cyprian Blamires and Thomas Harrison. Cambridge: Polity, 1993 (1980).

ADG   *After the Death of God*, with John D. Caputo, ed. Jeffrey W. Robbins. New York: Columbia University Press, 2007.

B   *Belief*, trans. Luca D'Isanto and David Webb. Stanford, CA: Stanford University Press, 1999 (1996a).

BI   *Beyond Interpretation: The Meaning of Hermeneutics for Philosophy*, trans. David Webb. Stanford, CA: Stanford University Press, 1997 (1994b).

BIS   *Being and Its Surroundings*, ed. Giuseppe Iannantuono, Alberto Martinengo and Santiago Zabala, trans. Corrado Federici. Montreal: McGill-Queen's University Press, 2021 (2018).

BS   *Beyond the Subject: Nietzsche, Heidegger, and Hermeneutics*, trans. Peter Carravetta. SUNY Series in Contemporary Italian Philosophy. Albany: SUNY Press, 2019 (1981a).

DN   *Dialogue with Nietzsche*, trans. William McCuaig. New York: Columbia University Press, 2006 (2000a).

DZ   *Deconstructing Zionism: A Critique of Political Metaphysics*, ed. Gianni Vattimo and Michael Marder. London: Bloomsbury, 2014.

EM   *The End of Modernity: Nihilism and Hermeneutics in Postmodern Culture*, trans. Jon R. Snyder. Baltimore, MD: Johns Hopkins University Press, 1988 (1985b).

FR   *The Future of Religion*, with Richard Rorty, ed. Santiago Zabala. New York: Columbia University Press, 2005 (2005).

FT   *A Farewell to Truth*, trans. William McCuaig. New York: Columbia University Press, 2011 (2009a).

HC   *Hermeneutic Communism: From Heidegger to Marx*, with Santiago Zabala. New York: Columbia University Press, 2011 (2013).

LIST OF ABBREVIATIONS FOR MAIN WORKS

N *Nietzsche: An Introduction*, trans. Nicholas Martin. Stanford, CA: Stanford University Press, 2002 (1985a).
NBG *Not Being God: A Collaborative Autobiography*, with Piergiorgio Paterlini, trans. William McCuaig. New York: Columbia University Press, 2010 (2006).
NE *Nihilism and Emancipation: Ethics, Politics and Law*, ed. Santiago Zabala. New York: Columbia University Press, 2004 (2003c).
OR *Of Reality: The Purposes of Philosophy*, trans. Robert T. Valgenti. The Gifford Lectures. New York: Columbia University Press, 2016 (2012).
R *Religion*, with Jacques Derrida, trans. David Webb. Stanford, CA: Stanford University Press, 1998 (1995).
RP *The Responsibility of the Philosopher*, ed. Franca d'Agostini, trans. William McCuaig. New York: Columbia University Press, 2010 (2000d).
TS *The Transparent Society*, trans. David Webb. Cambridge: Polity, 1992 (1989c).
WT *Weak Thought*, ed. Gianni Vattimo and Pier Aldo Rovatti, trans. Peter Carravetta. SUNY Series in Contemporary Italian Philosophy. Albany: SUNY Press, 2013 (1983).

Introduction

> Have called by their names many of those in Heaven
> For we are a conversation
> And able to hear from each other.
>
> Hölderlin, 'Versöhnender, der du nimmergeglaubt', 72–4

The notes that follow are based for the most part on Gianni Vattimo's own autobiography, *Not Being God*, written with Piergiorgio Paterlini (2016 [2006]); on Santiago Zabala's comprehensive introduction to *Weakening Philosophy: Essays in Honour of Gianni Vattimo* (2007); on the long interview Vattimo conducted with Luca Savarino and Federico Vercellone, 'Gianni Vattimo: Philosophy as Ontology of Actuality' (2009d); and on various other sources from the Vattimo Archive (Pompeu Fabra University, Barcelona) and as specified in the text.

A BIOGRAPHICAL-INTELLECTUAL PROFILE

Gianteresio (Gianni) Vattimo (b. Turin, 1936) is one of those rare philosophers who can claim the mantle of public intellectual, the *engagé* thinker called to comment on the political and social issues of his time while simultaneously developing an extremely sophisticated, complex and specialised branch of philosophical thought. He is a philosopher in the classic sense of the term: a well-rounded, inclusive figure who has embraced, in his mature years especially, the idea that philosophy is praxis – in the political sense as much as in any other – an approach we find in the origins of Western philosophy.

As Antonio Gnoli writes in his introduction to the 'Opera Omnia', *Scritti filosofici e politici*, '[Vattimo's] writings go beyond the theories that he professes and enter into the existence of a man who, after all, thought the way he lived. It is no small thing. And even though some may think it is, I would like his versatility and his contradictions to be seen as a singular form of coherence' (2021: 12, my translation). This 'singular coherence' may in part derive from Vattimo's status as a 'literate proletarian', as he loves to define himself (Gnoli 2021: 15), which is in marked distinction to most of his fellow schoolmates, and later, colleagues. Vattimo is the son of a Calabrese policeman who died of pneumonia when he was a year old, and of a Turinese tailor who worked from home. A precocious learner, he was always considered by his mother and his sister to be the 'educated' member of the family. His Catholic upbringing, although not strict by any means, marked him deeply. By the end of high school, he had become the diocesan representative of the student movement's Catholic Action Group.

Vattimo would later say that the church he frequented from the age of 10 formed his fundamental attitude towards the world and others, including his commitment to social and political causes. This variety of interests pushed him to study philosophy, moved as he was by the aspiration to form a new 'Christian humanism', free from both liberal individualism and Marxist determinism and collectivism. It was at the University of Turin that he began to study the 'integral humanism' of Jacques Maritain, a French neo-Thomist philosopher admired for his anti-fascism, whose critique of modernity inspired him to approach Nietzsche and Heidegger as radical anti-modern thinkers. Paradoxically, Vattimo admits, Nietzsche's critique of Christianity produced in him a 'return' to the Christian faith, or to something 'that very much looks like it' (Gnoli 2021: 16).

Between 1955 and 1959 Vattimo studied at the University of Turin, where he graduated with a thesis on the concept of *poiesis* in Aristotle that had been supervised by the well-known Italian philosopher Luigi Pareyson (see Vattimo [1961] 2007). This thesis was partly determined by Pareyson's own theory of aesthetics as a 'theory of production, of making and fashioning' (Vattimo 2009d: 315–16), along with his concept of *forma formante* ('forming form'), which would prove influential in the early writings on aesthetics by his young advisee.

The older philosopher also played an important role in Vattimo's academic career, first making him his assistant, and later backing him for a professorship after he won the competition for the chair in Aesthetics, passing over his friend and colleague Umberto Eco, who had also participated in the competition (*NBG*, 47). As Vattimo wrote, 'in 1964 I became a qualified university lecturer in Turin, which was my first official university teaching post. I believe that the first course I offered was on Nietzsche, then on Heidegger, and after that on Bloch and Schleiermacher' (Vattimo 2009d: 318). It was Pareyson who encouraged Vattimo to study Nietzsche after dissuading him from pursuing a study of Adorno and 'critical theory', both of which were quite fashionable at the time 'with the left-leaning intellectuals that Pareyson particularly distrusted' (Vattimo 2009d: 316), even though he himself, despite being an apolitical Catholic conservative, was well known and respected for his anti-fascist activity during the Second World War.

During his early years as a university student, Vattimo also had his first television experience, creating and hosting educational programmes (1955–57) together with Eco and Furio Colombo, the latter of whom would go on to become a well-known journalist and foreign correspondent. At the same time, Vattimo took up a teaching position at a vocational school to pay for his studies. He stayed in this role until 1959, when he was fired for taking his students to an anti-apartheid demonstration. He subsequently joined the faculty at Rosmini High School in Turin, where he continued to teach until 1962.

That year, at Pareyson's urging, Vattimo applied for and was awarded a Humboldt Scholarship and spent a couple of years in Heidelberg studying with Gadamer and Löwith. These were years of intense focus for Vattimo. He began the Italian translation of Gadamer's monumental *Truth and Method*, which he completed in 1969 and for which he also wrote an introduction. During this time he also wrote books on Heidegger (1963), Nietzsche (1967a) and Schleiermacher (1968), all while 'working on the second edition of the Sansoni *Encyclopaedia of Philosophy*, edited under the auspices of the "Centro studi di Gallarate", a monumental publication in several volumes' (Vattimo 2009d: 317). The book on Schleiermacher would earn Vattimo a full professorship at the University of Turin in 1968.

The narrative of these early years, which Vattimo recounts in numerous places, reveals a brilliant but not presumptuous young philosopher in the making, gifted with the humility to take teaching positions in modest schools and yet not afraid to try new and innovative experiences (such as public television) that most would have considered anathema to a traditional academic career. It also reveals the fundamental themes and passions that would accompany Vattimo throughout his long and productive career: the question of aesthetics as the experience of truth, the tradition of philosophical hermeneutics, the ways in which Nietzsche and Heidegger (and later, Marx and Hegel) can be read intertextually, and the discourses and practices of religion and politics.

As we have already seen, religion and politics were intertwined in Vattimo's life from an early age, but in the Heidelberg years, he went through 'a political shift from his former "Catto-communist" position to what he then called a "Catto-Heideggerian" mentality', in which the God of the Bible became the 'Heideggerian Being' (Zabala 2007: 8), that is, a matter of interpretation and not of dogmatic acceptance. Heidegger was later credited for bringing him closer to Christianity:

The dismissal of metaphysics, which is radically accomplished only in Heidegger, is of great importance for continuing to think as a Christian. Metaphysics, i.e., the objectivity, unfurled before the mind's eye, of structures of Being that are assumed to be given; in short, God as supreme Object that I cannot fail to recognize. A sort of violence because, among other reasons, where metaphysics leads me is never a god before whom we can sing and dance, nor a god that loves me (in *Letter on Humanism*, *möglich machen* also means to love, *mögen*). (*BIS*, 228)

In 1968 – a year considered pivotal by many intellectuals at the time due to the student uprisings that were taking place under the aegis of the workers' movement in Italy, France and other European countries, and in the United States as the civil rights movement and protests against the Vietnam war gained momentum – Vattimo describes the experience of convalescing from an ulcer operation and waking up a Maoist (*NBG*, 21). This was a position shared by many French artists and intellectuals at the time, including Michel Foucault, Julia Kristeva, Philippe Sollers, Alain Badiou, Jean-Luc Godard, Jean-Paul Sartre, Simone de Beauvoir and others who sympathised with the Chinese revolutionary movement as one way to declare their distance from the official Communist Party line of the Soviet Union.[1] As Badiou stated in a recent interview, 'In the 1960s and 70s, saying you were a Maoist – as thousands and thousands of militants from all over did between 1966 and 1976, during what I call the "red years" – meant precisely this: we think that the fundamental experience for pursuing communist politics is the Cultural Revolution and not the Soviet state.'[2]

A similar realignment among political leftist groups was taking place in Italy, informing many aspects of cultural production. As the writer and academic Edoardo Sanguineti declared in a 1993 interview, Maoism

represented the hope of a non-bureaucratic, non-tyrannical and dynamic socialism, and appeared as the only alternative for those who had little sympathy for capitalism and strong doubts about the Soviet Union . . . Mao was perfect, as a reference point, for those who wanted to change the world, beginning with the most disenfranchised areas, such as China was before becoming the legendary place of equality and justice.[3]

---

1 Maoist movements were also fuelling new approaches to feminism and homosexual rights in France in the years immediately following 1968. See, for example, Richard Wolin, *The Wind from the East: French Intellectuals, the Cultural Revolution, and the Legacy of the 1960s* (Princeton, NJ: Princeton University Press, 2018).
2 Miri Davidson, 'Alain Badiou: "Mao thinks in an almost infinite way"', Verso blog, 16 May 2016, <https://www.versobooks.com/blogs/2033-alain-badiou-mao-thinks-in-an-almost-infinite-way> (accessed 16 October 2021).
3 'Noi, cinesi d'Italia', *La Repubblica*, 11 November 1993, <https://ricerca.repubblica.it/repubblica/archivio/repubblica/1993/11/11/noi-cinesi-italia.html> (accessed 16 October 2021). My translation.

Although Vattimo has not elaborated on his 'Maoism' of those years, it seems apparent that for him Mao's communism offered a way to be 'a true revolutionary' (Vattimo 2009d: 319) and to denounce, as fellow leftist Luca Pozzi has observed, the 'current morality, the hypocrisy, the . . . stupidity of the capitalist system' and a 'world of injustice and exploitation'.[4] This is underscored by the fact that since the late 1960s Vattimo's philosophy and political engagement have clearly been motivated by a concern for the dispossessed and the 'weak' of the earth.

Despite the political affiliations Vattimo shared with his French colleagues, he was quite removed from the Paris of that time philosophically. His development and interests led him instead to German philosophy, not just the hermeneutic tradition that became his defining trait but also the 'political' thinkers such as Bloch, Lukács and Marcuse whose ideas provided material for courses he was offering at the University of Turin in 1968–69. The study of Nietzsche that Vattimo was developing in those years – which culminated in 1974's *Il soggetto e la maschera* (*The Subject and the Mask*) – owes little to the French interpretations of Nietzsche that were becoming fashionable at the time and that Vattimo knew well (as demonstrated by his introduction to the Italian translation of Deleuze's *Nietzsche et la philosophie* first published in 1962 [Vattimo 1978]). In his words, 'I have never really fully understood the importance that has been accorded to the Deleuzian reading of Nietzsche: even now, Deleuze strikes me as a modern Bergson translated into left wing terms' (Vattimo 2009d: 321).

Vattimo brought a similar scepticism to Foucault's version of structuralism, which remained for the Turinese philosopher too 'metaphysical in character' (Vattimo 2009d: 321), and to his interpretation of Nietzsche as a thinker who maintains the connection between truth and force. Even though he would borrow Foucault's expression 'ontology of the present', the French philosopher was, according to Vattimo, an epistemologist who revealed no ontological dimension in his thought (Vattimo 2009d: 321). Conversely, the 'ontology of actuality' in Vattimo starts by 'taking language as a point of departure, but also by bringing in something beyond language'. He continues, '[It] resembles a philosophical sociology . . . a kind of return to Adorno . . . If there is such a thing as an ontology of actuality in my work, it is contained, paradoxically enough, in the articles which I have written for the newspapers' (Vattimo 2009d: 342). This 'ontology of actuality' would come to fruition in the lectures on truth that Vattimo delivered at Louvain in 1998 and collected in *Of Reality*.

4 Ibid.

The 1970s were a time of intensive work for Vattimo on Nietzsche, Marx and nihilism. After the publication of *Il soggetto e la maschera*,[5] he took part in several lecture series on these topics, often paired with colleagues such as Massimo Cacciari, Pier Aldo Rovatti and Remo Bodei, who were active in leftist circles and in the city councils that were sprouting in many Italian cities at the time. As he recounts, 'philosophy was an enormously popular subject back then. We all thought that the political transformation of Italy should be accompanied by a democratisation of philosophical questions, without sacrificing the level of cultural discourse on such matters' (Vattimo 2009d: 323).

In the same year that Heidegger died –1976 – the Italian Communist Party (PCI) reached its peak in the national elections. It was the first time that 18-year-olds were allowed to vote in Italy. Vattimo was forty and had just finished editing and translating a collection of Heidegger's essays and speeches. Significantly, although without his consent, Vattimo had been listed as a candidate by the Italian Radical Party on its slate 'Fuori' (Italian for 'out'), an open reference to homosexuality, forcing a public 'outing' that was far removed from his own sensibility and cultural upbringing (*NBG*, 73).

Leftist politics in Italy would take an extremist turn along Marxist-Leninist lines in the late 1970s. It was a position that Vattimo could not endorse, even as some of his own students were embracing it and getting arrested as a result, because he could not accept its 'metaphysical and violent rhetorical subjectivity', which would soon give way to the terrorism of the so-called 'years of lead'.[6] He sympathised instead with the ideas that Antonio Negri was proposing at the time, which called for more autonomous and anarchic forms of community organisation that 'would escape and transcend the prevailing logic of power' (Vattimo 2009d: 324). *Al di là del soggetto*, published in 1981 (*BS*), operates a critique of subjectivity that draws on such premises and postulates that 'the true revolution would be an inner revolution, which would involve a dismantling of subjectivity' (Vattimo 2009d: 324–5).

The 1980s was a fertile decade for Vattimo, who published in close order some of the most significant reflections on modernity and postmodernity, subjectivity and difference, art and technology of the late twentieth century: *Le avventure della differenza: Che cosa significa pensare dopo*

---

5 This publication occurred in part due to the intercession of Umberto Eco at the publishing house Bompiani.

6 Vattimo recounted that when he became dean of the Faculty of Humanities at the University of Turin in 1977 (a position he held until the early 1980s) he was threatened by the Red Brigades and for a time had to leave the city (Vattimo 2009d: 327).

Nietzsche e Heidegger (1980, *AD*); *Al di là del soggetto: Nietzsche, Heidegger e l'ermeneutica* (1981a, *BS*); *Il pensiero debole*, with Pier Aldo Rovatti (1983, *WT*); *La fine della modernità* (1985b, *EM*); and *La società trasparente* (1989c, *TS*), cited by Jean-François Lyotard as being 'of major importance to the debate of the postmodern condition' (*TS*, back cover).

The concept of *pensiero debole* or 'weak thought' – one of the longest and most cited entries in this dictionary – is one of the central themes in Vattimo's hermeneutics, and it is the contribution for which he is best known in Italy and throughout the international community. At times, it has been widely misunderstood by the popular press and conveniently dismissed by colleagues who subscribe to different philosophical positions. Despite being tied to the emergence of the discourse around postmodernism in the late 1970s and early 1980s, the concept of 'weak thought' is still very current. In fact, according to Rovatti, who collaborated with Vattimo on the articulation of the theory, its full expression may still lie ahead and it is needed today more than ever.[7] 'Weak thought' starts by interpreting nihilism as a *weakening* of the structures of metaphysics and a dissolving of the concept of being as an 'objective foundation' (Vattimo 2009d: 337; *OR*, 213). It goes on to elaborate a very particular and convincing notion of postmodernity as the 'experience of the "end of history", not the appearance of a different, or newer stage of history itself' (Snyder 1988: xviii).

Vattimo also expanded his teaching and lecturing activities in the 1980s to include universities and institutions throughout Europe and the United States. He returned to Italian television in 1986 for a series of programmes for RAI 3 consisting of discussions with other Italian philosophers, including Francesco Barone, Remo Bodei, Italo Mancini, Vittorio Mathieu, Mario Perniola, Pier Aldo Rovatti, Emanuele Severino and Carlo Sini. These conversations were published in 1990 as *Filosofia al presente* (*Philosophy at Present*) (*NBG*, 124). Vattimo's television appearances continued in the 1990s with a series called *Atlante ideologico del Novecento* (*Ideological Atlas of the Twentieth Century*), broadcast on RAI 2 Nettuno (Network Teledidattico per l'Università Ovunque). It was a sort of Open University on video aimed at addressing key concepts from contemporary philosophy for a general audience. Vattimo presented each episode with the same clarity of exposition and communicative ease that have accompanied him throughout his teaching and lecturing career and have made him especially beloved by his students.

---

7 See intervention by Pier Aldo Rovatti in 'Three tenors tra filosofia e psicoanalisi: Gianni Vattimo & Friends' [09:45 ff], streamed live on 9 June 2021, <https://www.youtube.com/watch?v=1OIz8r4wogM> (accessed 2 September 2022). See also Rovatti 2007.

Between 1986 and 1995 Vattimo edited the Italian Philosophical Yearbooks, a series published by Laterza focused on significant issues in international philosophical debate. Some of the themes Vattimo chose are reflected in keywords in this dictionary, such as secularisation, history, language, hermeneutics and poetry. Among the contributors to the yearbooks were notable philosophers such as Alain Badiou, Jacques Derrida, Hans-Georg Gadamer, Jean-François Lyotard, Richard Rorty and Emanuele Severino. The European Yearbook series followed in 1992. Edited by Vattimo and Derrida, it consisted of two books, the first devoted to religion, the second to law, justice and interpretation. Stemming from his role as editor, Vattimo would next publish four books of his own, three on the theme of religion: *Credere di credere* (1996a, *B*); *Dopo la cristianità* (2002a, *AC*); *Nichilismo ed emancipazione: Etica, politica e diritto*, edited by Santiago Zabala (2003c, *NE*); and *The Future of Religion*, co-authored with Richard Rorty and edited by Santiago Zabala (2005, *FR*).

In these books, as elsewhere, reflection on religion is carried forward under the umbrella of Christianity not as metaphysical faith but as adherence to cultural tradition. The interpretation of Christianity through the 'weakening' effect of hermeneutics emphasises 'the incarnation, the kenosis, God that becomes man and therefore abandons his sacrality', leading to a philosophy of history in which 'human emancipation can only be thought of as a progressive reduction of natural violence', which is perhaps the most important legacy of 'weak thought'.[8] Vattimo's interpretation of religion in a 'weakened' state also reflects his disapproval of the Church's discipline, 'particularly when it dictated a "natural" sexual behavior for all believers' (Zabala 2007: 8). Although Vattimo's homosexuality is not central to his thought (and therefore did not warrant, in our opinion, a dedicated entry in this dictionary), it nevertheless plays an important role in his distrust of all forms of 'strong' thinking and normative ethical behaviour dictated by religious dogma.

In contrast to the international recognition he was accorded – Vattimo was awarded the Max-Planck Research Award for Humanities in 1992 – the 1990s marked a period of painful loss in the philosopher's personal life. Pareyson died in 1991. At the end of 1992 Vattimo's partner, Gianpiero Cavaglià, died from AIDS – a story narrated with disarming candour in *Not Being God*, where we also learn that less than ten years later, Sergio Mamino, his companion at the time, would die of a malignant tumour.

---

8 Maurizio Assalto, 'Gianni Vattimo: "I miei ottant'anni da estremista"', *La Stampa*, 3 January 2016, <https://www.lastampa.it/cultura/2016/01/03/news/gianni-vattimo-i-miei-ottant-anni-da-estremista-1.36545766> (accessed 2 September 2022). My translation.

Nevertheless, Vattimo's political engagement intensified during the 1990s, a period in Italy that was characterised by a new effort to fight political corruption known as *Tangentopoli* – a nod to the widespread bribery associated with local and regional mafias that was implicating functionaries and politicians in major cities and governmental institutions.

This period of political upheaval culminated in the dissolution of the First Republic and of one of the political parties that had governed Italy for most of the republican period, the Christian Democrats. Subsequently, Silvio Berlusconi, a former real estate developer in the Milanese suburbs and owner of private TV stations that made him a billionaire in the 1980s, took to politics and founded a centre-right party (which included elements of the historical fascist right and the emerging Northern League) that would see him take control of the government on and off in the decades between 1994 and 2012. Vattimo became increasingly active in the national press during these years, writing articles for the Turin-based *La Stampa* and the leftist newspaper *L'Unità*. In 1999 he won a seat as a deputy in the European Parliament, a position he held until 2004. The commissions he took part in were closely aligned with his philosophical and political convictions, including the Commission for Freedom and Citizens' Rights, Justice and Internal Affairs; the Commission for Culture, Youth, Education, Communication and Sport; and the Interparliamentary Delegation EU–China. Prior to Berlusconi's six-month term as president of the European Parliament, Vattimo notably took action against him. In addition, he successfully opposed the insertion of the term 'Christian values' into the European Constitution in order to protect secularisation, the most significant achievement of Christian culture in a non-metaphysical sense as he sees it.

The new millennium opened with the publication of *Vocazione e responsabilità del filosofo*, edited by Franca D'Agostini (2000d, *RP*), in which political life is articulated in philosophical terms as 'a choice for human liberation that places pedagogy before ideology, the transformation of individual minds before the transformation of the shape of society' (Robert T. Valgenti, foreword to *FT*, xiv). In the following decade, Vattimo would go on to develop his hermeneutical thought along more clearly delineated political lines, aiming to recast the idea of democracy in light of the end of metaphysics and renewing his interest in the possibilities of socialism.[9]

---

9 In 2003, for instance, Vattimo presented 'Heidegger: Philosopher of Democracy' at the twenty-first World Philosophy Congress, which he opened together with Jürgen Habermas.

Upon receiving the Hannah Arendt Prize for Political Thinking in 2002, Vattimo gave a lecture titled 'Globalization and the Relevance of Socialism'. In that lecture, he argued that Europe still had a critical role to play in distributing and rebalancing the global centres of power after the failure of monocentrism of the kind imposed by the United States following the collapse of the Soviet Union. Europe, for him, is a model and a symbol of dialogism and plurality grounded in the diversity of its constituencies – the locus of a contemporary revitalisation of the Kantian dream of cosmopolitanism. In 2004 he further elaborated these thoughts in *Il socialismo ossia l'Europa* (*Socialism, Namely Europe*), which he unsuccessfully put forward as a political platform for his re-election to the European Parliament. Although his political career came to a momentary close (he would go on to complete a second term in the European Parliament in 2014), Vattimo continued his political engagement by means of publications, public debates, interviews and a strong presence in the media.

Vattimo continued his philosophico-political investigation of socialism and communism through the lens of 'weak thought' with the publication of *Ecce comu: come si ri-diventa ciò che si era* (2007b; *Ecce Comu: How One [Re-]Becomes What One Was*), an obvious homage to Nietzsche's *Ecce Homo* and a reference to 're-becoming' communist in an anarchic sense, consistent with the pursuit of 'a politics of opposition on the margins' and a 'transformative Hegelian Marxism which contested any naturalistic conception of absolute principles and thus possessed a political vocation from the outset' (Vattimo 2009d: 343, 344). The connection between this renewed conception of Marxism and hermeneutics is even more evident in the book co-written with Santiago Zabala, *Hermeneutic Communism: From Heidegger to Marx* (2011). There, the authors take up Marx's famous statement, 'the philosophers have only interpreted the world in various ways; the point is to change it', from a hermeneutic-Heideggerian perspective, affirming that in order to change the world (and our interpretations of it) we must change the way we think. Once again, the goal is to let go of the pretence of overcoming metaphysics – in itself a metaphysical gesture – in order to *weaken* metaphysics. For Vattimo and Zabala, thinking particularly of communist democratic models in contemporary South America: 'a productive postmetaphysical philosophy will not only surpass metaphysics but also favor its discharge, that is, the weak who have become the vast majority of the population throughout the world' (*HC*, 1–2, 5).

In a paper titled 'From Weak Thought to the Thought of the Weak' presented in October 2008 at the Symposium on Religion and Science at Johns Hopkins University, Vattimo concerned himself with the distortion caused by technology and its contribution to the growing proletarianisation of society that brought him closer to Marx and his critique of globalisation. He 'alludes to the fact that "weak thought" was too ready to believe that the event of being already provided us with paths of emancipation, whereas such paths are still to be discovered' (Vattimo 2009d: 349).

Just a few days earlier, Vattimo had delivered his final lecture as a professor at the University of Turin. Focused on the issue presented in the title – 'From Dialogue to Conflict' – he stressed the point that 'philosophical discoveries are not independent of the actual present'. It continues to be the case that Vattimo's 'ontology of actuality' manifests itself not only in his attention to ongoing political and social events through an 'analysis of the sense of existence in the technologically oriented postmodern society' (D'Isanto 1999: 4), but also in the way he infuses his lectures and seminars with a sense of humour and a tendency to use humble and everyday examples to explain difficult concepts. In a 2008 article dedicated to the philosopher, the renowned Italian writer Alessandro Baricco, who is one of Vattimo's former students, remembers one of these examples: 'I think I understood Kantian ethics when you pointed out that at 3 a.m., in a deserted city, in front of a traffic light, you stop only if you are a fool: or if you are Kant.'[10] Humour and clarity are Vattimo's defining traits as a teacher, qualities that are also notably present in his interviews and philosophical writings; yet he has never made 'clarity' the end goal of his philosophy but rather 'the starting point, the precondition without which thought cannot get going'.[11]

It is not surprising, if one reflects on the meaning of 'weak thought', that Vattimo has always been fond of peppering his lectures and talks with jokes, ironic wordplay and witty examples: humour is a form of 'lightness' or 'lightening', a way to make ideas somewhat more concrete and digestible, which pedagogically is a formidable tool – and a very difficult one to use successfully. This process of 'lightening' occurs whenever metaphysical 'weight' is subtracted from ideas so that they do not operate dogmatically but, on the contrary, become open to interpretation and to being challenged. Santiago Zabala, who is another of Vattimo's former students and who remains one of his closest collaborators and interpreters, has declared that

Among the first things my teacher, Prof. Vattimo, taught me is that to be 'a philosopher means to be obsessed with the verb Being (concerning what is and what

---

10 Alessandro Baricco, 'Grazie, caro Vattimo, sei stato un maestro', *La Repubblica*, 14 October 2008, <https://torino.repubblica.it/dettaglio/grazie-caro-vattimo-sei-stato-un-maestro/1526873> (accessed 2 September 2022). My translation.
11 Ibid.

is not) because it invites you not to remain satisfied with your own identity and to seek the entire horizon of Being – in other words, to dialogue'.[12]

Other former students have gone on to develop their own philosophical careers, sometimes in very different directions from Vattimo's, as is the case with Maurizio Ferraris, who in recent years has supported the idea of 'new realism' in opposition to postmodernism. Others – including Franca D'Agostini, who wrote the entries on **weak thought**, **logic** and **truth** for this dictionary; Federico Vercellone, who wrote the entries on **aesthetics** and **art**; and Gaetano Chiurazzi, author of the entries for **Dilthey**, **hermeneutics** and **interpretation**; as well as Luca Savarino, Luca Bagetto and Gianni Carchia – have traced distinct philosophical paths while maintaining a robust dialogue with the work of their former teacher.

One can appreciate Vattimo's talent as a teacher and a public speaker – in addition to his brilliance as a philosopher – in the series of lectures he delivered in 2010 for the prestigious Gifford Lectureship (established in 1888), conferred on him in recognition of his stance as 'one of the foremost philosophers in the world today' and 'a major voice in European and world politics'.[13] Previous lecturers have included Hannah Arendt, William James, Jean-Luc Marion, Iris Murdoch, Charles Taylor and Alfred North Whitehead, and the award is rightly considered 'the Nobel Prize in philosophy', as Vattimo himself acknowledged with characteristic humility and wit in his opening lecture. Together, these lectures were collected with his previous Cardinal Mercier Chair Lectures given in Leuven and several other essays, and published as *Of Reality: The Purposes of Philosophy*. This book, in Vattimo's own words, 'presents a long and rather unsystematic work of reflection on the theme of the dissolution of objectivity or of reality itself, which began with the first expressions of "weak thought" in the early 1980s' (*OR*, 1).

While this was indeed the theme of the Leuven Lectures, in the Gifford Lectures Vattimo goes on to observe that 'the adversary to combat already (and today more than ever) seemed to me the return to order' that passes under the name of 'realism' or 'new realism' in philosophy today, and that constitutes a sort of return to metaphysical 'certainties' in which the difference between 'reality' (with quotation marks) and reality (without

---

12 Santiago Zabala, 'Interview with Santiago Zabala, Author of *The Remains of Being: Hermeneutic Ontology After Metaphysics*', Columbia University Press, 2008, <https://cup.columbia.edu/author-interviews/zabala-remains-being> (accessed 2 September 2022).
13 As stated by David Jaspers in his introduction to Vattimo's first lecture, <https://www.giffordlectures.org/lectures/end-reality> (accessed 2 September 2022).

quotation marks) is erased in the name of a presumed objectivity and neutrality on the part of the speaker. In the introduction to *Of Reality*, he passionately defends his own political commitment, starting with a lucid analysis of Heidegger's brief and tragic commitment to the cause of National Socialism in the 1930s, for which he provides no defence on substantive bases, but rather an understanding on historical grounds. The bottom line, for Vattimo, is that those for whom philosophy is an existential practice are called to engage with their particular epochal circumstance; and those philosophers who do not, often operate from a position of privilege. It could be that Vattimo's position derives in part from his own personal history, wherein his lack of 'pedigree' or family connections would make him a 'misfit' with the intellectual elite of his native city (see *NBG*, 95), with his particular ethical stance being defined by a secularised understanding of the doctrine of charity as love for one's neighbours and the community of one's interpreters (see D'Isanto 1999: 10).

Vattimo himself is not someone who avoids taking risks when circumstances demand that he take a position, and he is no stranger to controversy. The most recent of these controversies concerned his views on Israel's position in relation to the Palestinian cause, an outlook that became increasingly critical as he underwent a crisis of faith regarding the West and the so-called 'free world' under the aegis of NATO and the United States (*BIS*, 95). In the summer of 2014, following one of the heaviest bombing campaigns in the Gaza Strip in recent years (Operation Protective Edge), which raised international protests and condemnation, Vattimo made several controversial remarks on an Italian radio programme notorious for its provocative stance and specious interviewing methods. Vattimo later apologised for his more outrageous statements in an interview for Haaretz[14] – but not for his criticism of Israel's policies or for his sympathy for the Palestinian struggle, which he elaborated on most recently in his essay 'How to Become an Anti-Zionist' (*BIS*, 93–101). While this open involvement with intractable political issues might seem imprudent to some, it is entirely consistent with the notion that 'philosophy, if it does not want to be metaphysics (which is always just defending things as they are), must look at the general condition of the world and allow itself to be questioned by it' (*OR*, 227–8).

In 2015 Vattimo donated his archives to the Pompeu Fabra University in Barcelona, Spain, and they were inaugurated in the summer of 2016. The archives contain a vast trove of diaries, letters (including

---

14 Anna Momigliano, 'Italian Philosopher Apologizes for Saying He Wanted to "Shoot Those Bastard Zionists"', *Haaretz*, 30 July 2014, <http://www.haaretz.com/jewish-world/jewish-world-news/.premium-1.607992> (accessed 2 September 2022).

correspondence with Heidegger, Gadamer and Karl-Otto Apel), published and unpublished manuscripts, didactic materials, reviews, notes and audio-visual files. Although it is not at all uncommon for prominent philosophers to have their archives hosted at an institution other than their own, for Vattimo, having his papers at Pompeu Fabra University reinforces his ties to South America, whose intellectual climate has always been very receptive to the notion of 'weak thought' that he has cultivated over the decades.[15] Moreover, the fact that Vattimo's papers are not archived at an institution in Italy is indicative of the international scope of his philosophy, which was first nurtured by the German thinkers of the Continental tradition and then developed in a dialogue unequalled among his Italian peers with philosophers such as Jacques Derrida, Richard Rorty, Eugenio Trias Sagnier and Slavoj Žižek.[16] The multifaceted cosmopolitanism of Vattimo's thought, combined with his capacity to embrace various fields of philosophical inquiry – art, politics, ethics, ontology, religion – is ultimately what distinguishes it from that of his contemporaries and affords the opportunity for further scholarship in the coming years.

Being and Its Surroundings, published in 2021, allows English-speaking readers to familiarise themselves with some of the more salient aspects of Vattimo's thought. The book, a collection of essays, is presented less as a unified sequence of chapters than as 'variations on a single theme: the theme of a philosophy that is practised by testing perspectives and exploring occasions – we might call it a philosophy of occasions' (*BIS*, 3). Close to the spirit of an 'ontology of actuality' in a Vattimian sense, these essays were originally composed as lectures, presentations and invited talks. They revolve around the legacy of Heidegger's thought, particularly in light of the publication of the German philosopher's *Black Notebooks* (which prompted what Vattimo calls the 'diary of a crisis' [*BIS*, 4]), and touch upon various themes ranging from the dissolution of metaphysics, to hermeneutics and nihilism, to the role of art in the age of advanced technology, to politics and revolution, and to the possibility of emancipation left open by Christianity's overarching message. The original title of the book, according to Vattimo himself, was in fact *Questioni filosofiche-teologiche* (*Theological-Philosophical Questionnaire*).[17]

---

15 Gianni Vattimo, 'Nessuna polemica le carte di Derrida sono in California', *La Stampa*, 7 June 2016, 35.
16 See Santiago Zabala, 'Gianni Vattimo's Life, Philosophy, and Archives', *LA Review of Books*, 10 November 2016, <https://lareviewofbooks.org/article/gianni-vattimos-life-philosophy-archives/> (accessed 2 September 2022); and Claudio Gallo, 'Gli archivi di Vattimo a un'università di Barcellona', *La Stampa*, 7 June 2016, 35.
17 Assalto, 'Gianni Vattimo: "I miei ottant'anni da estremista"'.

To mark the publication of the first Italian edition of the book in 2018, a special event was arranged at the Circolo dei Lettori in Turin, where Vattimo received an honorary degree from the Institute for Doctoral Studies in the Visual Arts. The book was released by the publisher La Nave di Teseo (founded in 2015 by Umberto Eco and Elisabetta Sgarbi), which also published his most recent volume, a comprehensive anthology of his major books titled *Scritti filosofici e politici* (*Philosophical and Political Writings*, 2021), with an introduction by Antonio Gnoli and a presentation by Gaetano Chiurazzi. This ponderous volume – some 2,600 pages in length – is divided into three sections: 'The Philosophers' (including Vattimo's main writings on Heidegger and Nietzsche); 'Hermeneutics' (including key early texts such as *Poesia e ontologia* [*ACT*], and later writings such as *La fine della modernità* [*EM*], *Oltre l'interpretazione* [*BI*] and *Della realtà* [*OR*]); and 'Weak Thought' (including the titular essay, *La società trasparente* [*TS*], *Credere di credere* [*B*], *Dopo la cristianità* [*AC*], *Comunismo ermeneutico* [*HC*] *Essere e dintorni* [*BIS*]). A dedicated section on aesthetics is missing, which may seem surprising considering that so many of Vattimo's philosophical reflections, as well as the focus of much of his early academic career, have to do with questions concerning art and aesthetics. However, it is apparent that the discourse on art must be understood in the context of hermeneutics on the one hand and of 'weak thought' on the other. Even more radically, as Vattimo makes clear in the first paragraphs of his 1967 book *Poesia e ontologia*,[18] the question of art needs to be posed ontologically, and therefore such a question cannot be limited to the aesthetic sphere (a position that takes up the question posed by Heidegger in *The Origin of the Work of Art* [1936]). Indeed, to think of art in an ontological sense means to take the theme of 'ontological difference' highlighted by Heidegger as the central theme and to consider it in light of the hermeneutic practice such a thematic approach requires. The 'truth' of a work of art is thus revealed through a process of interpretation (Vattimo 2021: 951; Zabala, introduction to *ACT*, xiii).

By examining his complete works in the arc of a career that spans more than half a century, Vattimo seems to follow a contrary path to Heidegger – who, were we to oversimplify, goes from politics to poetry in his philosophy (beginning with the *Kehre* of the 1930s); the Italian philosopher, on the other hand, goes rather from poetry to politics, and from more specialised philosophical themes to an engagement with social concerns, including a renewed interest in religious issues.

---

18 Published in English with important updates and modifications as *Art's Claim to Truth* (2008).

In a recent conversation, Vattimo pondered the question of his apparent deviation from the discourse on art that characterised his earlier years, arriving at an answer having to do with his development of 'weak thought' in a political-religious direction. If he initially came to write about art and aesthetics through Pareyson's influence, it was by continuing to pursue the 'weakening' of metaphysics that he found himself focusing less on the art object and theorisations of art and more on the social facts informing them. Even when talking about art in a more conventional sense, it is not so much the individual experience that matters to him but a more generalised aesthetic experience on a collective level (Gadamer, for example, has spoken of Woodstock as a threshold in this sense). Referring to an early course he taught at the University of Turin, 'Art and Utopia' (1972a), Vattimo considers 'weak thought' a utopian thought because it points to a possibility not realisable or not yet realised.[19] And yet it is significant that a contemporary artist such as Francesco Clemente, whose paintings acquired international recognition during the same years that Vattimo was developing the concept of 'weak thought', would say in a recent speech:

of all languages I find that painting is the weakest and the most resilient, and it defies every notion we have about power and strength and this and that . . . it's so . . . not going to work out. The only thing that works is weakness, gentleness, and the perception of the . . . perfection of the imperfect.[20]

In reality, as Vattimo declares in the introduction to *BIS* (citing Rorty), philosophical systems themselves can be thought of as novels, and therefore, as art; and the reading of philosophy can indeed 'change one's life', which was for Gadamer the meaning of the experience of truth in art (*BIS*, 3–4). It is also worth noting that in 'From Dialogue to Conflict' (2008), Vattimo returns to Heidegger's essay on the origin of the work of art, where 'Heidegger defines the work of art as the "setting to work of truth"', and where the site of the truth as a happening 'is sought in the work of art' (*OR*, 225). 'What constitutes the basis of the inaugural force of the work of art, and this today seems to me more important than it had appeared to me in the past, is the fact that it keeps the conflict between world and earth open' (*OR*, 226). This conflict can be seen most clearly

---

19 Personal communication, 28 June 2021.
20 Francesco Clemente, from a speech delivered at the 2019 Skowhegan Awards Dinner (23 April 2019, New York City). From a recording courtesy of Skowhegan School of Painting and Sculpture. Vattimo is a friend of Clemente's, but he admitted that he does not 'follow contemporary art much' (personal communication, 28 June 2021).

in the work of the historical avant-garde, which has always occupied a central place in Vattimo's reflections on art and which provides a link to the political and social dimension not only of the aesthetic experience but also of 'weak thought' itself.

In the essay 'The Boundaries of Art', which favourably observes the dismantling of borders in the avant-garde projects of the early twentieth century and beyond, the philosopher further argues that 'today we are able to rethink more clearly and perhaps more reasonably the positive alternative that Benjamin called the "politicization of art"' (*BIS*, 134). Here, Vattimo compares the phenomenon of professionalisation in art to the restoration of specialisation in philosophy – which goes hand in hand with a renunciation of the latter's ties to the type of 'poetic' or creative thought that has always characterised philosophical inquiry centred on politics, ethics and existentialism, namely those that fall under the heading 'Continental philosophy'. The aestheticisation of social life that is in full swing today calls for a response by philosophy, 'not by restoring the "boundaries" of what is truly an aesthetic field but by asking itself what meaning the new social situation has or what valid (emancipatory) possibilities it opens up' (*BIS*, 137). The disturbing and troubling aspects of art – of avant-garde art especially – are, for Vattimo, the true foci of philosophy and politics and define an attitude towards the world. As he states with characteristic humour in a recent interview, 'The only type that I like today is the one who is a pain in the neck. Even Pope Bergoglio, when speaking to the youth, invites them to "*hacer lío*", to mess around, to make trouble.' This attitude comes from Vattimo's being a 'wrecked Marxist' and a Christian; philosophically, it is the opposite of practising the 'descriptive philosophy' that is now taught in academia (and that forms the basis for various kinds of neo-realism): 'The truth of being is the happening of projects, not the given structure.'[21]

Even though, as Vattimo says, getting old brings with it the realisation that one's personal life is no longer aligned with 'external' history,[22] he has not demurred from commenting on current issues in the press. He has, for instance, repeatedly expressed concerns over measures that the Italian government (and other governments around Europe) have adopted to contain the COVID-19 pandemic, measures that have, in his opinion, disproportionately affected the poor and marginalised segments of society – while at the same time highlighting the fact that many poor countries still need additional vaccine doses to protect their citizens, thus distancing himself from the more or less extremist positions embraced by

---

21 Assalto, 'Gianni Vattimo: "I miei ottant'anni da estremista"'.
22 Ibid.

some of his colleagues (including Agamben and Cacciari), who became controversial for their criticism of lockdown policies and other restrictions to limit the spread of the virus. Vattimo has also voiced concerns over the invasiveness of media and technology in people's lives, particularly in the educational field.[23] The spectre of a 'totally administered society' in which the boundary between public and private dissolves haunts our technologically advanced societies in a way that even Adorno could not have predicted. In this scenario, philosophy becomes necessary by virtue of its 'uselessness': 'It is known that Heidegger wrote "science does not think". Precisely because it is "useful", it works in view of goals that it does not even decide for itself . . . But of this uselessness we could not do without.'[24]

THE DICTIONARY IN CONTEXT

The Vattimo Dictionary presents an essential introduction in English to the philosophical thought of Gianni Vattimo, considered the most important Italian philosopher of the last fifty years and one of Europe's foremost contemporary thinkers. Vattimo is increasingly gaining recognition in the English-speaking world of philosophy, art theory and aesthetics, due to recent and upcoming publication of his works in English translation, as well as a growing secondary literature on his philosophy. His major works from the 1980s onward have appeared in English editions, although important gaps still exist in the translation of his voluminous production. These gaps in the nevertheless expanding bibliography in English translation contribute to the challenges that an English-speaking reader approaching Vattimo's thought for the first time encounters. In editing this dictionary I was especially thinking of graduate students of philosophy and art, but also scholars and creative thinkers at various stages of their careers who are not able to draw readily on the history of Continental and Italian philosophy during the nineteenth and twentieth centuries or to grasp the broad references to the cultural, political and historical milieu of post-war Italy in which Vattimo came of age.

One of the first volumes on Vattimo published in English was by Marta Frascati-Lochhead, *Kenosis and Feminist Theology: The Challenge of Gianni*

---

23 Raffaele Graziano Flore, 'Gianni Vattimo/ "Coronavirus? Le società moderne meno libere: troppo controllo e . . .'", Il sussidiario.net, 3 June 2020, <https://www.ilsussidiario.net/news/gianni-vattimo-coronavirus-le-societa-moderne-meno-libere-troppo-controllo-e/2031537/> (accessed 2 September 2022).

24 Vattimo, 'Nessuna polemica le carte di Derrida sono in California', 35.

Vattimo (SUNY Press, 1998). In keeping with Vattimo's exploration of religion, Thomas Guarino published *Vattimo and Theology* (Bloomsbury, 2009). *Weakening Philosophy: Essays in Honour of Gianni Vattimo* (McGill-Queen's University Press, 2007), edited by Santiago Zabala, a Festschrift marking Vattimo's seventieth birthday, features critical essays by Umberto Eco, Jean-Luc Nancy, Richard Rorty, Charles Taylor, Jean Grondin, Pier Aldo Rovatti, Reiner Schürmann and other important thinkers. On the topic of hermeneutics, it is worth mentioning *Between Nihilism and Politics: The Hermeneutics of Gianni Vattimo*, edited by Silvia Benso and Brian Schroeder (SUNY Press, 2010); Andrzej Zawadzki's *Literature and Weak Thought*, edited by Ryszard Nycz and Teresa Walas (Peter Lang, 2013); and *The Routledge Companion to Hermeneutics*, edited by Jeff Malpas and Hans-Helmut Gander (Routledge, 2015). The latter contains the essay 'Pareyson and Vattimo: From Truth to Nihilism' by Gaetano Chiurazzi and 'Conclusion: The Future of Hermeneutics' by Vattimo himself (additionally, Vattimo is cited throughout the book). *Making Communism Hermeneutical: Reading Vattimo and Zabala*, edited by Silvia Mazzini and Owen Glyn-Williams (Springer, 2017), explores the political aspects of Vattimo's thought, and *Hermeneutic Communism: From Heidegger to Marx*, written with Santiago Zabala (Columbia University Press, 2011), presents an original recuperation of Marxian ideas in a hermeneutic key. Finally, an entire issue of *Philosophy Today: An International Journal of Contemporary Philosophy*, edited by Peg Birmingham and Ian Alexander Moore (60[3] 2016), was dedicated to Gianni Vattimo in honour of his 80th birthday. The issue includes contributions from such notable figures as Stefano Azzarà, Michael Marder, Silvia Mazzini, Ian Moore, David Rose, Robert T. Valgenti and Ashley Woodward, many of whom are also contributors to this dictionary.

In the coming years, this secondary literature is likely to grow even further, given Vattimo's stature and the relevance of his thought to contemporary philosophy and to intellectual discourse more broadly. Some themes in his work are just starting to be explored in more depth, such as the religious implications of 'weak thought' in theological studies.

STRUCTURE AND FORMATTING

The Vattimo Dictionary consists of 101 entries arranged in alphabetical order and written by 52 contributors from around the world – the highest number of collaborators ever featured in this series. This fact alone testifies to the importance of Vattimo's thought and to the vitality of the growing body of literature dedicated to his philosophy. The entries vary in length based on their relevance and the extent to which they are examined in Vattimo's work. They include specific philosophical concepts and philosophers who have influenced his thinking, as well as terms of biographical interest, such as **Turin** and **Europe/European Parliament**.

The entries shed light on concepts and figures relevant to Vattimo's thought who may not be as familiar to English-speaking readers because of missing translations of seminal texts, such as the study on Schleiermacher that Vattimo published in 1968 (*Schleiermacher: il filosofo dell'interpretazione*) or his influential book on Nietzsche first published in 1974 (*Il soggetto e la maschera*), or because the work of certain philosophers who have been instrumental to Vattimo's thinking, such as Pareyson or Bonhoeffer, has historically had a more limited audience.

In the interest of preserving the individual authors' styles and approaches, some differences are to be expected in the way the key terms have been developed. However, the focus throughout the articles remains Vattimo's understanding and interpretation of each given term within his work, and not the personal take of the contributors of each entry.

Given the nature of this publication as a reference tool and a gateway to the philosopher's main concepts, we thought it preferable to keep the entries reasonably brief by providing key definitions and bibliographical references in order to facilitate further research of a given term. The list of entries also includes terms that are strictly cross-references (e.g., 'CHARITY [*CARITAS*] [see CHURCH; ONTOLOGICAL DIFFERENCE; THEOLOGY]'). Some cross-references are given within individual entries (except for terms that might be expected to be found throughout the articles, such as Heidegger, Nietzsche or weak thought). An index at the end of the volume lists the terms and related entries as they appear throughout the dictionary within and across specific articles.

Whenever possible, we have indicated bibliographical references based on the English translations of the original Italian texts, listed as abbreviated entries in the prelims. In the articles, a Vattimo text available in English is cited with an abbreviation; author–date formatting is used for all other cases (titles in Italian or in languages other than English have not been abbreviated).

The bibliography includes a comprehensive – though not exhaustive – list of publications by Vattimo in Italian in chronological order, followed by a list of works written collaboratively with other authors. The 'Critical Works on Vattimo' section lists a selection of texts that are useful for an in-depth exploration of Vattimo's thought within the context of scholarly critique – whether cited in the dictionary or not – while the 'Other Works' section is limited to works by other authors who have been cited in one or more entries.

A

ADORNO, THEODOR WIESENGRUND

Giovanni Giorgio

With Adorno, but beyond Adorno (1903–69): this is how Vattimo's relationship with Adorno's thought could be summarised. This, in fact, remains the term of reference, 'for the most part unspoken' (*AD*, 5) that goes with the Vattimian reflection, especially when it becomes clear that his personal development goes from an initial vision, marked by dialectics, to a more clearly hermeneutic vision (Giorgio 2006: 18–23). He would later say that 'a revised "Adornism", very deeply revised' was needed (Vattimo [1989c] 2000: 115).

Adorno, as is well known, finds in Auschwitz the event from which to pose the question of the failure of Western metaphysics (Adorno 1973 [1966]). Auschwitz represents not only the extreme consequence of a certain rationalistic vision of the world, but also and above all the anticipated image of the current unfolding of metaphysics (Horkheimer and Adorno 1969 [1947]), since 'a fully rationalized society is a prison precisely when it becomes a reality' (*BIS*, 152): it is the place where the 'link between metaphysics and violence' emerges (Vattimo 2007d: 403; see **violence**). By metaphysics, following Heidegger's line, we mean that Western tradition of thought for which, from Plato onwards, the idea of being is that of an order that organises the multiplicity of entities into unity. This order enjoys a stable presence, as it is founded on a *Grund*, accessible to reason, which anchors the totality of reality to itself and makes it depend on itself. Although there have been many *fundamenta inconcussa* in which Western reason wanted to anchor the truth (Antiseri 2003: 51), 'god' remains the figure that identifies them all.

But the most serious question of this tradition of thought is the one raised by Adorno and the reference to Auschwitz, since the 'given' metaphysical order does not only exist as a structure of reality, but also as an ethical-social discipline that legitimises a dominant power which is capable of deciding, as in the Shoah, who is worthy to live and who to die. This is why metaphysics is violent, because disciplinary power, legitimised by the knowledge of the foundation, puts the freedom of each individual, contingent and transient, as Adorno calls it, out of the question. The individual, in fact, is expropriated of his or her own freedom, and lives alienated because the meaning of his or her own existence, the one given within the choice of a life project, does not come from himself or herself, but from the possibilities 'given' by the current metaphysical order. Every contingent and transient entity, therefore, remains a function of that totalising order which is completely indifferent towards its needs, since – as happens exemplarily in Hegel – every detail is cancelled as a moment of the whole, leaving the latter to dominate as an unfolded totality. Auschwitz is the consequence of all this and the anticipation of that 'society that Adorno later called the "total organization", and which Chaplin represented in *Modern Times*' (Vattimo 2003c: 81). The result of this situation is clear for Vattimo: 'metaphysics is discredited also and above all because indifference to the life of the individual, to the rights of the contingent and of the transient, is what has always constituted its essential core: Auschwitz, somehow, only highlights all of this, unfolding its intolerable violence' (Vattimo 1987b: 76).

For these reasons Vattimo agrees with Adorno that the distrust of metaphysics 'and the program, variously enunciated between the nineteenth and twentieth centuries, of its "overcoming", has not, in the final analysis, [mainly] "theoretical" motivations, but rather ethical reasons' (Vattimo 1987b: 71). For the same reasons Vattimo appreciates Adorno's speculative effort to formulate a negative dialectic that preserves the freedom of the contingent and the transient (Giorgio 2006: 151–6). And yet he cannot help but notice that Adorno's thought does not seem to be completely consistent. This is evident in his aesthetic theory (Adorno 1970), where the work of art is characterised as a place of criticism of the existing world and, at the same time, of the appearance (*Schein*) of an alternative utopian world to the existing one, in which every alienation is overcome in a conciliation between existence and meaning. This is the *promesse du bonheur* that announces itself in the work of art, even if only as a utopia: what 'the finite, in its ephemeral and accidental nature rightfully aspires, is [therefore] the dialectical reconciliation that is also the telos of Hegel's absolute spirit' (*OR*, 152).

Right here, according to Vattimo, lies the unsolved problem of Adorno's philosophical proposal: it sees the emancipation from alienation as a reconciliation of the fracture between existence and meaning, albeit transferred to a utopian future, according to the metaphysical ideal, 'that is, [according to] the idea of true being as presence' (Vattimo 1987b: 81). In short, Adorno retains the idea, albeit utopian, that only when a new order, the 'true' one, is present and unfolded, will the freedom of the individual be reconciled with the necessity of the whole, without any conflicts.

The difficulties of the notion of negative dialectic, thus, only seem to express a more serious and radical problematic nature: that which encounters every attempt to go beyond metaphysics without abandoning the conception of being as an unfolded presence that determined it in its development, and which still dominates the thought of Hegel and Marx, to which Adorno remains attached. (Vattimo 1987b: 81)

In the end, according to Vattimo, the goal in Adorno's thought is always to establish a new 'true' order that replaces the current one, rather than getting out of this dynamic and assuming the idea of being not as a presence, but as an event (Vattimo 1983a; *WT*). Thus, even if Adorno is placed in the horizon opened by Nietzsche and Heidegger, for the identification of the link between metaphysics and violence, 'his remaining tied to the dialectic, and to the idea of being that it implies, makes him a still pre-Nietzschean and pre-Heideggerian thinker' (Vattimo 1987b: 81).

See also **aesthetics**; **death of God**; **Marxism/Italian Marxism**; **overcoming** (*Überwindung*).

AESTHETICS

Federico Vercellone

Aesthetics, the discipline that Gianni Vattimo taught at the University of Turin from 1964 to 1981, constitutes one of the main interests and focal points of his work, starting with his first book, *Il concetto di fare in Aristotele* (1961), and culminating in *Poesia e ontologia* (1967b; *ACT*), where one of the fundamental themes of his aesthetic research emerges: the relationship between the latter and the artistic avant-garde, within which he sees the possibility of an ontological interpretation of the work of art. It is a theme that runs throughout Vattimo's philosophy and connects Nietzsche with Heidegger. This is evidenced by two volumes following the one dedicated to Aristotle, *Ipotesi su Nietzsche* (1967a) and *Il soggetto e la maschera* (1974). Central to this is the theme of decision, which breaks into the time *continuum* and alters its course due to the intervention of the subject, graphically symbolised by the biting of the serpent's head. The episode in *Thus Spoke Zarathustra*, 'The Vision and the Enigma', proposes the reason for a decision that interrupts the linear course of time (and therefore the underlying traditions), and grafts within them the interruption, the very reason and moment of the decision. Here, for Vattimo, a route of communication and exchange opens up between Nietzsche and Ernst Bloch, a fusion of Nietzschean thought and utopian Marxism. The new utopian is linked here – as an aesthetic motif – to the theme of the mask, and thus to the theme of an appearance that is a manifestation of truth. From this point of view, Nietzsche's philosophy leads to a 'liberation of the symbolic', which in this context takes on an almost subversive (though not violent) scope, in keeping with the political-spiritual climate of those years. For Vattimo, the positivity of the mask and thus the stance in favour of appearance, brings into play a profound connection between Nietzsche and hermeneutics that had not been recognised by his mentors Luigi Pareyson and Hans-Georg Gadamer. In this context, Nietzsche becomes the one who revises, from a hermeneutic point of view, Heideggerian metaphysics as the 'oblivion of being', opening the way to its overcoming through the infinitude of interpretations. This previously unexplored link opens up a new path in Vattimo's thought that leads us in the direction of an 'ontology of decline', as expressed in *Beyond the Subject* and the idea/project of 'weak thought'. The ontology of decline presents this theme in the form of an indefinite liberation of being from the shackles of metaphysics, which creates a melancholic and ultimately positively aestheticising tone in Vattimo's thought.

From the great essay on Nietzsche to the idea of an ontology of decline as formulated in *Beyond the Subject*, a path opens up that leads towards 'weak thought'. It is a project that first took shape in the collective volume *Weak Thought* in which, through the mediation of postmodernism, a positive vision of the weakening of being is proposed that recalls the idea of a positivity of aestheticisation (against which Vattimo had instead argued in *ACT*). Aestheticisation combined with a positive view of nihilism constitutes the founding core of Vattimo's thought through *The Adventure of Difference*, *The End of Modernity* and up to *The Transparent Society*, in which aesthetic appearance is revealed almost as the positive characterisation of contemporary society dominated by the media and thus as an element that defines a much wider sphere than that of art. It is evident, in this context, that Vattimo is revising, in a theoretically decisive key, the analysis and negative evaluation of aestheticisation elaborated by Benjamin in an essay very important to Vattimo, 'The Work of Art in the Age of Its Technological Reproducibility'. Thanks to this passage, the political declination of Vattimo's thought also changes direction, acquiring a less radical and more confident dimension with regard to the present. The journey through postmodernity, as outlined in *The Adventure of Difference*, *The End of Modernity* and *The Transparent Society*, shapes a thought that relies on postmodern hope in a present that has opened up to differences, to an effective pluralism embodied in the many different media. Here, the positive declination of appearance, as revealed in Nietzsche's interpretation through the concept of the mask, is substantiated by immersing itself in the new pluralism of postmodern society, which is realised by virtue of the infinitude of interpretations permitted by the media itself. Benjamin's diagnosis of the aestheticisation of politics is almost overturned in this context, and there even seems to be a more intense transition, mediated by the positive interpretation of nihilism and of aesthetics in politics, which constitutes one of the salient motifs of Vattimo's thought.

See also **postmodern art/aesthetics**.

ANALYTIC AND CONTINENTAL PHILOSOPHY

Davide Monaco

According to Vattimo, the conceptual opposition, which is widely diffused in contemporary debate, between an analytic philosophy of Anglo-Saxon origin and a Continental philosophy of European origin constitutes, more than a simple historiographic schema, the enunciation of a central and decisive problem for today's philosophy. The task before philosophy is to reconstruct or mend the split between analytic and Continental philosophy, between 'truth' and 'actuality', between structure and event (Vattimo 1997a: xv).

The dichotomy between the analytic and Continental philosophers is overlaid by similar, though not perfectly corresponding, dichotomies, such as the Rortyan dichotomy between a Kantian, epistemological line and a Hegelian, hermeneutical line in contemporary thought. The Kantian line is made up of all those philosophies that, interested primarily in seizing the transcendental conditions of the possibility of knowledge and of rationality in general, focus their attention on logic, epistemology and the forms of scientific knowledge or even of ethical action with the aim of identifying their universal and structural elements. The Hegelian line, instead, constitutes those philosophies that are attentive above all to the historical concreteness of forms of life, language and scientific paradigms, and that therefore place the question of the historicity of knowledge and of philosophy itself at the centre of attention.

Another way of formulating the antithesis is the one used by the later Foucault when he spoke of one philosophy as an 'analytic of truth' and another as an 'ontology of actuality'. Aside from Foucault's hypothesis, for Vattimo the ontology of actuality opens up a divide within the Continental group between those thinkers who, more faithful to Heidegger, believe that one should still try to talk about being, and those who, like Derrida, think that this would make one a prisoner of a metaphysical perspective.

Vattimo underlines the profound analogies linking the linguistic outcomes of Continental philosophy, especially the later Heidegger and hermeneutics, and the developments of analytic philosophy, in particular Wittgenstein's *Philosophical Investigations*. The analogy is not only about the priority assumed by the dimension of language, but also the emergence of a 'hermeneutic' or 'reflective-transcendental' need. There is a 'semiotic transformation of philosophy' that reclaims some of the traits of the existentialist and hermeneutic critique of the Kantian transcendental subject, through the underlining of its finiteness and historicity. The shift from the centrality of the transcendental subject to language does not occur without profound consequences for the way reason and subjectivity are conceived. Language is not something that is exercised by the subject as a representative of universal reason, as the a priori activities of Kantian reason were, but as an intersubjective historical phenomenon. The world is formed of language games that are essentially dialogical and thus intersubjective and historically becoming. The individual is immersed in a web of intersubjective relations that he or she does not enter into by choice, but which for him or her constitute the condition of possibility of any level of access to objectivity.

See also **Derrida, Jacques; language; ontology of actuality; truth; Wittgenstein, Ludwig.**

ANARCHY

Ian Alexander Moore

At the end of his interview with Jeffrey Robbins ('A Prayer for Silence'), Vattimo imagines the possibility of slowing down the reproduction of capital, a process that would involve, not violent uprising, but (positively) creating independent centres and (negatively) boycotting and 'simply working against' it. 'This is why', he concludes, 'I sometimes call myself an anarchist' (*ADG*, 112–13).

Vattimo goes on to reference Reiner Schürmann's seminal reading of Heidegger (Schürmann 1987), as he often does when discussing anarchy. With Schürmann, Vattimo agrees that Heidegger marks the site at which metaphysical principles collapse and thinking can no longer secure unshakable foundations for action. In contrast to Schürmann, however, Vattimo does not believe that this interpretation of Heidegger is a truer account of Being or results in closer proximity to it, an aspiration Vattimo denigrates as 'mystical' (*FT*, 32; *DN*, 188; 2008b: 10; 2009d: 340).[1] Instead, on Vattimo's reading – and even against the letter of Heidegger's text – the dissolution of principles means nothing short of a dissolution of Being (*DN*, 189; *EM*, 19 and *passim*). Being is nothing other than its dispensations (Vattimo 2008b: 9–10). This affords new possibilities for conceiving of anarchy.

Vattimo uses 'anarchy' and its cognates in five different ways, to describe 1) postmodernity, 2) hermeneutics, 3) Christianity, 4) post-metaphysical political practice, and, in stark contrast to the foregoing, 5) populist reaction.

1) Postmodernity is itself an age of anarchy, which we should take literally as 'without' (*an-*) 'ultimate ground' (*archē*), not as violent. Violence, rather, is always based on absolutes (*OR*, 116; see also *ADG*, 43, 93).

2) Hermeneutics is essentially anarchic, not because interpretation is altogether baseless – it must necessarily draw on the traditions it inherits – but because it can never find an absolute foundation that would justify a claim to absolute certainty. (See especially the chapter 'Interpretation as Anarchy', co-authored with Santiago Zabala, in *HC*, 79–87, as well as Zabala 2009.) Furthermore, this anarchic hermeneutics involves attention to the silenced voices of history (*FT*, 32).

3) For Vattimo, Christian *kenosis* – God's 'emptying out' of himself in the Incarnation and on the Cross, along with the concomitant confounding of worldly power – can be understood in terms of the weakening of Being and of reality. But, with Novalis, it can also be understood as 'true anarchy', which 'is the fertile element of religion' (*AC*, 80, quoting Novalis).

4) 'Anarchy' can also signify autonomous existence and practice 'on the margins' of the hegemonic order (Vattimo 2009d: 343; see also 324; *EM*, 162; *FT*, 129–30; *NBG*, 84–5). The left should create a society that would increasingly tolerate and allow for the expansion of these anarchic margins (*NE*, 113).

5) Finally, Vattimo occasionally (and inconsistently) uses 'anarchy' to signify violent reaction. For example, in 'Globalization and the Relevance of Socialism', he analyses two possibilities for resistance to economic globalisation. The first he calls 'populist anarchism', which marks 'a violent impulse of revolt against a global hegemony that no longer meets

---

[1] Schürmann, for his part (2003: 550), contests Vattimo's critique. See also Schürmann (2007 [1984]).

any external checks' (*NE*, 123, 126).² It resembles Durkheim's theory of anomie, where one curtails freedom in order to safeguard it from incursion from without (*NE*, 129). The second possibility Vattimo calls federalism.

For more on the role of anarchy in Vattimo's work, see Birmingham 2017; D'Angelo 2016; and Ginev 2016; see also **globalisation**; *kenosis*; **postmodernism/postmodernity**; **Schürmann, Reiner**.

ANDENKEN (REMEMBRANCE)

Andrzej Zawadzki

Vattimo develops the concept of remembrance (*Andenken*) most extensively in his earliest text devoted to this idea: '*An-denken*: Thinking and the Foundation' (*AD*), and later on also in *The End of Modernity* and *Etica dell'interpretazione* (1989a). His ideas are essential to the contemporary reflection on the phenomenon of remembering in history and culture, in which *Mnemosyne* and *Lethe*, memory and forgetting, are treated not as opposites, but complementarily (Weinrich 1999; Ricoeur 2004). The fundamental concepts by which Vattimo considers *Andenken* are the following: representation, difference as opposed to identity and totalisation, hermeneutics and interpretation, tradition and transmission.

Andenken is a concept very close to *Verwindung* (see **convalescence** [*Verwindung*]). Both are drawn from the writings of the late Heidegger. In *What Is Called Thinking?* Heidegger characterises memory as consciousness, attentiveness, concentration, an ability to 'recall', that is, to restore that which is past and unendurable, which is in the most proper sense given to be thought and must be preserved as a gift. However, this preserving is also forgetting, but interpreted not as deficiency, but as concealing, an inevitable dimension of memory. Therefore, memory in *What Is Called Thinking?*, being far removed from the colloquial usage of the term, becomes a model for authentic thinking (*Denken*) which also constitutes a thanksgiving (*Danken*) for thinking itself, which is a gift entrusted to humankind (Heidegger 1968).

In Vattimo's interpretation, *Andenken*, together with *Verwindung* and, to some extent, *pietas*, is a basic concept to describe the post-metaphysical and post- (late) metaphysics, as well as the *grand récit* of modernity (see *pietas*). *Andenken* plays the same role in post-metaphysical thought as

---

2 In his book on Vattimo, Guarino (2009: 5, 33, 36, 45) uses 'anarchy' only in this last, pejorative sense.

the idea of the foundation, or ground, has in metaphysics, being close to the Heideggerian *Ab-grund* (*AD*, 134). *Andenken* means a rejection of philosophy as representation: since Being (*Sein*) is not beings (*seienden*), or something present (both in the spatial and temporal sense), thinking about it as remembrance must be opposed to presence (in the Heideggerian sense) and re-presentation (as the doubling of an original presence). *Andenken* is not limited to the ability to present what is absent since in this case it would remain limited to the horizon of instrumental, objectivising thought: 'The *An-denken* to which Heidegger summons us cannot be conceived as a re-memoration that "recuperates" Being as something we can meet face to face. Re-memoration recalls Being precisely as that which can only be recalled, and never re-presented' (*DN*, 188). Therefore, thinking as *An-denken* is a thinking of what thought does not fully have at its disposal and cannot fully possess.

Thinking as *Andenken* differs from critical philosophy, too. In another essay from *The Adventure of Difference*, 'Dialectic and Difference', Vattimo contrasts Heideggerian *Andenken* with Hegelian *Erinnerung* (memory, remembering). The latter has a metaphysical character, since its essence is the internalising or appropriation of what is external with respect to the subject in the process of reaching absolute self-knowledge. In contrast, *Andenken*, as thinking based on a conception of being as transmission (trace), *Geschick* (Heidegger 1991; see also Derrida's concept of *envoi*, Derrida 1980: 71; 1987a: 109–44), leaves the past as passed without any attempt to reappropriate and unify it, thus undermining any possibility of identity (contrarily, '*Andenken* thinks Being as *difference*'; *AD*, 125) and totalisation. In this sense, it can be called a 'weak' memory and functions as a model for weak thought in general. Here we may clearly perceive Vattimo's attempt to connect the two traditions from which weak thought emerges: post-Heideggerian philosophy of difference and the negative tendencies in dialectical philosophy, especially those of Benjamin and Adorno (*WT*, 41–3).

Andenken can be easily identified with hermeneutics, specifically the radical version, which emphasises the open and infinite character of interpretation, as never constituting a final sense of being, existence or the text. Vattimo defines this aspect of hermeneutics with the term *sfondante* (literally 'breaking down' or 'undermining'; *sfondante* is the opposite of *fondante* – that which builds, grounds – and is close to such ideas as *dislocazione*, dislocation, or *spaesamento*, disorientation), which in his later conceptions becomes the point of departure for the building of a nihilistic hermeneutics.

On the other hand, *Andenken* has also a more 'constructive' aspect, because instead of a 'strong' foundation it nevertheless provides a certain, even if 'weak', ground of understanding and mediation. This 'weak' hermeneutic ground is based on the idea of *koiné*, a common language, which is spoken by a historical, concrete society and which is opposed to the abstract and formal language of science. Thanks to this, it facilitates understanding between the atomised outcomes of particular sciences, fulfils regulating functions in reference to human choices concerning the future, and, most importantly, ensures continuity between the past and the present, as an 'inscription' into tradition, which is also understood as a process of transmitting (Gadamer 2006 [2004]: 291) and response to it. Hence Vattimo, this time referring more specifically to Gadamer and the Hegelian conception of objective spirit, speaks of the 'classical' conception of truth as a belonging to a defined cultural horizon of collective experience.

ANIMAL

Felice Cimatti

Animality should not always, nor mainly, be looked for where 'animals' are explicitly mentioned. In particular, this applies to Vattimo's philosophy. When he explicitly deals with animality he highlights the now customary problem of animals suffering in biomedical experimentation or industrial exploitation. In the recent essay 'On Politics and Love' he writes that 'we need, first of all, to see the suffering of "others" [. . .] the forgotten of all kinds (third or fourth world, the marginalized and exploited, animals subjected to biomedical experiments)' (*BIS*, 91). The question of animality is not treated as a main philosophical problem but as a particular case of the general ethical question of the 'suffering' of the 'forgotten others'.

However, if one takes into account Vattimo's whole theoretical trajectory, the question of animality appears as an implicit point of arrival of his philosophy. Such a question places itself at the extreme end of the process of self-emptying of Western metaphysics. In this context, animality represents the complete realisation of the process of *kenosis*, that is, the self-renouncing to the will to power on the part of the subject. In *Il soggetto e la maschera* (1974), the question of animality appears when Vattimo discusses the meaning of the controversial Nietzschean figure of the *Übermensch*, which Vattimo does not translate as 'super-man' (that is, a human endowed with more than human powers) but as *oltreuomo* (beyond the man, or 'overman'). Therefore the *Übermensch* is the living being who leaves behind the 'metaphysical' humanity made up of resentment, violence and the will to dominate the entire world. In this sense such an *Übermensch* is no longer human, but rather is a post-human animal. The key characteristic of the metaphysical subject is the dualism between the human being on one side, and the rest of the world on the other, a world that is at his or her own complete disposal. Such a dualism digs a ditch (Western metaphysics is nothing but such a ditch) between the mind of the subject and the body and nature. In particular, it is a dualism between the actual life and the meaning or value of such a life, a value that lies outside the ground level of existence. It is exactly such a dualism between immanence and transcendence (body and mind, life and essence, subject and object) that the *Übermensch* as a post-human animal leaves behind. For this reason, into this life there will be 'first of all [. . .] identity of existence and value' (Vattimo [1974] 1994: 285); that is, it is a way of living that completely adheres to actual life, therefore it will be beyond metaphysics and dualism.

According to this line of thought, the post-human animal is not to be sought in the untamed past of humanity, as has been done in many interpretations of Nietzsche. On the contrary, according to Vattimo, the animality of the *Übermensch* lies after and beyond 'metaphysical' humanity: in fact 'the Nietzschean "return" to nature [. . .] properly is not a return, but rather a first effective access to it' (Vattimo [1974] 1994: 344). Therefore, if the question of animality can pose itself only at the end of metaphysics and anthropocentrism, in Vattimo one can find it at least implicitly when he discusses the extreme outcomes of our age; for example, when he asks himself whether future human life must

> be founded/ungrounded on a naturalness, an animality, or maybe even a silence that is more than the silence between words which makes possible the differential play of the signifier? This is the real *animal silence* which is the pro-venance of human words and to which, in some as yet still-to-be-discovered sense, these words refer. (*AD*, 155)

What is such an 'animal silence' if not a condition that is at the same time before and beyond humanity? Before, because it refers to the always removed animal origin of humanity; beyond, because such a condition can only be attained by a human being who voluntarily renounces the arrogance of humanism and anthropocentrism. From this point of view, as Vattimo himself explicitly admits, animality will be the theme of the future philosophy:

> The weakened subject should thus also be open to a less melodramatic relation with his own mortality. That is also the reason why I allude at a certain point in these essays to 'animality' [. . .] Through animality [. . .] possibilities of dialogue

seem to open up between the heirs of Heidegger and other theorists of human reality [. . .] But for the present these avenues still remain to be explored. (*AD*, 6)

APEL, KARL-OTTO

Eduardo Mendieta

Karl-Otto Apel (1922–2017) was one of the important post-war German philosophers and unquestionably Jürgen Habermas's most important philosophical partner, ally and colleague (Mendieta 2003; Nascimento 2019; see **Habermas, Jürgen**). Apel was key to the 'linguistic turn' in German philosophy. He introduced into the Heideggerian-dominated German philosophical world ordinary-language philosophy, Charles Sanders Peirce and Charles M. Morris's semiotics, as well as Wittgenstein's ideas about 'language games' and 'forms of life'. Apel, however, was one of the few German philosophers to study closely Italian philosophy. His 1963 *Habilitationschrift, Die Idee der Sprache in der Tradition des Humanismus von Dante bis Vico* (*The Idea of Language in the Tradition of Humanism from Dante to Vico*) (Apel 1963) remains a major contribution to the study of the development of the philosophy of language out of the sources of humanism. In the introduction to this book, Apel argues that modern hermeneutical and phenomenological theories of language owe their foundations to the Italian Renaissance philosophers.

Apel developed his unique philosophical position, which he called alternatively 'transcendental pragmatics' and 'transcendental pragmatic-semiotics' (Mendieta 2003), in long systematic essays, which he published from the mid-1950s until the end of his life (Apel 2017). His monumental two-volume collection of essays, appropriately called *Transformation der Philosophie* (*Transformation of Philosophy*) (Apel 1973, and 1980 in partial translation) called for the convergence of semiotics, hermeneutics and pragmatics in order to develop a normative philosophy of language that would depart from what he called the 'a priori of the communication community' (Apel 1980: 225–300), which would also serve as a foundation to what he called discourse ethics (Apel 1988). Apel, along with Habermas, developed the conception that language, both as communication and action (meaning that we do things with words and that human action is always linguistically mediated), entails a basic set of normative commitments: to truth, to truthfulness (or authenticity) and to rightness (or justice).

Apel, like Habermas, was influenced by Heidegger and Gadamer's phenomenological hermeneutics, but he was also very critical of the historicising and thus relativising of reason. Both, therefore, also repudiated Heidegger's Nazism as a consequence of the decisionist character of his phenomenological hermeneutics. It is for this reason that Vattimo frequently refers to and criticises them jointly, notwithstanding their differences (see *EM*, 113–14, 146; *TS*, 18–21, 24, 109–10; *FT*, 39). For Vattimo, Apel attempts to escape the consequences of the 'hermeneutic *koiné*' by retreating to Kantian transcendentalism, a position that is no longer tenable after the Heideggerian phenomenological-hermeneutic transformation of philosophy (*EM*, 114). Vattimo also criticises Apel's implicit conception of the 'self-transparency of reason', which disavows the hermeneutic task of clarifying reason to itself though language (*TS*, 18–21), as well as Apel's modelling discourse on the community of researchers and scientists, with its attendant scienticisation of human communication (*TS*, 24).

Apel, unlike Habermas, read Vattimo and criticised him for following Heidegger and Gadamer in the direction of Rortyan pragmatic historicism, Derridean irrationalist postmodernism and a Nietzschean reduction of reason to the 'will to power' (Apel 1988: 382, 384, 389). Apel, most importantly, criticises Vattimo for following uncritically Heidegger's project of de-transcendentalising philosophy, which resulted in the post-metaphysical, and thus post-philosophical, and consequently post-rational, if not irrational, tenor of postmodern philosophy (Apel 1998: 508).

ARISTOTLE

Giovanni Giorgio

The interpretation of Aristotle proposed by Vattimo in his earliest works focuses on the hermeneutic character of 'doing'. Vattimo starts from a well-known notion, when he argues that, according to Aristotle, the *téchne* is to operate orderly in view of an end. Precisely this last feature allows Aristotle to unite *téchne* and *phýsis*, in a 'similarity between the *process* of nature and the *process* of art' (Vattimo [1960b] 2007: 226). The *téchne*, in fact, imitates the *phýsis*, in the sense of '*a doing as, a producing in the manner of*' (Vattimo [1961] 2007: 42), as it produces substances by operating in an orderly and finalistic manner, organising the multiple moments and aspects of the production process in view of the particular shape to be created. Relevant for Vattimo is the fact that the *téchne* does not submit to the natural 'given': 'it is not a question of recognizing the nature of the thing as given once and for all, limited to where nature, *physis*, wants to take it' (Vattimo [1961] 2007: 128), but rather of taking it beyond this alleged necessity. Brought back into the sphere of human finalistic doing, things take on ever new possibilities, without a necessary essence, defined once and for all.

In this sense, the primacy of the theoretical-descriptive attitude declines in favour of the hermeneutic-practical one. Through the *téchne*, humans, entering upon an interaction with things, reveal these things in unexplored possibilities, starting from their world projects (Vattimo [1963] 1989). So, thanks to the making of the *téchne*, humans shape themselves while giving shape to a world of nature. They discover and live their freedom, they know themselves not to be defined once and for all according to a 'given' essence; in fact, 'man' does not exist, but only historical 'men' and 'women', that is, determined historical humanities. By transforming the world, human beings transform themselves and discover themselves as a nexus of possibilities, as a project and not as a 'given' (*datum*).

The question that arises at this point is, if humankind is a project and not a 'given', does this project aim at an ultimate goal, or does it remain an open planning? Vattimo answers the question, via the idea of an accomplished work of art (Pareyson 1960 [1954]), which provides an aesthetic pleasure that derives from its perfection as a finished form, organically structured in a complete unity. From this point of view, he returns to Aristotle to address the *vexata quaestio* of catharsis in the tragic work of art (Vattimo [1960a] 2007). This is given, Vattimo explains, due to the fact that pitiful and terrible events, insofar as they are included in the structured construction of the tragic plot, receive their own explanation: existence receives a meaning (Vattimo [1977b] 2010: 23–6). It is precisely here that Vattimo bends to the dialectical position, since the work of art, understood in this way, represents precisely the place of that reconciliation of all conflicts, which closes the historical planning of humankind in a sense that is fully deployed in presence. The metaphysical vision of being is thus re-proposed as an unfolded and necessary presence, from which the whole previous path instead pushed to leave.

See also **aesthetics**; **metaphysics**; **overcoming** (*Überwindung*); *poiesis/poesis*.

ART

Federico Vercellone

Vattimo brings art into the equation above all in the first and second phase of his theoretical journey, the one that begins with *Il concetto di fare in*

Aristotele (1961) and culminates with *Il soggetto e la maschera* (1974), then continues with *The Adventure of Difference* to arrive at *The Transparent Society*. For the most part, this is the long period during which he taught aesthetics at the University of Turin. In marked contrast to many aspects of aesthetics during this phase of the second half of the twentieth century, Vattimo's philosophical reflection on art is never defined as a philosophy of art, and is never considered in his thought as an autonomous and decontextualised component. Vattimo takes his cue from an original interpretation of 'the concept of doing in Aristotle'. In the course of his work he identified, above all through his journey through Nietzsche and hermeneutics, an emancipatory and liberating scope of art that also comes from his association with Ernst Bloch. His emphasis on the hermeneutic circle in Schleiermacher's work, as seen in *Schleiermacher filosofo dell'interpretazione* (1968), also falls within this framework. And it is from the centrality of the circle that a liberating dimension of artistic activity emerges, through Schleiermacher's and Gadamer's analyses, as outlined in Nietzsche's interpretation in *Il soggetto e la maschera*.

Thus, two different approaches arise that also connect the two authors to whom Vattimo's work most extensively refers: Nietzsche and Heidegger. In his thought, the idea of the hermeneutic circle and Nietzsche's idea of the 'will to power as art', understood as the metaphysical superabundance of symbolic production that establishes reality itself, are thus intertwined. These are themes that were hotly discussed in Italian philosophy, in particular with regard to the concept of the 'will to power', a notion about which the long-distance confrontation between Vattimo and Massimo Cacciari was particularly lively. The will to power – interpreted by Vattimo not as a doctrine but as a hermeneutic model – becomes the organ of a deconstruction of the symbolic in an anti-metaphysical key. This is an activity that closely resembles the work of the artistic avant-garde, who Vattimo sees as prophetic representatives of bourgeois rebellion, almost allegories of a time to come that these artists are unable to fully understand because of the historical conditioning, defined from a Marxist perspective, of their point of view. The idea of a liberating scope of art linked to its hermeneutic connotation and its symbolic potential, which unfolds as an infinite interpretation, is combined with the ontological scope of the work as is revealed, on the basis of Heideggerian theory, in *Poesia e ontologia* ([1967b] 2008; *ACT*). This path is further developed in *Il soggetto e la maschera*, the book in which Vattimo develops his interpretation of Nietzsche, starting with *The Birth of Tragedy*. With regard to this first book by Nietzsche, Vattimo overturns the literalness of the German philosopher's initial Schopenhauerian attitude by reading tragedy not as a liberation from the Dionysian but as a liberation of the Dionysian, and thus of the Schopenhauerian 'will to live'.

The tone of Vattimo's aesthetics, resonant with the avant-garde, is manifested again in later contributions such as the one on Benjamin and Heidegger, who are approached, despite their apparent differences, on the basis of the affinity between and quasi-homology of the concepts of Benjamin's *shock* and Heidegger's *Stoß* (*TS*). It is precisely this dimension of shock or transformative 'impact' – to echo Heidegger – that makes the conceptions of the two philosophers, who are in fact very different from each other, similar, and implies and generates the idea of an aesthetics of oscillation. What emerges here very strongly is a political engagement with art that follows up on one of the most significant features of the thought of Vattimo, who increasingly interprets art in a hermeneutic key. From this point of view, it becomes an application that undermines the conservative foundation of Gadamerian hermeneutics, that *Wirkungsgeschichte*, that 'history of effects' that eliminates the new radical from its own existence, which is instead negated by the transformative role of art.

See also **postmodern art/aesthetics**.

BEING

Rogi Thomas

Vattimo's discourse on Being is shaped by his reading of both Nietzsche's 'eternal return' and Heidegger's 'overcoming of metaphysics' discourse on the end of the modern era and on postmodernity (*EM*, 3). Postmodernity, thus, is a transformation of Being as such (*NE*, 3). His approach to Being is, in fact, a coming to earth of being because he sees Heidegger's critique of humanism and Nietzsche's announcement of an accomplished nihilism as positive moments for a philosophical reconstruction (*EM*, 1), resulting in 'the negation of the stable structures of Being' (*EM*, 3). Being is not understood as that which *is* but as that which *becomes*. Being occurs according to necessary and recognisable rhythms which nevertheless maintain a certain identifiable stability. As an alternative, they radically conceive of Being as an event 'to understand at what point "we are" and at what point Being itself is' in its unfolding (*EM*, 3).

For Vattimo, 'ontology' is the interpretation of the 'present situation' (*NE*, 3–4), and since Being is nothing apart from its 'event', it occurs when it and when we historicise ourselves (*EM*, 3). Therefore, Being 'events' itself through history and in numerous other domains: existential, ethical, epistemological, aesthetic, linguistic and theological. Consequently, there is no disclosure of Being that is final or ultimate, but Being maintains itself through its perpetual self-interpretation. Through 'weakening' of the traditional structure of metaphysics, 'Being' allows 'thought to situate itself within the post-modern and post-metaphysical condition' (*EM*, 11). The genuinely hermeneutical and postmodern revelation of Being is through its broken transmissions. Being links us to our mortality through the handing down of linguistic messages from one generation to another (*EM*, 12). The perpetual death and resurrection of Being discloses itself as 1) 'an event', 2) 'as weakening', 3) 'as secularisation', 4) 'as forgetting', 5) 'as being toward death', 6) 'as language', 7) 'as epochality' and 8) 'as charity'.

1) Being as an 'event' (existential): The *eventual* nature of being supports metaphysical nihilism. It reveals the nature of Being as always disruptive but renewing at the same time, which presents a further theological and existential motif, that is, the continual disclosure of infinite being. For Heidegger, the objects of our experience are given only within a horizon which is not objectively visible. Being is a horizon of self-disclosure and not a general structure of objects. Since it is not an object, it does not have stability: 'the event of Being lies in the double sense of the genitive: the horizon is the opening belonging to Being, but it is also that to which Being itself belongs' (*AC*, 21). Being manifests itself through us as an event by virtue of us being interpreters, forever uncovering new ways of being 'on the way' (*AC*, 22). The 'eventing' similarly demonstrates 'the weakening of Being': it shakes all claims to 'peremptoriness advanced by metaphysics'. Vattimo also talks of a 'leap of being'. Being does not manifest itself abstractly, the *Ereignis* is an event that happens daily. This daily continuity of events establishes the 'thread of the tradition, onto which we leap' (*AC*, 22; *NE*, 16).

2) The weakening of Being (theological): For Vattimo, the post-metaphysical reflexive re-engaging with religion and associated rebirth of the spiritual is a consequence of the destiny of Being as weakening, that is, of Being divesting itself of its absoluteness and becoming ever more worldly. The process reflects, for Vattimo, the *kenosis* (*AC*, 22–4; see *kenosis*).

3) Being and secularisation (theological): Vattimo hermeneutically links the secularisation of modernity with the end of metaphysics and the 'discovery' of Being as weakening (*AC*, 34–5). The conception has

its foundation in the doctrine of redemption through giving. It offers a positive side to Nietzsche's and Heidegger's nihilism, characterising it as a positive historical process of secularisation. If the weakening of Being realises itself as the *kenosis* of God, secularisation cannot be considered the abandonment of religion but as a paradoxical realisation of Being's religious vocation (*AC*, 24; see **secularisation**).

4) Being as forgetting (eschatological and theological): For Vattimo, the 'forgetting of Being' – that is, metaphysics – advanced because philosophy mistook language as a criterion of things rather than a clarification of what emerges in experience. It is possible to overcome the oblivion of the 'forgetting' of Being if reflection on the ontological 'significance' of the present situation is prioritised. Vattimo observes that Being is never totally forgotten: not wholly dissolved or vanished (*EM*, 19–20). When Being is 'annihilated and forgotten' it is actually transformed into an entirely new value (*EM*, 20), that is, reduced to 'exchange value' (*EM*, 21).

5) Being towards death (theological and ethical): For Vattimo, the 'showing' and 'shattering' (*Zeigen*) of the 'word' reflects Heidegger's 'being-toward-death'. The link between 'language' and 'mortality' 'flashes before us', but in an 'unthematised' manner. It suggests that 'the shattering of the word' in 'originary saying' and poetry should be understood in relation to the constitutive mortality of Dasein (*EM*, 69). The 'truthfulness' of Dasein's being is always revealed by its orientation towards death. The connection between Dasein and being-toward-death is brought out by posing the problem of the totality of the structures associated with Dasein. Dasein becomes thinkable as a totality only by anticipating, and resolving upon, its own death. 'Among all the possibilities that constitute Dasein's project, that is, its being-in-the-world, dying is the only possibility that Dasein cannot avoid' (*EM*, 116). Death would render impossible all the other possibilities for which humanity in fact lives. Precisely through its remaining a permanent possibility, death acts as the factor that allows all other possibilities to manifest themselves as possibilities. The hermeneutic totality of Dasein exists only in relation to the constitutive possibility of no longer being (there) (*EM*, 116). Historicity, the opening up of human existence, and the refusal to let it be subsumed within Being metaphysically understood signifies mortality. Since the world is given as world only to the gaze of Dasein and its 'thrown project', and since this project is endlessly finite, it can be concluded that Being is not a fixed timelessness but the infinite passage of finite projects. Being is the event of its ahistorical historicity (*NE*, 74).

6) Being and language (linguistic): Vattimo connects Being and language. The analysis of Dasein as a 'hermeneutical totality', and the effort to free thought from the limits of metaphysics by appeal to the notion of 'rec-

ollection' provide two elements that link Being and language (*EM*, 115). Like Heidegger and Wittgenstein, Vattimo regards language as the house of Being. For Gadamer, Being that can be understood is language. For Heidegger, this dissolution of Being into language resolves Being into the events of language. For Vattimo, this renders language the locus of a total mediation of every experience of the world. In consequence, every occurrence of Being is characterised as that which speaks to the individual, rather than being that of which the individual speaks. Thus, language is the locus, the concrete realisation of the collective ethos of a 'historically determined society' (*EM*, 130–2). Language is the emergent being of that society (see **language**).

7) The epochality and aperture of Being (existential): Being's permanent difference from beings signifies that philosophy cannot know Being through beings. Both the ontological difference and the epochal character of Being prevent us from establishing a positive relationship between Being and beings. However, for Vattimo, the self-concealing of Being cannot be conceived as a 'being-present' somewhere outside of the world of beings, as if Being really were something or someone that is given somewhere. 'Being is not, except as *epoché*: Being is nothing but its history, its epoch' (*ACT*, 23). Thus, 'Being is the illumination of the realm within which beings appear'. Epochality is the authentic path of access to Being to the extent that it cannot be reduced to beings or stand outside an epoch (*ACT*, 23). Vattimo also suggests that the philosophical thought of Being has no legitimation beyond the aperture of Being in which it finds itself thrown (*NE*, 11). The 'throwness' in which existence is always already found is explicitly historical. Being is the aperture within which humankind and the world, subject and object, can enter an ever-changing relationship.

8) Being, charity and value: For Vattimo, the Christian teaching of charity is not exclusively an ethical consequence of accepting the objective truth of God. Rather, it is a call that arises from the historical event of Incarnation, and it speaks of the nihilistic vocation of Being. It is a teleology in which every ontic structure is weakened in favour of ontological Being, namely the *Verbum*, a shared dialogue (*Gespräch*) that constitutes our historical being (*AC*, 112). Nihilism is characterised by the death of God, and the reduction of Being to commodifiable values (*EM*, 20). This reduction of Being to value places Being in the power of the subject who manipulates such commodities for its own ends. Nihilism entails the illegitimate claim that instead of existing in an autonomous, independent and foundational way, Being is subjugated to the subject (*EM*, 21). The subject and not Being is placed at the centre of things.

BELIEF

Eduardo Mendieta

Belief (*credere*), most immediately, refers to the English title of Vattimo's book *Credere di credere* (1996a). In the sequel to this book, Vattimo notes that the expression *credere di credere* (believing that one believes) sounds paradoxical as much in English as in Italian (*AC*, 1). To believe means to have faith, conviction or certainty in a *credo*. One's belief is one's faith, one's confession. To believe also means to opine, to have a view about something, to hazard an opinion. While the former sense of belief seems unconditional and peremptory, the latter is tentative and abstemious. It is the tension between these two senses that Vattimo has sought to reconcile over nearly a half a century of philosophising on what can and should be believed in the aftermath of the end of metaphysics, secularisation, the metaphorisation of ritualistic and natural violence, the de-religionisation of Christianity, and the weakening of Being – in a sentence, what remains of Christianity in our post-metaphysical and post-secular age.

'Belief' also refers to a complex of interpretations and ideas in Vattimo's thinking that are in evidence as early as his essay 'Metaphysics, Violence, Secularization' from 1986 (Vattimo 1988d: 45–61). In this essay, Vattimo articulates the links between the Western metaphysical tradition, violence, the most recent attempts to overcome this complicity in the works of Nietzsche and Heidegger, and the failed attempts by Adorno and Levinas to overcome metaphysics and its violent inheritances. Vattimo argues that the overcoming of Western metaphysics, as best articulated in Heidegger's call to deconstruct the tradition so as to overcome the violence of reducing Being to beings, is related to the project of secularisation. The entwining of metaphysics and theology that is evident in the work of Levinas reveals how the task of overcoming metaphysics is entangled with secularisation (Vattimo 1988d: 61).

Since then, in a series of important works (*ADG*; *B*; *AC*; *FR*; *R*; and Vattimo and Girard 2010), Vattimo has expanded and deepened a series of related interpretations that could be called his post-religious philosophy of Christianity (*ADG*, 37). At the centre of this philosophy is the claim that weak ontology, or the ontology of weakening, ought to be understood as the culmination of a theology of secularisation (*B*, 63, 65). For Vattimo, secularisation is the essence of modernity, which came about because of Christianity, and thus secularisation is the essence of Christianity. Vattimo makes a distinction between a 'negative' and 'positive' secularisation, which parallels the distinction between 'negative' and 'positive' nihilism. While 'negative' secularisation is to be understood as the dispossession and delegitimation of all religious claims, leading to the disempowerment, abolition and evaporation of these claims, 'positive' secularisation means the liberation and acceptance of a weakened, de-laicised, de-theologised, non-religious Christianity (*B*, 43, 65). Christianity lives on precisely because of secularisation; or, secularisation is one of the means by which Christianity preserves itself. The end of metaphysics, which is loudly announced with Nietzsche's proclamation of the 'death of God', is at the same time the announcement of the gods to come. This is the 'nihilistic rediscovery of Christianity' (*B*, 33–4).

For Vattimo, this means that 'weak ontology' must be understood as a 'transcription' of the Christian message, perhaps its most faithful inheriting interpretation (*B*, 42), insofar as 'weak thought' also inherits the Christian tradition of a disempowered Christianity. This claim is based on a more fundamental argument, namely that the core doctrine, principle, interpretation of Christianity is that of *kenosis*, namely the doctrine of God's incarnation in human flesh, or God's abasement to the level of humanity, which catalysed a gospel and theology of a 'non-violent and non-absolute God' (*B*, 39). The God of the 'Book', which is revealed in Holy Scripture and belongs to the history of the interpretation of that 'Book', is a *kenotic* God, a God whose revelation takes place in salvation history, the history of the liberation of humanity. *Kenosis* is understood as the ongoing event of salvation by God's abasement, which is understood philosophically as the weakening of Being (*AC*, 38, 53, 80, 91). This weakening of Being, qua *kenosis*, means that the abasement of God must also be understood as the weakening of reason qua the secularisation of reason, that is, reason without universal guarantees, references, grounds or divine alibis (*B*, 92).

What remains of Christianity for Vattimo is the key message of the Gospel, the call to 'charity' and the love of one's neighbours (*B*, 92). In an essay from 2005, Vattimo links his arguments about Christian charity to Christian anti-authoritarianism (see *ADG*, 27–46). Christianity is understood by Vattimo as a 'faith' that is predicated in the freedom of believers, the freedom of the community of faith. Thus, secularisation as the telos, the goal of Christianity, is grounded in the Christian affirmation of the freedom of the believer. This entails that Christianity dissolves its link from religion, understood as a practice of subordination to either doctrines or rituals (*ADG*, 37). In recent dialogues with René Girard, the thinker who has contributed most to untangling the links between Christianity, religion, violence and victimology, Vattimo has linked his earlier arguments about metaphysics, violence and secularisation with Girard's argument that Christianity ought to be understood as a religion that disavows natural, sacred violence, by turning it into symbolic and metaphorical violence. For Vattimo, the Christian *kenotic* God is a God that renounces and seeks to abolish violence. Consequently, the Christian doctrines of incarnation and salvation ought to be understood as the 'dissolution of the sacred as natural-violent' (*B*, 61; see also Vattimo and Girard 2010: 85). To this extent, Christianity seeks to dissolve the links between absolutes, authority, religion and violence through the sacrifice of the Son, Jesus Christ, who is also God. *Kenosis* is thus also the uncoupling of salvation from violent sacrifice. For Vattimo, the 'believing that one believes' is the remnant of the end of metaphysics and the ontology of the weakening of Being. This weakened sense of belief means that Christianity lives on as a message of pure love, and a call to a non-violent ethics of charity (*ADG*, 45).

See also *kenosis*; **kenotic sacrifice; religion; weak theology.**

BENJAMIN, WALTER

Giovanni Giorgio

Vattimo argues that, as has happened throughout the modern age (*EM*, 31–47), it is probable that even today 'the distinctive character of existence [. . .] appears first and most clearly in aesthetic experience' (*TS*, 45). In this lies the interest that Benjamin's aesthetic thought (Benjamin 1974–89a) assumes in the philosophy of Vattimo, who underlines the central idea: 'the new conditions of artistic production and appreciation that obtain in the society of mass media substantially modify the essence of art, its *Wesen*' (*TS*, 46).

In the era of its technical reproducibility, the conditions of production of the work of art change, as art suffers the loss of what constituted it as a *monumentum aere perennius* (*TS*, 57):[3] its aura. This sort of religious sacredness is removed from the work of art, since it is precisely the technical means – Benjamin refers above all to photography and cinema and Vattimo, more generally, to mass media – that allow us to detect aspects of the work that are accessible only through the technical instrument, and according to the possibilities of the latter. Thus, the original loses its cogency and, thanks to technology, the work reveals aspects otherwise imperceptible, multiplying its ontological richness at will, in ever-changing contexts. Therefore, art no longer appears centred on 'the *work*, but [on the] *experience*' of it (*TS*, 58).

---

3 Editor's note: misspelled as *momentum aere perennius* in the English translation, but correctly spelled in the Italian version (Vattimo [1989c] 2000: 80).

In this sense, on the side of fruition, the user's experience can no longer be considered in the manner of classical aesthetic theories, which, from Aristotle to Kant to Hegel, describe it 'in terms of *Geborgenheit* – security, "orientation" or "reorientation"' (*TS*, 52): humanity sinks into the work of art to find itself. Today what happens is the opposite: the work of art sinks into the contemporary mass-individuals, producing a shock, as Benjamin calls it, an effect of 'uncanniness', since art is able to lead them to live experiences that are different from the consolidated ones. The analogy with the Heideggerian *Stoss* is pointed out and developed by Vattimo (*TS*, 47). But, going back to Benjamin, it is true that, according to his thought, the current aesthetic perception is characterised by distraction (*Zerstreuung*), that is, a sort of unawareness, as when one is immersed in a film or moves in an architectural environment. But it is precisely in this way that the work of art penetrates us almost without us noticing it, and produces a shock effect. It puts the natural familiarity with the world in a state of suspension, to open us up to new horizons of meaning and, with them, to new possibilities of life: 'reality presents itself as softer and more fluid' (*TS*, 59) and no longer peremptory. And the same is true for the subject, since it as well, like every reality, is discovered not as 'given' once and for all and forever, but, as Heidegger puts it (Vattimo [1963] 1989), as a living project *of itself*, as an opening to new possibilities of meaning.

However, once this hermeneutic horizon of which the work of art is a forerunner has been defined, a question remains open, which has pestered Vattimo for some time, and to which Benjamin manages to give an answer. As is well known, Heidegger characterises the world unfolded by technology as *Gestell*, in which the history of metaphysics, understood as the progressive oblivion of Being, is fulfilled (Heidegger 1990 [1957]: 49). However, Heidegger himself underlines, in an *apax* that Vattimo often takes up, that in this time there is also a first, pressing flash of the *Ereignis* (1990 [1957]: 27), that is, something happens that has to do with the passing (*Verwindung* – see **convalescence** [*Verwindung*]) of metaphysics, by virtue of some remembrance (*An-denken* – see *Andenken* [**remembrance**]) of Being (Vattimo 1983a; *WT*). The question that Vattimo wants to answer is the following: what is the Being that the history of metaphysics has forgotten and that, in the time of the fulfilment of metaphysics, calls us to go beyond it? The later Vattimo, the more political one (Giorgio 2009), who rediscovers the ideality of Marxist thought, is clear: it is not a matter, once again metaphysically, of researching 'the "objekt" of Being, but rather a recollection of the oppressed history of metaphysics, what [. . .] Benjamin called "the tradition of the oppressed." It is in this forgotten, defeated, and different history that one can find the victims' (*HC*, 16), those victims who are inspirational to revolutionaries, who 'feed on the image of enslaved ancestors, not on the ideal of liberated descendants' (Benjamin 1974–89b: 700). In this way Benjamin – as for the work of art – emphasised the importance of looking at history from another perspective, telling another story, repressed and forgotten, the history that is not of the victors and oppressors, but of the defeated and oppressed. 'But, as an oppressed history, it encourages the defeated and weak to come forward' (*HC*, 41) because it is precisely that which can reveal unexplored possibilities of life and emancipation.

Compared to a conservative metaphysics of the existing order, which legitimises the dominators in their political power thanks to the 'truth, as the reflection of a given objective order' (*HC*, 18), hermeneutics sets itself in opposition, therefore, by not proposing itself as a further metaphysical theory. By virtue of a historical rationality (Vattimo 1992b: 100–1), it claims its validity as

(strong) theory of weakening as an interpretive sense of history, a sense that reveals itself as emancipative because of the enemies it has attracted. Weak thought can only be the thought of the weak, certainly not of the dominating classes, who have always worked to conserve and leave unquestioned the established order of the world. (*HC*, 96)

See also **aesthetics; hermeneutic communism; information technology/*Gestell*; Marxism/Italian Marxism; politics; subject/weak subject.**

BLOCH, ERNST/UTOPIA

Silvia Mazzini

The concept of utopia is present in Vattimo's reflections from the time of his early writings. Following the development of his thought, it takes on two meanings and connotations. The starting point for this development was one of the first courses taught by Vattimo, given in 1969/70. Analysing Ernst Bloch's *The Spirit of Utopia* (published in 1918), Vattimo understands utopia not as an abstract dream or as a 'castle in the clouds' but as a 'projection into the future' (Vattimo 1972a: 28). As he conceives of them, utopian projects can be achieved if they draw on concrete possibilities rooted in historical processes. Thus, the concept of utopia assumes political and emancipatory value: by anchoring their activities to realistic tendencies, human beings can transform and create themselves and the world.

In a second step, however, Vattimo reflects critically on the utopias of the past: drawing 'their model of a perfect, ideal and final order' (2005: 18), they acted according to the systematic will of metaphysics, which imposes, with more or less explicit violence, a single principle as the foundation of reality. It is for this reason that, in the era of postmodernism, we encounter 'counter-utopias'. Novels such as George Orwell's *1984* and Aldous Huxley's *Brave New World* feature dystopian worlds produced by the same tendencies of the actually existing present era (Vattimo 1989a: 63). Taking up Adorno and Horkheimer's arguments in *Dialectic of Enlightenment*, Vattimo argues that this reversal from utopia into dystopia is due to the human being's consciousness of the collapse of reason. As a matter of fact, the catastrophic scenarios of these counter-utopias were brought about not because of possible failures and misjudgements of Western rationality, but precisely because of its (functioning) mechanisms (see **Enlightenment**).

Yet, for Vattimo, this does not imply that the emancipatory and political connotations of utopia are altogether lost. On the contrary, as with metaphysical categories that can be remembered (see *Andenken* [**remembrance**]), utopia should not be forgotten, but instead needs to undergo a 'dissolution – a *Verwindung* in the Heideggerian sense – which effectively will enable it to be re-expressed in a new form, with characteristics more in conformity with our post-metaphysical era' (Vattimo 2005: 18). In this distortion, utopia takes its distance from modernity's linear and progressive conception of history. In particular, utopia must disengage from the idea of unity that underpins metaphysical thought.

In this way, Vattimo comes to his formulation of the concept of heterotopia: a 'distorted and transformed' realisation of utopia (*TS*, 69). Heterotopia is utopia under the sign of multiplicity. Indeed, if the modern conception of history implies the idea of a single utopia, it also means that the end of the modern concept of history leads to the end of unitary utopias.

Heterotopia is the liberation of multiplicities and differences: its *Verwindung* (distortion) is also the reappropriation or secularisation of utopia, with its political and emancipatory components: a multiplicity of projects, each of which, in hermeneutic dialogue between themselves and the realisable tendencies of the historical processes, can tend towards different, constantly changing, multiple transformations and creations.

BONHOEFFER, DIETRICH

Carmelo Dotolo

Bonhoeffer's perspective is represented by secularisation as the expression of a change in direction of religious experience (see *AC*, ch. 2; Vattimo 2012: 202, 205; *OR*, part IV, 'Title'; *BIS*, 143). It stands in relation to an interpretation of religion unburdened by dogmatic weight. Specifically, it is the weakening of the onto-theological substance of religious contents in view of a reproposing of Christianity in non-religious terms. The only possible itinerary is that of a thought capable of thinking 'God without God'. This line of thinking embodies the critique of the tragic thought that seems to represent 'the last great metaphysical misunderstanding of Christian thought' (*B*, 80). Such an emphasis on the living of Christianity does not, in the unsuccessful recognition of the role of the negative, isolate the arbitrariness of a thought and of faith as simplistically friendly in the face of humankind. Rather, it points to the consequence of the principle of incarnation whose *Weltanschauung* avoids a natural-metaphysical guarantee hardened by the violence of dogmatism and punishment. The temptation to mask religious experience in relation to an impossible reality, because of the unbearableness of evil and the tragic nature of the finite, seems again to follow the idea from Christianity either of the 'leap' or of the *deus ex machina*. Christianity here, that is, seems to follow yet again a stop-gap (recalling Bonhoeffer) that, facing the impediments of reality, cannot avoid returning to God in order to bring an end to the trial of failure and defeat. Such a resolution would remain within an interpretative error, one that is surely possible, but one that is insufficient because of a neutralisation of *kenosis*, within which 'perhaps I can endure and secularize evil insofar as it concerns me, but I have to take it seriously when it has to do with the neighbor who calls for my help, or at least for my understanding of his suffering' (*B*, 96).

CAPITALISM/LIBERALISM

Mike Grimshaw

Vattimo's thought occurs within, and as resistance to, the anti-teleological experience of capitalism and consumption (*EM*, xix), within a larger frame of the death of God wherein everything is reduced to exchange-value. Due to the mass media, capitalism no longer exists as a single reality: 'by a perverse kind of internal logic, the world of objects measured and manipulated by techno-science (the world of the *real* according to metaphysics) has become the world of merchandise and images, the phantasmagoria of the mass media' (*TS*, 8). Therefore, to understand capitalism, we need to understand the role of 'Western techno-scientific culture . . . [and how it is] inextricably bound to the system of capitalist exploitation and its imperialist tendencies' (*TS*, 31).

Vattimo has always opposed 'the oppressive functioning of positivist capitalism' (*NBG*, 62). In modernity, capitalism occurs as the status quo where continual renewal is a physiological requirement 'for the system to simply survive' (*EM*, 7). Therefore, nothing is new in capitalism in a revolutionary or subversive sense; rather what is new is what allows 'things to stay the same' (*EM*, 7).

Vattimo and Zabala's argument for hermeneutic communism critiques the metaphysical system of liberalism's ideal of objectivity, wherein truth and freedom are legalities 'within the established, recognized and framed democratic order' (*HC*, 52). The problem with liberalism is not its defence of individual liberties but rather that 'its particular view of freedom . . . has already decided who we are' (*HC*, 53). Liberalism is therefore both a metaphysical problem and a metaphysical violence to be opposed and overcome because it is not an alternative or opposition to capitalism, but part of the larger metaphysical problem (*HC*, 52), including violence imposed on non-liberal states and beings. This metaphysical and physical violence is imposed by the framed democracies of liberal capitalism and their financial system which is aimed at perpetuating a global status quo (*HC*, 64). Capitalism is therefore part of 'the logic of domination' (*HC*, 93) that exists and is conditioned as ideology (*FT*, 105).

Drawing on Max Weber, Vattimo situates capitalism as the 'transformed application' of 'the medieval Christian tradition' (*TS*, 41; *NE*, 31) which needs to be understood as a new form of religion, belief and myth. The success of liberalism in 'the reduction of religion to the private sphere, or at most to the realm of civil society' (*AC*, 94) has also enabled the expansion and dominance of capitalism. Liberalism therefore supports and justifies capitalism.

Yet capitalism is failing precisely because of the unified nature of the world due to how information and commerce operate. The reason is that 'now it becomes difficult to organize a global power with the capacity to exploit or take advantage of the inequality of capitalism' (*FR*, 75). Not only do we have politics governed by the economy, we have politics governed by the information techno-science economy. This means that not only do we 'need to restore the independence of politics from economics' (*NE*, 128), we also need to recognise that capitalism 'has never concealed the fact that it prospers by virtue of the periodic crises it undergoes' (*NE*, 128).

See also **hermeneutic communism; modernity; Weber, Max**.

CHARITY (*CARITAS*) (see CHURCH; ONTOLOGICAL DIFFERENCE; THEOLOGY)

CHAVEZ, HUGO

Claudio Gallo

'I am definitively a Chavist', said Vattimo in an interview with an Argentinian website in 2010 (Goldman 2010).[4] Hugo Chavez (1954–2013), the former president of Venezuela, was in the first decade of the twenty-first century a political hero for a large sector of Western radical leftists who saw the Spanish of Latin America as the current language of the 'working men of all countries'. Vattimo met the president three times in Caracas, also taking part in a radio debate with him.[5] Chavez was the leading representative of the 'weakened communism' that Vattimo (with Santiago Zabala) proposed as the newest model of rethinking Marx's ideas

---

4 It is not possible to find on the web the interview quoted on Vattimo's blog, <https://giannivattimo.blogspot.com/2010/07/sus-lideres-estan-del-lado-de-los.html> (accessed 2 September 2022)
5 Vattimo met Chavez during the I (2005), II (2006) and V (2010) International Forum of Philosophy in Caracas, as confirmed by Professor Carmen Bohórquez, who was on the Forum's board.

(*HC*, 113).[6] This means a politics of social reforms favouring the poor while maintaining some cornerstones of democracy such as elections and pluralism. More specifically, 'Communism's promise of a society "without classes" must be interpreted as "without dominion," that is, once again, without an imposed unique truth and compulsory orthodoxy' (*HC*, 116). Vattimo interpreted Chavez's populist communism through a classical anarchist attitude, envisaging the elimination of 'the polluting weight of ownership' or at least its reduction to a minimum (*HC*, 117; Mazzini and Glyn-Williams 2017: 188).[7] However, this radical approach is mitigated by the philosopher's anti-metaphysical stance, to which one must perhaps add the president's political pragmatism: in the end, hermeneutic communism 'can never present itself as a revolutionary radical force' (*HC*, 118). Facing a Chavism still in evolution, this is Vattimo's bet. The Western-'framed' democracies saw (and still see) Venezuela's model as the devil because it might become a viable alternative to their neoliberal systems, especially in Latin America:

> Chavez, together with his allies, provides an alternative and a model we could follow. However, our attention has been drawn not only by South American social politics but also by the excessive interest that the Obama administration [. . .] is putting into improving, consolidating, and establishing the U.S. military presence in South America. (*HC*, 132)

In the first decade of the 2000s Vattimo was one of the first to give a favourable judgement of leftist populism (see Laclau 2005), having in mind mainly the Venezuelan experiment: 'If Chavez is a Populist, then long life to Populism!' (López San Miguel 2009).

---

[6] Note that the book is dedicated not only to Chavez but also to Castro, Lula and Morales.
[7] This volume also includes Vattimo and Zabala's assessment of Chavez's politics after his death.

CHRISTIANITY/CATHOLICISM (see CHURCH; RELIGION; ONTOLOGICAL DIFFERENCE)

CHURCH

Thomas G. Guarino

The 'Church' in Vattimo's work almost always refers to the Roman Catholic Church, an institution that often serves as a polemical foil for his thought. On the one hand, Vattimo likes to cite Benedetto Croce's essay, 'We Cannot but Call Ourselves Christians' (*NE*, 30; *ADG*, 36), implying that, particularly in Italy where citizens are surrounded by Catholic institutions and artwork, the Church is an omnipresent reality. On the other hand, Vattimo is relentlessly critical of the Church's understanding of truth and morality.

What role does the Church play in Vattimo's philosophy? Can there be a dialogue between Catholicism and an author who has stated that 'postmodern nihilism constitutes the actual truth of Christianity' (*FR*, 47)? And how does this statement elucidate Vattimo's understanding of the Church?

Central to Vattimo's 'weak thought' (*il pensiero debole*) are the ideas of contingency and provisionality. Men and women must learn to live with endless vicissitudes – historical, social and cultural – rather than with the stable and secure foundations provided by allegedly 'objective' truths. In fact, there exist no enduring and unchanging truths; truth itself is a 'constructed' reality, deeply influenced by a variety of conditions. This is what Nietzsche meant when he declared, in a statement often cited by Vattimo, 'there are no facts, only interpretations' (*NE*, 155; *DN*, 74).

Of course, the Catholic Church is known for making dogmatic claims, assertions that it regards as universally and perpetually true. But it is precisely this kind of thinking that Vattimo regards as illegitimate given that all truth-claims, as Heidegger and Nietzsche have convincingly shown, are socially, historically and culturally conditioned, deeply enmeshed and embedded within determinate forms of life.

To illustrate this point, Vattimo frequently mentions Nietzsche's parable, 'How the World Became a Fable' from *The Twilight of the Idols* (*AC*, 111; *OR*, 18). Over time, Nietzsche argued, the ideas of 'truth' and 'the real' became progressively more unattainable. Plato held that 'the real' was accessible to the wise man, while Christianity promised it to those who were virtuous. Kant radicalised this viewpoint, teaching that 'the world itself' was beyond humanity's cognitive grasp. This gradual slipping away caused Nietzsche to conclude that the very idea of the 'true world' served little purpose. It was best abolished.

Vattimo's purpose in citing this fable is to show that forceful claims to certitude and finality – to knowing the *ontos on*, the really real – fail to recognise the profound ambiguity accompanying all such assertions. And the Catholic Church, with its insistence on dogmatic truth – indeed, even infallibly taught truth – needs to recognise this honestly. Reality itself is never objectively 'given'; it is constituted by the play of endless interpretations (*BI*, 7; Vattimo 2007d: 402).

Similarly, the Catholic Church speaks of 'natural law', meaning by this that there is a moral law inscribed by the Creator in the very structure of the universe – a 'law' visible, at least theoretically, to all men and women. For example, Pope John Paul II insisted that this moral law 'can also be known in its essential traits by human reason'. In other words, one need not be a Christian, or a religious person of any kind, to recognise – using an example adduced by the Pope – fundamental truths about the defence and promotion of human life (Guarino 2009: 86–7).

But it is precisely this position – that moral norms are 'given' rather than created – that Vattimo is at pains to refute. For the philosopher, emancipatory freedom means that a human being, in his or her sovereign autonomy, exercises creativity regarding life and morality. Men and women have the right to mould and shape their lives in new ways, apart from predetermined structures and assertive claims about eternally valid moral norms and unchanging human nature. Anything less than this kind of freedom unduly restricts human creativity and fails to recognise the deeply historicised nature of existence (*ADG*, 92–3; *AC*, 117).

Despite Vattimo's strong antipathy towards the dogmatic and moral claims of the Church, he is not entirely opposed to religion. He makes clear, however, that 'dogmatic and disciplinary Christianity ... has nothing to do with what I and my contemporaries "rediscover" when speaking of faith' (*B*, 61). For Vattimo, Jesus Christ invited men and women to universal friendship, not to 'our last idolatry: the adoration of Truth as our god' (2007a: 218). The Church, then, should preach more about *caritas* and less about *veritas*. *Caritas* or charity is here understood as tolerance towards every non-violent point of view.

For all of Vattimo's sharp criticisms of the Catholic Church, one might argue that he also has something of love–hate relationship with it. Again and again, he comes back to the issue of God, faith and the Church, like a moth drawn to a flame. His work represents an attempt to sketch how a postmodern thinker, whose eyes have been opened to the contingency, provisionality and historicity of human life and thought, might rediscover some faint semblance of Christian belief today.

COMMUNISM (see HERMENEUTIC COMMUNISM)

CONVALESCENCE (*VERWINDUNG*)

Robert T. Valgenti

Verwindung is a key concept in Vattimo's interpretation of the history of metaphysics. Vattimo reclaims the German word from Heidegger's scant use of the term in *Identity and Difference*, *Off the Beaten Track* and his essay 'Overcoming Metaphysics' (Vattimo 1987c). In contrast to an *Überwindung* (overcoming) of metaphysics, a *Verwindung* of metaphysics would mean a declination/distortion of it (*WT*, 46); to accept and to recover it – also in the sense of recovering from an illness, recuperation; 'to resign oneself to something, or to accept (another's judgment)' (*EM*, 39). It is a twisting, wrenching and distorting; a convalescence, a resignation (as to a loss or a pain) and an ironic acceptance of the heritage of metaphysics, the West and its notion of universality (*NE*, 27–8, 73, 160). It is 'a going beyond' metaphysics that is 'both an acceptance and deepening' (*EM*, 172) yet still to be fully comprehended (*EM*, 180). For Vattimo, *Verwindung* thinks the truth of Being as a handing down and transmission/destiny (*WT*, 46), making it synonymous with '*An-denken*, Heidegger's term for the post-metaphysical thinking of Being as a sort of remembrance or recollection' and more generally, as hermeneutic ontology (*WT*, 47; also *EM*, 176; *NE*, 160; Vattimo 1987c: 13; see **Andenken [remembrance]**).

Vattimo's interpretation of *Verwindung* is consistent with his more general interpretation of the history of metaphysics through both Heidegger and Nietzsche. What for Nietzsche is 'convalescence', 'good temperament' and the 'philosophy of morning' is captured and improved in Heidegger's notion of *Verwindung* (*EM*, 171). In Vattimo's interpretation, thought 'has no other "object" than the errancy of metaphysics, recollected in an attitude which is neither a critical overcoming nor an acceptance that recovers and prolongs it' (*EM*, 173; Vattimo 1987c: 12–13).

The term first appears in *The Adventure of Difference*, where Vattimo reflects on Heidegger's suggestion that the overcoming of metaphysics is either impossible, or possible only after a long *Verwindung*. Vattimo returned to the idea a couple of years later in his watershed essay, 'Dialectic, Difference, Weak Thought' (*WT*, 39–52). The essay reveals the uniqueness of Vattimo's interpretation of *Verwindung*: rather than simply exploring the origin of the term in Heidegger, he proposes it as a way to engage with the historical and conceptual tension between difference and dialectic he identifies in postmodern thinking. *Verwindung* provides a way forward without repeating the logic of metaphysics. It marks the declination of difference into weak thought through an engagement with 'the heritage of dialectics' (*WT*, 45–6) – that is, metaphysics traditionally understood as overcoming or sublimation. The thinking of difference still bears the marks of dialectics and thus marks a *Verwindung* – a declination, distortion and recovery from metaphysics that is simultaneously a 'taking account' and a 'taking leave of' Being as a 'stable structure or end of a logical process' (*WT*, 46).

In *The End of Modernity*, Vattimo examines Heidegger's critique of humanism, the crisis of which is the unavoidable outcome of metaphysics as *Gestell*. Technology does not overcome the values of humanism but presents a call for humanity to recollect, distort and accept the destiny of humanism, technology and the metaphysical structures of Being (*EM*, 41). Such thinking is not without an authentic programme: we inherit from the history of Being, 'the traces of an illness or a kind of pain to which we are resigned' (*EM*, 173), and 'both Metaphysics and the *Gestell* are twisted in a direction which is not foreseen by their own essence' (*EM*, 173). The reception and interpretation of this destiny establishes Vattimo's distinct approach to post-metaphysical thinking, which charts a path between hermeneutic relativism and strict historicism, offering a 'revised (*verwunden*), distorted form of historicism' (*EM*, 76).

Verwindung is also a central feature in Vattimo's broader discussions of the 'post-' in postmodernism and the 'general aestheticization of experience' (*EM*, 164) accompanying the event of Being as the *koiné* of hermeneutics. To say that Being is event is to announce 'the resigned resumption-distortion-acceptance of metaphysics and nihilism' (*BI*, 77) in the very language of metaphysics, now consciously accepted and *verwunden*. Vattimo challenges prevalent correspondence theories of truth by accepting their 'resumption and distortion' as examples of 'a secondary moment of the experience of truth' (*BI*, 88). Such truths display aesthetic experience 'as it is given at the end of metaphysics . . . in the form of *Verwindung*' (*BI*, 89). In this context, art endures a decline or a weakening, but not its own death, given that art (as theorised by Heidegger and Benjamin) depicts truth in the era of Being's decline (*EM*, 51–64). For Vattimo, this event of Being ripples throughout contemporary culture. In *The Transparent Society*, *Verwindung* appears in the pervasive irony and distortion of modernisation (*TS*, 41) and the twisting of utopian ideals (*TS*, 69). In Vattimo's interpretation of Christianity as the history of its secularisation, 'emancipation is reached only by means of a radical transformation and distortion of its very contents' (*EM*, 179) such that an '*Überwindung* (overcoming, realization and thus setting aside) is no more than a *Verwindung*, a long convalescence that has once again come to terms with the indelible trace of its sickness' (*R*, 79). And in Vattimo's more recent political works, *Verwindung* is invoked in passing to reflect on justice reform (*NE*, 169, 172), and to interpret a weakened form of communism or political revolution (*HC*, 1; *OR*, 150).

See also **overcoming** (*Überwindung*).

CONVERSATION (see RORTY, RICHARD)

DANTO, ARTHUR (see DEATH OF ART/END OF ART)

DEATH OF ART/END OF ART

Alessandro Bertinetto

According to Hegel, 'art, considered in its highest vocation, is and remains for us a thing of the past. Thereby it has lost for us genuine truth and life, and has rather been transferred into our ideas *instead of maintaining its earlier necessity* in reality and occupying its higher place' (Hegel 1975: 10). The 'pastness' of art means that it is no longer a guide for modern humanity, the understanding of whose complex form of life is rather entrusted to philosophy. In the Anglo-Saxon world, Hegel's thesis is known as the 'end of art' thesis and Arthur Danto (2014) interpreted it as meaning that art history had come to an end because contemporary art is not self-sufficient and needs a philosophical justification. Instead, since in the Italian context the thesis is known as the 'death of art' thesis, Vattimo re-proposed it in the light of his general view of the 'death' (or end) of metaphysics, of modernity and of God (see **death of God**).

This task is accomplished in three ways. First, Vattimo interprets the Hegelian thesis as meaning that art is no longer essential for us: as testified by Marxist aesthetics, 'the more art is considered a serious fact rather than pure play, the more it is resolved into philosophy and reflection'

(*ACT*, 41). Hence, 'art reveals its own truth only by emptying itself of the specific characteristics that distinguish it from philosophy and reflection': its 'lack of seriousness and its ludic character' (*ACT*, 41). In other words, only when art is overcome is it made true. Which is testified by the dissolution of art in literary criticism and poetic manifestos of the avant-gardes. Art dies since 'reflection and self-justification ultimately prevail over the creative spirit' (*ACT*, 112).

However, this is still a metaphysical interpretation of art's death. While 'the problem to which the poetics intend to respond is [. . .] the question of whether and how art as original creation can still exist' (*ACT*, 34), Vattimo finds secondly in Nietzsche's notion of the 'will to power' a different postmetaphysical way to see how art is possible after Hegel's declaration. The point is that 'art is a past [. . .] but it is also a future, if we take seriously the assertion that there is no such thing as happiness without the pleasure of nonsense, i.e. without artistic travesty, invention and mask'. Art '*exceeds* the decline which is the destiny of the forms of metaphysical "lying", and it does so precisely to the extent that it differs from them in being play and exception' (*AD*, 90–1). In other words, the death of art actually is a rebirth of art: a creative form of the will to power that emancipates art from the objectivistic-representational dimension of traditional aesthetics.

Thirdly, Vattimo resorts to Heidegger's essay on *The Origin of the Work of Art* to take the final step beyond the metaphysical (historicist and rationalist) idea of the death of art, now understood in terms of the decline or 'sunset' of art: an event of truth that art itself sets to work and that, as Gadamer famously argued (Gadamer 2006: 103), is capable of changing those who experience it. In this framework, 'the death of art is a phrase that describes or, better still, constitutes the epoch of the end of metaphysics as prophesied by Hegel, as lived by Nietzsche and as registered by Heidegger' (*EM*, 52). Rather than a description of a certain state of things, it is 'an event that constitutes the historical and ontological constellation in which we move' (*EM*, 52). It concerns us in that it is 'destined' to us. Art declines as a specific phenomenon, 'as a specific social form (subjected to the law of the division of labor)' (*ACT*, 138) and it is 'suppressed and ablated – in a Hegelian way – through a general aestheticization of existence' (*EM*, 52).

The death of art is, then, 'an explosion of aesthetics' (*EM*, 54; see **aesthetics**). In a utopian sense, this 'indicates the end of art as a specific fact, separate from the rest of experience, thanks to the renewal and reintegration of existence' (*EM*, 56); in a weak sense, this 'points to aestheticization as an extension of the domain of the mass media' (*EM*, 56; see **media**). In these conditions the artwork is like the Heideggerian 'Being': 'it arises only as that which at the same time withdraws from us' (*EM*, 57). Hence, although art in the traditional and institutional sense of the world of artistic products still survives, authentic art is silent. On the one hand, this corresponds to the death, or the loss of meaning, of traditional philosophical aesthetics and its values (in particular, the new); on the other hand, the thesis of the death of art also acquires the sense that the perishable and declining temporality of the artwork itself (taken as ornament and monument) becomes symbol of factuality, of birth and death, of Dasein's mortality (*EM*, 126). This is 'the post-modern experience of art [. . .] the way in which art occurs in the era of the end of metaphysics' (*EM*, 106).

See also art; Bloch, Ernst/Utopia, Gadamer, Hans-Georg; Hegel, Georg Wilhelm Friedrich; metaphysics; modernity (end of); *sensus communis*.

DEATH OF GOD

Frederiek Depoortere

The death of God is one of the core elements of Nietzsche's philosophy. Given Nietzsche's importance for Vattimo, it is not surprising that the death of God is present in his work. Vattimo goes beyond Nietzsche, however, by explicitly identifying the latter's death of God with the death of God on the Cross (*AC*, 104; *ADG*, 90; *FT*, 58). This identification evidently raises the question of how Vattimo links the death of God as announced by Nietzsche with the Crucifixion. As a first step in reconstructing the link between both, we need to mention that Vattimo considers Nietzsche's proclamation of the death of God to be equivalent to Heidegger's announcement of the end or dissolution of metaphysics (see, for instance, *B*, 39; *ADG*, 91). The God who is declared dead by Nietzsche is the God of the philosophers, the highest Being, the first cause, the ultimate source and guarantor of all being, order, truth, value and hope. The dead God is, in short, the God of metaphysics or onto-theology. However, this God is also the God of natural religion, Girard's 'natural sacred' (*B*, 38). Vattimo understands Girard as talking about a dissolution of the sacred that was initiated by the Incarnation. At the moment that Vattimo encountered the work of Girard, he had already developed his interpretation of Heidegger as offering an ontology of decline, interpreting the history of Being as showing a tendency towards weakening, and he had begun to use the notion of 'secularisation' in this regard. Inspired by Girard, Vattimo started to interpret the Incarnation (understood as *kenosis* and abasement) in terms of 'weakening' (*BI*, 48) and secularisation as its destiny (*BI*, 50). Thus, by reading Girard through Heidegger, Vattimo concluded that Heidegger's ontology of weakening was a 'transcription' of the doctrine of the Incarnation, and the doctrine was 'an announcement' of that ontology (*B*, 36). In this way, Vattimo portrays weakening and secularisation (only limited by charity) as Christianity's destiny. Given the identifications he makes, it becomes clear why Vattimo can see the Incarnation culminating in the death of the God of metaphysics and natural religion. However, this still leaves unanswered the question of how the death of God, as announced by Nietzsche, is identical to the death of God on the Cross.

Overall, the Crucifixion plays no significant role in Vattimo's work. His Heideggerian-Girardian reading of Nietzsche's announcement of the death of God does not, in fact, need the identification of Nietzsche's death of God with the death of God on the Cross to make sense and be intelligible. Therefore, the identification seems to be an alien element in his thought, and this suggests an influence on it that he does not sufficiently acknowledge. A clue to this influence is Thomas Altizer's *The Gospel of Christian Atheism*, in which the Crucifixion amounts to 'the death of the original sacred, the death of God himself' (1966: 54). There are several striking similarities between Vattimo's thought and *The Gospel of Christian Atheism* (as outlined in Sciglitano 2007: 535–6). Anthony Sciglitano even claimed 'that Vattimo reprises nearly step by step, influence by influence' that book (2007: 535). Whether there was any direct influence from Altizer on Vattimo is unlikely, however. Vattimo admits having met Altizer twice, but they did not have sustained contact (*NBG*, 102). He also concedes that he never studied 'death of God' theology intensely and emphasises that he is different in using the death of God in the context of the history of Being (*ADG*, 92–3). Therefore, the most likely explanation for the similarities between Vattimo and Altizer is a shared source of inspiration. As Altizer reads Nietzsche's death of God through Hegel (see Harris 2021: 54; Sciglitano 2007: 537), the similarities between Vattimo and Altizer suggest to Sciglitano that, in fact, Hegel is Vattimo's 'prime influence' (2007: 528). Sciglitano even posits that Vattimo's entire thinking is invaded by him (2007: 537) and that this makes any claim of having moved beyond metaphysics highly suspect (see, for instance, 2007: 528).

In contrast, Matthew Harris, while acknowledging Hegel's influence on Vattimo, underlines that his is a 'weakened' Hegelianism (2021: 59), and he emphasises the difference between Altizer and Vattimo. Altizer offers a modernist approach to Nietzsche's death of God and conceives it as a true state of affairs. Vattimo, in contrast, is postmodern. For him, the Hegelian process that is a fact for Altizer can only be an interpretation. Yet even when Vattimo's Hegelianism is a weakened one, some of the problems connected to Hegel's philosophy remain present in his thought. In this regard, we can refer to the seven points listed by Sciglitano (2007: 537) and Caputo's concern that philosophers influenced by Hegel remain indebted to the latter's anti-Judaism and supersessionism (*ADG*, 79–80).

DECONSTRUCTION (see DERRIDA)

DEMOCRACY

Silvia Mazzini

For Vattimo, democracy is neither an ancient model to conform to, nor an idea to realise: it is a collective hermeneutic practice, animated by a 'weak conflict of interpretations'. As a matter of fact, hermeneutics is understood not as a literary method that involves tracing or developing a certain interpretation, but as a praxis that generates multiple different interpretations and perspectives. For Vattimo, conflicts between ideas, truths and desires are essential components of life in a *polis*. This has to do with democracy in the proper sense of the word, where the clash and confrontation of different *Weltanschauungen* is part and parcel of the normal order of things. It involves conceiving of a democracy in which elections and decisions are not made according to a single absolute truth but are based on a decision achieved collectively. Therefore, paradoxical as it may sound, the goal of democracy is not to find consensus but to avoid it.

A just society is not a perfect society, quite the contrary. It is a society where conflicts, as well as differing opinions about which path to choose, are fought out, and in which interests are not necessarily shared by all actors, in which decisions are not simply determined by differences between classes, wealth, power, or success. (Vattimo 2007b: 108)

In this sense, democracy can be defined as an 'adventure of difference' (see *AD*), or rather, 'differences'. These differences proliferate and make their competing claims to legitimacy after the end of history (see **postmodernism/postmodernity**), that is, after the end of the 'metanarratives' that had proclaimed themselves as the only true interpretations. The reason why hermeneutics is a model for democracy today is therefore not related to a theoretical necessity but to a historical one: that is 'the result of the end of metaphysics', the fall of the Berlin Wall and 'the end of Eurocentrism and its pretence to universal Western rationality' (*HC*, 110–11). In a situation characterised by anti-foundationalism (but not by absolute relativism: *HC*, 98), dialogue and conversation (see **Rorty, Richard**) offer the democratic opportunity to dialogue openly without being governed by one imposed, absolute truth, but rather through procedures that can themselves be continually discussed and questioned, in order to find different interpretations (and not, again, absolute truths) that are able to change reality.

Taking up a famous phrase from Walter Benjamin, Vattimo highlights the fact that history, as it has been told to us, is simply 'one' version of the facts that we have at our disposal. It is the history of 'winners', of those who were in power and who left their mark on what we call civilisation (for example, Eurocentric, male historiography following the criteria and interests of occidental rationality, etc.). Claiming the 'monopoly of truth', that is, the one, exclusive way to interpret reality, the winners have determined (and still determine) the existence or non-existence of facts, events, ideas and cultures, and they have neglected the 'narratives' of those who have hitherto been excluded from *this* history: the enslaved, the poor, women, subcultures, LGBTQ+s, among others.

In other words, for Vattimo, democracy should evolve from one of the anarchic origins of hermeneutics (see **anarchy; Schürmann, Reiner**): the end of truth. In this sense, hermeneutics reflects the democratic ideal, albeit in a radicalised form, since decisions are not taken in the name of absolute truth and necessity, but rather on the basis of dynamic encounters between different interpretative frameworks. This is why 'the end of the truth is the beginning of democracy' (*HC*, 23), and in particular, the beginning of a participatory, more direct, yet 'weak' democracy.

A hermeneutic democracy is the only way to oppose what Vattimo, together with Santiago Zabala, calls the 'politics of descriptions', one that sees the world through the lens of the impositions of positivistic realism: what is possible and realistic always coincides with the interests of the most powerful segments of the global order. Thus, 'description', as opposed to interpretation, here means the claim to a supposed objectivity, rooted in the 'conservative nature of realism' (*HC*, 17) that does not recognise any form of rationality or political project that diverges from dominant thought – the thought of dominant groups. This is what happens in 'framed democracies', which for the two authors are only formally democratic since they seek to systematically foreclose any genuine conflict of (different) interpretations.

This is why Vattimo refuses to dictate in advance what a proper democracy looks like. To do so would mean simply replicating the imposition of 'truth' carried out by what he calls the 'politics of description'. For Vattimo, we rather need a politics that refuses to formulate an (absolute) system, an (untouchable) constitution. We can clearly see a parallelism between this refusal of a foundation in political as well as ontological terms (see **nihilism**). In this sense, we can consider the whole philosophical and political production of Vattimo as weakly democratic, since it renounces normative claims and rather invites others to respond, engage, diverge and reinterpret his or her own interpretations.

DERRIDA, JACQUES

Alberto Martinengo

The success of Vattimo's hermeneutics is due, on the one hand, to his original interpretation of German philosophy from Hegel onwards and, on the other, to his specific focus on French thought in the second half of the twentieth century. In the first case, his contribution comes from his reinterpretation of Friedrich Nietzsche, who Vattimo ranks alongside Heidegger and Gadamer as one of the key authors of contemporary hermeneutics. On the other side, the case of French philosophy presents a more complicated picture, involving different names and movements: from Foucault to Lyotard and from Ricoeur to Derrida. From them Vattimo derives the – not always peaceful – coexistence of postmodernism and hermeneutics of symbols, as well as of certain philosophical legacies of psychoanalysis and structuralism.

The exchange with Jacques Derrida (1930–2004) is certainly the most profound. It consists of a frequent dialogue that also covers shared initiatives such as the creation of a *European Philosophical Yearbook*: a short-lived project that we can nonetheless thank for the publication of *Religion* (1998). More broadly, however, the main issue from their decades-long exchange lies in the notions of difference and the end of metaphysics. Vattimo views Derrida's central focus on the theme of language as a positive confirmation of the true territory in which metaphysics is rooted. In line with late Heidegger, metaphysical ontology is first and foremost a structure of the languages we speak: more than just a mirror of reality, the thought of being is the result of our syntax and grammar. Hence Derrida's emphasis on writing and its function of preservation – as well as of alteration or dissemination – of meaning (Derrida 1981; 1978).

Vattimo shares this interest in the textuality of philosophy. In Derrida he identifies another version of the attention that Gadamer's hermeneutics pays to tradition, understood as a repository of resources that have been handed down – in textual form, among others – and that never cease to influence the present. It is precisely due to this influence on the present that traditional texts should be thought of as living resources, rather than eternal forms: that is, as content destined to be altered and even manipulated, as Derrida (1978) explains through the notion of *différance*.

In spite of these shared assumptions, their positions diverge on the prognostic front, that is, on the end of modernity. Derrida reinterprets Heidegger's destruction of metaphysics as the still defective form of a more radical project that he refers to as deconstruction: at the margins of the textuality of philosophy, Derrida (1982) shows that meaning (that is, onto-theology: truth, essence, God) is altered to the point of becoming empty and thus shows the deception of metaphysics. For Vattimo, by contrast, deconstruction is illusory in its goal of overthrowing the onto-theological regime: he considers leaving the metaphysical tradition through a leap towards its margins as a sort of 'throw of the dice' that not only abandons onto-theology but also the need – for philosophy – to argue its own positions. Contrary to Derrida's deconstruction, in *Beyond Interpretation* Vattimo supports the idea that convalescence (*Verwindung*) should be understood as a form of reconstruction of rationality: a weak rationality (see **convalescence** [*Verwindung*]; **weak thought** [*pensiero debole*]), whose goal is not to erase the concepts of metaphysics, but to redefine them from an emancipatory, rather than oppressive, perspective.

See also **difference**; **language**; **metaphysics**; **Ricoeur, Paul**.

DIALECTICAL REASON/HERMENEUTICAL REASON
(see **OVERCOMING** [*ÜBERWINDUNG*])

DIFFERENCE

Silvia Marzano

In *Being and Time*, Heidegger investigates the constitutive temporality of Being and examines difference as a philosophical issue, asking why the question of difference has been forgotten. As Vattimo observes, as soon as we merely recall the fact that there is a difference between Being and particular beings, we are already forgetful of Being itself. Indeed, this would still be a 'metaphysical' discourse on the 'object' Being; instead, the question of difference concerns difference as such, and not its terms. Hence, we need to consider this question in its eventuality, namely to recollect the 'question of' difference as such, in the double sense of the genitive (*AD*, 65). Accordingly, this also invites consideration of such a question in the objective sense of the genitive, as Heidegger does in the *Letter on Humanism* with respect to the thought of Being.

The expression 'the event of Being' is to be understood not only in its subjective meaning – that is, 'the event belongs to Being' – but also in its objective meaning – that is, 'Being belongs to the event'. The same goes for difference problematised as such in its eventuality: 'forgetting difference does not mean losing sight of the fact of difference: it means forgetting as a fact. This is not failure to keep in mind *that* difference does actually dominate and condition *our* historical existence; it is to forget the question "why difference?"' (*AD*, 78).

Since Being, in its temporality, belongs to the event, it wholly belongs to Western metaphysics, conceived of as the history and destiny of Being. Even for this idea, Vattimo recalls the ambivalence of the genitive, namely its (also) objective sense, according to which the end of metaphysics coincides with the decline of Being, 'in the sense that it behooves Being to set' (*BS*, 18). Being itself is not something or someone that has a history, but rather it wholly belongs to metaphysics and its history because 'it is only in metaphysics that Being is given, happens, eventualizes itself' (*AD*, 79). The history of Western metaphysics 'is the arising of a given epoch of Being, one dominated by mere presence at hand, by the ideal of objectivity, by language as a pure tool for communication. Is it therefore also an epoch of difference?' (*AD*, 76).

Hence, is the eventuality of Being also the eventuality of difference? In what sense are metaphysics, Being and difference finite? What is the meaning of Heidegger's insistence on the overcoming of metaphysics, and of his very well-known expression – somehow implicit to the being-toward-death in *Being and Time* – 'we must leap away from the *Grund* to the *Ab-grund* which is at the bottom of our being mortal'? Here arises Vattimo's 'third way': it is necessary to grasp together both difference as event – also in the objective sense – and the overcoming character that Nietzsche attributed to his thought, namely to his proclamations that 'God is dead' and that 'nothing remains of Being'; such statements are to be understood as findings of an event, that is, of metaphysics' loss of its strong characters. According to Vattimo, difference is eventual, since it does not apply to every possible history; it is not about becoming aware of difference, but about recollecting it as an event eventualised in the horizon of the history of metaphysics. If this eventuality is denied, difference would still be a metaphysical principle; that is to say, it would be a metaphysical rejection of stable Being (*AD*, 67), as if one were to interpret Nietzsche's claim that God is dead as a statement of God's inexistence.

Thus, difference belongs to a specific epoch and character (*Prägung*) of Being. Neither can it be said that metaphysics is overcome, nor can its end be conceived through a representative discourse; instead, its end is an overcoming process, in the Nietzschean sense of a *Zwischen*, that is, of a 'being in between' (*AD*, 80). Difference is not structure but event, which in turn is internal to that metaphysics that is to be overcome. According to Vattimo, 'being in between' means that Being itself never ends its ending; the history of Being is a history of 'consumption', of an endless weakening, a manifestation of Being's temporal essence: ephemerality, caducity, birth-death (*WT*, 45, 47–8).

The problem of difference is related to the nihilistic outcomes of Heidegger's thought, to being-toward-death, to the abyss, and to the question of the overcoming of metaphysics. According to Vattimo, the Dasein thinks Being as difference when it projects itself towards its own death. However, death is not 'the shrine of nothingness', as it is for Heidegger, but a process of decline and of the disappearing of the violent structures of metaphysics towards a 'weak ontology'. For Vattimo, being-toward-death is at once grounding and ungrounding (*sfondamento*). It is grounding because it keeps open – for the Dasein – the continuity of a 'text-texture' that 'lets the possible be as possible, stripping it of the mask of necessity imposed on it by metaphysics' (*AD*, 125); in this sense, it already differs. Moreover, it is also ungrounding because it grounds such continuity on a discontinuity that is the ungroundedness of the abyss (*Ab-grund*) and of our being mortal (*AD*, 154).

For Vattimo, the 'leap' (*Sprung*) from the *Grund* towards the *Ab-grund* or absence of foundation (*AD*, 119; *BS*, 30) is also a relation with the past (*Überlieferung, Geschick*) from which the Dasein comes. This 'leap' enables a positive access and a 'grounding' (even though a 'weak' one) that coincides with difference as 'recollective thought' (*Andenken*) (*AD*, 125) (see *Andenken* [**remembrance**]). Hence, *Andenken* leaves behind Being as foundation and *properly* thinks Being as Difference. Recollective thought turns back to our provenance, not through making the past present, but through a 'taking leave' that thinks its object as 'differing'; such thought grasps the occurrence of disclosing 'in a differing contrasted to the presence of the *objectum* of re-presentation' (*AD*, 121). By doing so, it ungrounds the metaphysical stiffening of presence (*AD*, 116).

Thinking as recollecting means grasping the disclosure in which we are thrown as an event, and corresponding to the *Schickung*, to the transmission, that is to stand before it 'as a historical possibility and not as Being itself' (*AD*, 123). Being does not identify itself with any of the horizons that it opens, but it 'suspends' the opening and puts it in an indefinite oscillation, displacing and differing it. Being, characterised as weak, is not one of the poles of the oscillation, but is 'the horizon [*ambito*], or the oscillation itself' (*BS*, 30). Indeed, its 'paradoxical positivity' lies precisely in its not being any of the alleged foundational horizons (*BS*, 26).

Since it is connected to the abyss of our being mortal and to the historical and finite condition of the Dasein, the *Andenken* is a hermeneutical grounding, namely, a retracing *in infinitum* in relation to the *Grund* (*BS*, 27–33). Thus, this endless and inexhaustible analysis 'constructively' ungrounds the peremptoriness of each of the different contexts into which historical existence is thrown, liberating Dasein for other contexts (*AD*, 128).

The overcoming (*Überwindung*) of metaphysics (see **overcoming** [*Überwindung*]) is therefore a 'twist' (*Verwindung* – see **convalescence** [*Verwindung*]), a distortion (*AD*, 113). The plexus *Überwindung/Verwindung* still lies in metaphysics, taking off from it the character of the *ontos on*. According to Vattimo, *Verwindung* is the declension of difference in weak thought. Indeed, 'Being *is not*: entities or beings [*enti*] are what can be said to be. Being, on the other hand, befalls, or occurs [*accade*] [. . .] All we can say about Being at this point is that it consists in trans-mission, in forwarding [*invio*]: *Überwindung* and *Geschick*' (*WT*, 44).

See also **ontological difference**.

Translated by Daniele Fulvi

DILTHEY, WILHELM

Gaetano Chiurazzi

The name of Wilhelm Dilthey (1833–1911) is linked to a fundamental stage in the history of philosophical hermeneutics, namely that of its determination as the general *organon* of the human sciences and the tracing of its origin to the Protestant Reformation. Dilthey's reflection is set within a cultural context characterised by positivism and the debate around the opposition between the natural and human sciences, which animated the academic and scientific community at the end of the nineteenth century. Dilthey, as Kant had done before him with regard to modern natural science, tried to epistemologically ground the sciences of the spirit by identifying for them an appropriate object (historical reality) and method (understanding). However, the reference to the concept of life in this foundation is implicitly presented as an attempt to overcome the opposition between the natural sciences and the human sciences.

Dilthey's life-philosophy ultimately yields the recognition of the historical character of reason. This recognition enables Dilthey to critique the way Kant (and together with him Locke and Hume) had conceived of the transcendental subject, in whose veins 'no real blood flows', but rather the rarefied sap of a reason understood as pure activity of thought. Initially, in the wake of Schleiermacher, whose biography he wrote, Dilthey identified psychology as the *organon* of the human sciences, conceiving understanding as a process of empathic identification that leads to 'reliving' the experience (*Erlebnis*) of a foreign life. Later, Dilthey would instead assign the role of *organon* of the human sciences to hermeneutics. The object of understanding, in fact, is not so much the individuality of a 'Thou' but the objective productions of the spirit, what Hegel summed up under the title of 'objective spirit', which for Dilthey also includes the cultural manifestations of art, religion and philosophy. These products of the spirit are signs that demand to be understood and interpreted. Hermeneutics has the task of mediating between the handed-down objectuality (the historical datum) and the subjectivity of the author or interpreter, between the outside of the symbols and the inside of the subjectivity that expresses itself in them or that understands them.

Vattimo certainly appreciates the fact that Dilthey recognised hermeneutics as the method of the human sciences. However, following in the footsteps of Heidegger and Gadamer, for him Dilthey's investigation does not fully unveil the ontological foundation of this methodological choice, which is instead made explicit by Heidegger as well as by Gadamer in the notion of temporality as the horizon of being. Even more important, however, is the fact that Dilthey, starting from the Protestant Reformation, understands the history of hermeneutics as the history of liberation from dogma: an idea that Vattimo extends to the entire history of Western civilisation as a progressive movement of emancipation from every metaphysical foundation and from the violence it entails.

See also **hermeneutics**.

DUSSEL, ENRIQUE

Eduardo Mendieta

Enrique Dussel (b. 1934) is an Argentinian-Mexican philosopher, emeritus professor of the Metropolitan Autonomous University in Mexico and distinguished chair in the faculty of Philosophy and Letters in the National Autonomous University of Mexico. He is unquestionably the most important Latin American philosopher of the second half of the twentieth century and the early part of the twenty-first century (see Allen and Mendieta 2021). He is one of the founders of the Latin American philosophy and liberation theology, and a major figure in the development of (decolonial) world philosophies. He has contributed to the fields of the history of the Latin American Church, world history, Marxology (the study of the evolution of Marx's thinking), history of Latin American philosophy, ethical theory and (world) political philosophy. He is the author of over fifty books, among them *Philosophy of Liberation* (1985), *Ethics and Community* (1988), *The Invention of the Americas: Eclipse of 'the Other' and the Myth of Modernity* (1995), *The Underside of Modernity: Apel, Rorty, Taylor, and the Philosophy of Liberation* (1996), *Politics of Liberation: A Critical World History* (2011), *Ethics of Liberation: In the Age of Globalization and Exclusion* (2013) and *Filosofías del Sur. Descolonización y Transmodernidad* (2015).

Dussel and Vattimo share many philosophical inspirations, above all Heidegger and Gadamer. Vattimo's 'weak thought' and Dussel's 'philosophy of liberation' could be understood as forms of 'left Heideggerianism', namely as methods of reading Heidegger in radical and liberatory ways. Dussel's early work from the late 1960s and early 1970s was an attempt to develop an 'ethics of Latin American liberation' using Heideggerian and Gadamerian concepts (Dussel 1970–72). In the early 1970s, however, Dussel discovered Emmanuel Levinas, and made what he called his 'analectic turn', by which he meant a turn away from the sameness of the totality of Being towards the distinction of the 'Other', who irrupts from the beyond the ontology of what is (Dussel 1973; see also Allen and Mendieta 2021).

While they shared political views, and were supporters of Hugo Chavez's Bolivarian Democratic project in Venezuela, which they often visited in the last year of Chavez's government in 2013, Dussel and Vattimo diverged on how to read the aftermath of the dissolution of the Heideggerian destruction of Western metaphysics. Dussel wrote a series of essays to introduce Vattimo on the occasion of his visit to Mexico (13–18 September 1993), which were subsequently published as a book (Dussel 1999). This book offers one of the most sympathetic, synoptic and useful overviews of the evolution of Vattimo's thought, from his dissertation through the mid-1990s. It also offers severe critiques, three of which are noteworthy: first, he claims that Vattimo failed to fully appreciate the ways in which Levinas propelled the Heideggerian project of de-transcendentalising philosophy towards an ethics of liberation; secondly, he states that Vattimo's hermeneutical idealism fails to incorporate the materiality of the community of dialogue and understanding, thus failing to properly incorporate economics within his own 'ethics of interpretation' (Vattimo 1989a); thirdly, and perhaps most severely, Dussel accuses Vattimo of not overcoming the Graecophilia, Eurocentrism and (post-)modernism of Euro-American philosophy. According to Dussel, Vattimo is still caught in what he calls Heideggerian and Nietzschean 'ontological Eurocentrism'.

See also **ethics; weak thought** (*pensiero debole*).

E

ECO, UMBERTO

Daniel Gamper

Gianni Vattimo was 19 years old when he first met Umberto Eco (1932–2016), four years his senior, while they were apprentices at the Italian television station RAI. In those days, Eco was one of the leaders of the Catholic student association Azione Cattolica. Vattimo's first published text was a review of Eco's *Il problema estetico in S. Tommaso* (*The Problem of Aesthetics in Saint Thomas Aquinas*), which Eco had written under the supervision of Luigi Pareyson, whom he introduced to the young Vattimo. Eco became from then on a friend and 'a kind of comrade or vice-maestro in the school of Pareyson' (Zabala 2007: 5) from whose friendship Vattimo learned all kinds of jokes.

Eco applied for the chair of Aesthetics at the University of Turin which Vattimo won. Apparently, as Vattimo recalls in his autobiography *Not Being God* (*NBG*, 47), Pareyson had some doubts about Eco's Catholicism and his relations with the phenomenological group around Enzo Paci in Milan.

Vattimo has always recognised in Eco's main novels, *The Name of the Rose* and *Foucault's Pendulum*, the spirit of weak thinking (Vattimo 2009d: 328). It is noteworthy that Eco also participated in the seminal *Weak Thought* anthology that Vattimo and Rovatti edited in 1983, proposing a way to unite reasonableness (intersubjective control) and contextuality (weakness), slightly distancing himself thereby from the radical postmodernism of Vattimo.

They kept disagreeing about realism in an extended discussion, in which Eco defended the position according to which, for there to be an interpretation, there must be some facts to be interpreted (Eco 1994 [1990]). In his last decade, and as a reaction to the revival of realism, Eco proposed a 'negative realism': it is not possible to establish that an interpretation is correct, but rather it is possible to identify when it is incorrect (Eco 2012). Eco tried to find a convergence between his and Vattimo's philosophical positions in the thesis that 'every knowledge cannot be but conjectural' (Eco 2007: 56), expounded in his contribution to Vattimo's seventieth birthday anniversary.

EMANCIPATION

Paolo Diego Bubbio

The term 'emancipation' first appears in Vattimo's works in relation to Nietzsche's nihilism. Other sources are Jean-Paul Sartre (see **existentialism**), for whom emancipation is 'the reappropriation of the meaning of history on the part of those who actually make it' (*EM*, 29), and then Max Weber, Norbert Elias and René Girard: for these thinkers, 'emancipation is reached only by means of a radical transformation and distortion of its very contents' (*EM*, 180).

In *Belief*, Vattimo argues that, according to Heidegger, the social transformations that seem to threaten modern subjectivity are possible 'chances of emancipation from metaphysics' (*B*, 51–2): emancipation consists in 'recognising that Being is event', and this enables us to 'enter actively into history, instead of passively contemplating its necessary laws' (*B*, 78). Truth and evangelical charity cannot be kept apart; Vattimo also argues that Habermas's notion of 'communicative action' is similar to this notion of 'lived charity' (*RP*, 97). For Vattimo, 'philosophy, project, historicity, emancipation [. . .] all mean the same thing' (*RP*, 108).

In *After Christianity*, the identification of emancipation (as the weakening of strong structures) with *kenosis* (as the abasement and weakening of God) is made explicitly – an identification that, in Vattimo's view, was already articulated in similar terms by Hegel and Dilthey; also, while Heidegger rarely addresses morality, interpreting his overcoming of metaphysics as a process of emancipation is 'a valid extrapolation' (*NE*, 18). Emancipation entails a 'move away from the sacral horizon of the beginnings'; this is not, however, the 'extirpation of religion', because such a process of weakening is entirely consistent with the core message of Christianity (*NE*, 31). 'This is the only emancipation I know, with nihilism to dissolve the absolutistic elements' (*NBG*, 157; cf. Vattimo 2009c: 32). In this sense, 'emancipation actually consists in pursuing secularization', conceived as the process of desacralisation, which is also the transformation from the natural to the spiritual, which was addressed by Hegel (*ADG*, 41); emancipation lies 'in taking secularization further, in the sense of grasping better and better the spiritual sense of Scripture' (*FT*, 75).

In *Hermeneutic Communism*, Vattimo and Zabala argue that Marx shares with Heidegger a 'project of emancipation from metaphysics' (*HC*, 4). Emancipation is also political emancipation, 'that is, the realm within which freedom is effectively possible' (*HC*, 41); 'emancipation means openness, transformation, and projected interpretation instead of what already is' (*HC*, 94; cf. *OR*, 152).

Guarino (2009) developed Vattimo's notion of emancipation in the field of theology, arguing that emancipation occurs when nihilism is embraced. Benso focused on Vattimo's philosophy of history, pointing out that 'Vattimo's theoretical commitment to history (and the political) finds a correlate in the concrete project of emancipation, which inspires the content of his philosophy' (Benso 2010: 205–6). Harris (2016) addressed Vattimo's notion of emancipation in the context of a discussion of *kenosis*, arguing that instead of recovering a sense of identity, it is a matter of grasping nihilism as a chance of emancipation.

EMERGENCY

Ian Alexander Moore

In *Contributions to Philosophy*, Heidegger claims that the greatest emergency of his times is the lack of any sense of emergency (*die Not der Notlosigkeit*) (1999: §§50, 54, 60). One could also translate Heidegger's phrase as the 'plight' or 'distress' of 'being without plight or distress', although Vattimo follows Heidegger's translators in rendering it as 'absence of emergency' (*OR*, 215–16 n.5). Vattimo (along with Santiago Zabala, who is better known for his work on emergency) takes up Heidegger's diagnosis in several works. In *Of Reality*, for example, he stresses that conflict is necessary for what Heidegger calls the 'happening of truth'. Conventional hermeneutics, pragmatism, the theory of communicative action have largely become anodyne. These movements, as well as the trends towards realism in both post-analytic and Continental philosophy, share with many today the impression that 'nothing ever happens any more'. Indeed, they are complicit in this sense of eventlessness. Yet, as Heidegger saw a century ago, the 'lack of emergency', in Vattimo's synopsis, 'means lack of liberty, the identification of Being with the present order of entities and of thought as the mirroring of the world as it is'. It means siding with the status quo and the 'winners of history', in Walter Benjamin's sense of the phrase. What we need, rather, is to think of Being as an event and to participate actively in the conflict of its interpretation (*OR*, 108–12; see also Vattimo 2014). We need to be rescued, not 'from' the emergency, but, as Heidegger puts it in the *Black Notebooks*, 'into' it (Heidegger 2017: 219). Art and religion can help in this endeavour. But it is above all Heidegger himself – and '[p]erhaps only he' – who 'can provide the foundation from which to refute [. . .] the leveling of every political discourse to make the system "work well"', a levelling or, as Vattimo also calls it, a 'neutralization' that is sustained by the absence of emergency (Vattimo 2015a: 584). Perhaps, we might say then, it is only Heidegger who can save us now.

Vattimo and Zabala develop these thoughts on the absence of emergency in *Hermeneutic Communism* and in their response to commentators in Mazzini and Glyn-Williams (2017). See also George (2020), Polt (2006) (which Vattimo references in *OR*, 215–16 n.5), Vattimo (2015a) and Zabala (2015).

ENLIGHTENMENT

Silvia Mazzini

In Vattimo's work, the term Enlightenment or *Aufklärung* extends far beyond the historical delineation of an era. It points to the goal of modernity: the desire for the liberation of humanity through a universalising use of reason. The hope of emancipating the world by rational means corresponds to the systematic will of metaphysics, to the near-total domination of instrumental reason, and to the idea of linear progress. All these elements are put into crisis by the end of modernity and metaphysics. And this crisis is, for Vattimo, a precious opportunity to recover them, even if in a distorted form, and to become open to new forms of communal life and thought.

In particular, *Aufklärung* is for Vattimo the idea of a reality that aims to become progressively transparent (see **transparency/transparent society**), that is, completely and 'objectively' explicable through the use of a single *logos*, a single way of intending and applying reason. In these terms, *arché* should be understood in its double etymological meaning as the 'foundation' of a system of thought, and also as beginning, origin: a beginning of a linear, progressive history. But with the end of modernity, we are witnessing the end of history as a unitary process (see **postmodernism/postmodernity**): the category of novelty, the engine of the idea of progress, becomes routine; with the end of colonialism and the coming of globalisation, we instead witness the multiplication of histories and narratives, which can no longer be reduced to a unitary and universal use of reason.

In conjunction with these considerations, Vattimo argues that the category of the subject has also been dismantled – and in particular, the category of consciousness as the supreme instance of personality, which had been the basis of the ideas of the Enlightenment. In fact, Vattimo notes how Kant's definition of Enlightenment as coming out of a state of minority implies the conception of a subject who is master of herself (the same cogitating consciousness is at the foundation of the Cartesian system). After Freud and Nietzsche, however, the subject is no longer to be understood as an individual, but as a consequence of the disintegration of the unity of the foundation. Along with the subject, the category of the object, considered as what is in front of or opposed to the perceiving consciousness, also loses its legitimacy. Thus, with the crisis of the categories of subject and object, the Enlightenment's claim of an objective being and reality crumbles.

However, Vattimo notes, this does not happen as a result of a logical or rational refutation of the tendencies of Enlightenment. On the contrary, as Adorno and Horkheimer argued in their *Dialectic of Enlightenment*, all this goes along with an awareness of the collapse of reason itself. In fact, it is precisely when instrumental rationality reaches its completion (when the world is organised in a totally rational way), that dialectical totality is realised. But this realisation of reason goes against the original goal of Enlightenment itself: it does not lead to emancipation, but to the systematic organisation of the world, to what Heidegger calls the *Gestell*. This is the paradoxical situation described by Adorno and Horkheimer: Enlightenment leads to a form of incompatibility between freedom and the rationalisation it sought to achieve.

This crisis point, however, can be a valuable opportunity. Even the Enlightenment's categories and goals, in fact, despite losing their claims to validity, can be distorted (see *Andenken* [**remembrance**]) and subjected to a weakened recovery (see **weak thought** [*pensiero debole*]). Vattimo takes as a paradigmatic example aesthetic experience, and in particular the idea of the universality of beauty in Kant's Third Critique. What for Kant was the appeal to the universal human community 'is realized for us only in the form of multiplicity' (*TS*, 69). For Vattimo, the function of recognition within groups, which Kant attributed to art, is thus not dependent on a single model of the beautiful, a model that is imposed universally on all humanity. Today, universalism paradoxically consists instead in plurality. Hence, the recognition of different groups and communities through models and canons of beauty consists in the existence of different models and different communities. This form of belonging to a community, already present in Kant, takes on 'a form of objectivity very *sui generis*', that is, something can be considered universally valid (albeit in a distorted way) only in reference to the community that shares a certain aesthetic experience (*FT*, 136).

Therefore art, with its ability to 'open new worlds' (Heidegger), with its exposure of elements that are irreducible to the schemata of rational organisation or universalistic discourses, can point to new ways out of the Enlightenment. Indeed, it is by distorting the very tendencies of the

Enlightenment that art actually embodies the emancipatory scope that was its original goal.

EREIGNIS/APPROPROPRIATION (see BEING; ONTOLOGICAL DIFFERENCE)

ETHICS

Davide Monaco

For Vattimo, hermeneutics is a philosophy endowed with a decisive ethical vocation in the sense that the reasons for its constitutive anti-metaphysical application are not of a theoretical nature but of an ethical one (*BI*). The rejection of the conception of truth as conformity is not motivated by an attempt to rediscover a description of the meaning of being and of the idea of truth that is more suited and faithful to our experience, but rather stems from the rejection of metaphysics as a constitutively violent thought, in the sense that it is dominated by a conception of being as a *Grund* beyond which one does not go and which silences all questions (*BI*). Metaphysics is essentially a violent thought insofar as it is a thought of the peremptory presence of being as the ultimate foundation in the face of which one can only remain silent or adopt an attitude of religious adoration. The foundation that gives itself with no room for new questions, like a complete presence, is an authority that silences all further questions and imposes itself without further explanation, putting an end to dialogue (*BI*; see also **violence**).

Here emerges the particular notion that Vattimo uses of violence as the 'breaking off of the dialogue of question and answer', a notion that is intended to be radically anti-metaphysical in that it does not resort to concepts such as essence, nature and structure (*NE*). For Vattimo, even this definition of violence is not a true definition but is an interpretation that is not intended to be definitive, and indeed is exposed to dialogue and refutation, aware of its own historicity, which cannot be traced back to a stable structure, but to a history, that of the critique of metaphysical thought made by Nietzsche and Heidegger, but also by Levinas and Adorno (*BI*).

In Vattimo, the ethical application not only motivates the rejection of metaphysics, but also marks the transition, and its obligatory nature, to the 'weak' narrative-interpretive rationality, having as its object metaphysics itself, understood as the history of being and its nihilistic fulfilment in modernity. Continuity seems to be the only sense of rationality in the age of nihilism: if for metaphysics it was a question of establishing itself on the ultimate and certain basis of the early foundations, then for nihilistic hermeneutics it is a question of arguing in such a way that each proposed new interpretation dialogues with the previous ones, and does not constitute an incomprehensible dia-'logical' leap. The imperative of continuity is that of a rationality that is not defined in relation to objective structures that thought should and could reflect, but in relation to respect and *pietas* for one's neighbour. For this reason, too, continuity cannot be defined abstractly, but must refer to a neighbour, to specific neighbours (*BI*; *NE*). The imperative of continuity expressed by the criteria of coherence and shareability thus finds its rationality in the same ethical intentions that motivate the rejection of metaphysics, that is, in the rejection of the violence of the foundation as a silencing of questioning in favour of an openness to dialogue. The necessity of the transition to the weak rationality of hermeneutics once metaphysics has been rejected is thus revealed to be founded not on theoretical reasons, but on ethical ones.

The ethical inspiration behind the rejection of metaphysics also motivates the transition from metaphysics to hermeneutics in its Vattimian form of 'weak thought', allowing the reconstruction of a rationality in the age of nihilism, taking the latter as its guiding thread. The need for the fulfilment of nihilism, of taking it to its extreme conclusions, is thus revealed in Vattimo to be based on the same ethical reasons that are at the origin of nihilism. Nihilism, on the other hand, remains incomplete when it experiences the death of God – the dissolution of every ultimate foundation and stable structure of being – as a new delirious absolutisation of this situation or as a fall into a desperate human situation, self-referential, forever destined to failure. In so doing, in both cases, it forgets its ethical and ontological reasons and implications, and is not brought to what for Vattimo is its fulfilment: hermeneutics (*NE*).

EUROPE/EUROPEAN PARLIAMENT

Giuseppe Iannantuono

Political Europe, according to Vattimo, is a largely artificial construction that has the advantage of not identifying with a territory or a pre-existing national spirit, of not being based on the values of 'blood and soil'. Its identity is created by opposition, by contrast, by comparison with other models of development and political organisation. It is crossed by a kind of mass historicism that considers and suspends values and identities in a process of weakening metaphysical structures and emancipation from strong authorities. The very idea of identity, Vattimo emphasises, can only be interpreted with reference to the European tradition of modernity and the development of the human sciences, which placed at the centre the question of the identity and difference of cultures, epochs and societies. The specific character of Europe is that it is both the continent of national identities and the place where identities and multiple spiritual forms are always problematised.

But although Europe is trying to resist the habituation and homologisation produced by the intensive process of globalised mercantile relations, it is unable to reverse the technological drift of politics. It is now in the hands of technicians and experts obsessed with numbers and fiscal balances, who govern with procedural engineering rules and regulations laid down by institutional bodies that appear increasingly distant and mysterious to the will of the people. In fact, Europe, Vattimo states, increasingly relies on a model of governance that neutralises the political space of public debate into a pure management technique based on the model of technological rationality, where a rationally organised bureaucracy dominates. The centre remains invisible to the citizens. The normative core of European politics, according to Vattimo, is aimed at making the economic space work at its best and regulating the play of interests of economic and financial actors, according to the principle of the mercantilely useful or useless. This principle organises the running of society and things in managerial terms, where natural and human resources and political choices are resolved in agreeing on the best technique for directing processes.

When the economic vector, the main driving force behind the consolidation of government in Europe, tends to jam, the process of integration also grinds to a halt, leading to the current deadlock in political Europe and the explosion of the regressive phenomenon of Eurosceptic parties. It suffers from a twofold weakness: the lack of a public sphere of consensus and an institutional architecture imposed from above on the body of societies. It is indifferent to the symbolic and media models needed to succeed in uniting the peoples of Europe. On the other hand, the nation-states can count on the immediate appeal of the aggregating force of a common language, the evocative powers of a shared culture, and emotional participation in symbols of collective identification.

In the imaginative/symbolic void and in the absence of a European public opinion, interpretative elements, economic factors and institutional choices have been articulated in ways that have failed to harmonise the heterogeneity of economic resources and the political and cultural aspects of the different member states, making their relations anything but fluid, indeed worsening rivalries and differences, unable to mend the fracture between the interests of global finance and the difficulties and sufferings of the popular classes. At the very moment when it should be speaking with one voice, Europe is experiencing the risk of splitting and conflict, so that values and major issues, such as globalisation, the pressure of migratory flows and the COVID-19 pandemic, no longer find a suitable place for their consideration. European identity therefore no longer seems to have a point of arrival, torn apart on the religious, political and social fronts in a perpetual oscillation between universalist claims and nationalist withdrawal.

EVENT/OCCURENCE (see BEING)

EXISTENTIALISM

Mike Grimshaw

Vattimo's postmodern existentialism arises from the emancipation of diversity: 'If in this multicultural world, I set out my system of religious, aesthetic, political and ethnic values, I shall be acutely conscious of the historicity, contingency and finiteness of these systems, starting with my own' (*TS*, 9). The central existential act is to accept the Nietzschean statement that 'there are no facts, only interpretations', and to recognise the validity of 'the discourse of truth as aperture as opposed to the discourse of truth as correspondence' (*FT*, 8).

This repositioning and questioning of truth, linked to the death of God, creates the 'crisis of Humanism' (*EM*, 32), because the death of God, as 'the culmination and end of metaphysics' (*EM*, 33), means that existentialism has had to overcome the crisis of humanism as 'a process of the *practical* decadence of a value that is, humanity – which nevertheless remains *theoretically* defined by the same traits traditionally assigned to it' (*EM*, 34). That is, existentialism stands in defence of human values against the rise of the natural sciences. Now, via Heidegger and Nietzsche, in postmodernity Being is recognised as an existential event because 'a different possibility of existence for man emerges, a positive possibility and opportunity' (*EM*, 11), a decision of 'the accomplished nihilist' who is able to understand the 'sole opportunity' of nihilism (*EM*, 19).

Existentialism is part of the hermeneutic experience of truth that represents 'the outcome of not only early twentieth century existentialism but also earlier neo-Kantianism, phenomenology and even neo-positivist and analytic thought' (*BI*, 5). Hermeneutics is linked to existentialism, not only in relation to the continuation but also the critique of a neo-Kantian 'pre-understanding', but also because, via Heidegger, we need to interpretatively articulate that pre-understanding via 'existing as Being-in-the world' (*BI*, 5). Heidegger's ontology of the history of Being is, for Vattimo, the 'message that summons me' (*RP*, 91) and does so as 'an ethico-political demand' that is 'an existential discomfort' (*OR*, 42). The result is that we experience 'the problem of temporality as an existential category' (*DN*, 4). Hermeneutics is therefore a type of existential nihilism arising out of the emancipation offered by nihilism; this emancipation occurs out of 'Kierkegaard's intolerance of Hegelian rationalism [and] the revolt of the philosophical life versus positivistic science' (*BI*, 28), and continues as opposition to the world of scientific-technological phenomenology.

One expression of this existentialism is the return of religion, arising out of the fear 'of losing the meaning of existence', coupled with the fear 'of the widespread and profound boredom' that accompanies consumerism (*R*, 80). Existentialism is both an act of resistance and a desire for emancipation within modernity and capitalism, and opposes the philosophical and political totalitarianism of positivism (*NBG*, 34–5). The basis of Vattimo's existentialism is 'the Christian commandment of charity' (*FR*, 54); therefore, our being-in-the world is an existential decision and act in relation to this commandment of charity: 'the only emancipation I can conceive is an eternal life in charity, a life of heeding others and responding to others in dialogue' (*RP*, 97).

FREEDOM

Davide Monaco

The question of freedom in the age of the techno-scientific rationalisation of the world constitutes for Vattimo, even when it does not appear explicitly, the decisive issue of twentieth-century philosophy (Vattimo [1997b] 2002; 2000b: ix–xvi). Indeed, what unites the 'demonisation' of technology carried out by most of twentieth-century culture – by the artistic avant-garde as well as by existentialism, by phenomenology as well as by hermeneutics, by the *Kulturkritik* from the beginning of the century of the right as well as of the left – is a vision of technology as a negator of human freedom (*BIS*, 110–11).

However, the technical dominion against which that culture rebelled – Heidegger among them – was that of engine technology, in which from a central unit all the mechanisms subservient to it were deployed on the basis of the need for productivity, which through functionalisation gave meaning to every part of the system. This model of technology could only give rise to a society of total organisation, in which a central power sent orders to a purely passive periphery made up of citizens who increasingly took on the character of functional elements for the reproduction of the system and of simple cogs in an assembly line (*NE*). If we look at the roots of the anti-modern and anti-technology attitude of philosophers who are so different from each other, such as Heidegger and Adorno, we find this fear everywhere, namely that the free character of human existence, with its spontaneity and unpredictability, transcendence and incoercibility, planning skill and openness, is destroyed by the rational organisation of society, which needs planning, predictability and coordination, in other words the unchallenged domination of a central element (*AC*).

For Vattimo, on the contrary, the emergence of the hegemony of a new form of technology (of information and communication), whose image is effectively summarised by that of a network without a centre, allows us – adopting a suggestion by Joachim of Fiore (*AC*; see **Gioacchino da Fiore**) – to think of our era as a new age of the spirit, one of freedom (*NE*). According to Vattimo, the new technology of information and communication leads to a weakening of the principle of reality insofar as the experience we have of it gradually loses its realistic features: the world increasingly takes the shape of the image we are able to create of it – a becoming-image of the world that is, however, closely connected to it, giving itself as a multiplicity of images (Vattimo 2006: 191–3; *NE*). The establishment of the network allows us to think of freedom no longer metaphysically as a liberation beyond appearances and inauthenticity, in an alleged domination of the authentic being, but as a mobility between 'appearances', which, with Nietzsche, can no longer even be called such now that the real world has become a fable (Vattimo 1981a: 30; *BS*). Freedom is thought of by Vattimo as the liberation of differences and diversities, of the plurality of messages, images, languages, references and connections without a centre, in which we find ourselves living and which are transmitted to us, who become active and personal interpreters of them, oscillating between belonging and disorientation (*TS*).

GADAMER, HANS-GEORG

Jean Grondin

The founder of contemporary hermeneutics, Hans-Georg Gadamer (1900–2002) was a crucial inspiration for Vattimo's hermeneutic philosophy. In his major work *Truth and Method. Outlines of a Philosophical Hermeneutics* (1960), Gadamer challenged the notion that the truth experience of the humanities could only be ascertained through a methodology that would assure their objectivity by keeping in check the input and prejudices of the interpreter. Rather, he relies on the truth experience that occurs in the encounter with an artwork and on the guiding notions of humanism, geared towards the education of common sense, judgement and taste, to argue that the interpreter is productively and positively involved in the truth experience of the humanities. He relies in so doing on the insistence of his teacher Heidegger on the constitutive anticipatory structure of understanding and the hermeneutical circle in every interpretation. This leads Gadamer to highlight the historical and linguistic nature of the 'event' of understanding. Vattimo was attracted by Gadamer's overcoming of modern positivism, his reliance on the art experience, his insistence on the historicity, the event character and the linguistic nature of understanding as well as his effort to develop a hermeneutical ontology.

It was from his teacher Pareyson that Vattimo first heard of Gadamer. In the early 1960s a fellowship from the Humboldt Foundation enabled him to travel to Heidelberg to conduct research in the vicinity of Gadamer (*NBG*, 27). Both became close over the years and there is a correspondence between the two which will hopefully be published one day. One of the fruits of this encounter was Vattimo's translation of *Truth and Method* into Italian which, when it appeared in 1972, was the first translation of this book into a foreign language. Vattimo wrote a substantial 30-page introduction to his translation titled 'The Hermeneutical Ontology in Contemporary Philosophy' (Vattimo 1972b), to which he added an afterword in 1983. It can be seen as Vattimo's first and most basic account of his enormous debt towards Gadamer.

Constantly referring in this introduction to Gadamer's philosophy as a 'hermeneutical ontology', he wholeheartedly endorses Gadamer's famous dictum 'Being that can be understood is language', which means for him, in 1972 and beyond, that ontology can only be a meditation on language, since every encounter with the world, even that with things in their immediacy, can only be a linguistic encounter (see **language**). In Vattimo's view, this transforms philosophy itself, which becomes hermeneutics through and through, thus relinquishing the notion that there could be a Being beyond language. This notion leads Vattimo to his conception that hermeneutics has become the new *koiné* of our time. This *koiné* corresponds by and large to Gadamer's philosophy, at least in the way Vattimo interprets it: replacing the *koiné* of Marxism in the 1950s and 1960s, and that of structuralism in the 1970s, the hermeneutical *koiné* would underline the historical and linguistic nature of our understanding, hence the notion that truth is always a matter of interpretation. Vattimo likes to understand this hermeneutical *koiné* out of Nietzsche's declaration 'there are not facts, only interpretations' (*OR*, 16), which frames his understanding of Gadamer's own dictum 'Being that can be understood is language'. Vattimo thus promotes a more Nietzschean reading of this thesis which was perhaps less germane to Gadamer.

If Vattimo admired and defended Gadamer's hermeneutics, he could not hide his conviction that it ultimately lacked radicalism and in his view coherence, in that it did not take sufficiently into account Heidegger's critique of metaphysics and the need to break with the inherited understanding of Being and truth as something that would be beyond interpretation. This showed itself, Vattimo suggests, in Gadamer's unbroken and too optimistic reliance on the reason of history and tradition, hence Vattimo's push for weak thought and a more radical hermeneutics that would recognise its nihilistic vocation. This entails that a postmodern hermeneutics should do away with the classical notion of truth as a correspondence with some reality out there. This is an influential reading of Gadamer that Vattimo shared with Richard Rorty. It did not escape Vattimo that Gadamer did not embrace this postmodern turn of hermeneutics or this nihilist ontology (*OR*, 16). Yet Vattimo felt that a hermeneutic ontology that takes seriously the identification of Being and language, that is, in Gadamer's terms, of reality (*Wirklichkeit*) with the history of its understandings (*Wirkungsgeschichte*), provided a more consistent philosophy of interpretation.

GIFFORD LECTURES

Santiago Zabala

When Vattimo received the invitation to deliver the Gifford Lectures (Vattimo 2010d), he was not only honoured but also quite excited, even though he had already lectured throughout the world. This excitement had nothing to do with his being the only Italian philosopher ever invited to give these lectures, which had been established in 1888 by Lord Adam Gifford, but rather was stirred by those who had preceded him. These include, among many others, John Dewey, Hannah Arendt and Paul Ricoeur, whose Gifford Lectures Vattimo had read. This is probably why during the inauguration – after David Jaspers introduced him as 'one of the foremost philosophers in the world today' – he compared these lectures to the Nobel Prize as he thanked the Gifford committee for inviting him.

The lectures took place during four days in June 2010 at the University of Glasgow and were later published as the third part of his book *Of Reality: The Purpose of Philosophy*. Each lecture was introduced and moderated by a different university faculty member and was followed by a dinner where the Italian philosopher enjoyed fine Scotch whisky. Titled 'The End of Reality', the lectures' main objective was to combat the 'temptation of realism' and the 'return to order' that had been asserting itself since the beginning of the twenty-first century. What preoccupied Vattimo was the dominant feeling that the 'war against international terrorism' and 'the financial crisis' could only be defeated with a 'new realism' (*OR*, 2), which inevitably implies a number of philosophical problems that he confronts in these illuminating lectures.

In the first lecture – titled 'Tarski and the Quotation Marks of His Principle' – Vattimo begins by underlining the political nature of the Tarski theorem of truth. Following Rorty, who argued that this principle is proof of the uselessness of a certain type of philosophy, Vattimo believed that one must also question whom it is actually useful for. This not only proves Rorty right but also reveals the use the theorem is put to by those who favour the ongoing return to order and realism. According to Vattimo, whoever 'says, claims or affirms that P should stand outside of quotation marks is probably somebody who benefits from its being stated in this way' (*OR*, 83). But in order to reap these benefits, others must also accept the statement; they represent the paradigm that can verify it. Vattimo considers this principle 'reactionary' because most of its proponents will not acknowledge that there is always a 'community that professes and applies the paradigm', rendering its validity a matter of 'negotiation' rather than of 'rain' (*OR*, 90). The Tarski principle is useless for those who are dissatisfied with the current order because it ignores their demands. This is why Vattimo concludes this lecture by pointing out that being 'antirealist today is perhaps the only way to still be "revolutionary"' (*OR*, 91).

In the second lecture Vattimo continued to provide arguments in favour of anti-realism, but this time through Heidegger's opposition to Husserl's phenomenology. According to Vattimo, we must follow the former when he moved 'Beyond Phenomenology', as the lecture is titled, to oppose realism. Heidegger could not accept grounding 'regional ontologies in the transcendental I', as Husserl suggested, because doing so disregarded its historicity, becoming a 'vision *from nowhere*'. The problem with this vision, as with the Tarski principle, is that it doesn't 'put into play the existence of the philosopher who speaks and formulates the theories' (*OR*, 101). What inspires Heidegger's and Vattimo's rejection of objective metaphysics and realism is not the drive for a better vision or greater truth, but the need for freedom that is constitutive of any authentic existence. But how can we achieve greater freedom in a metaphysically organised society where existence is annihilated through objectivity?

The third and fourth lectures – 'Being and Event' and 'The Ethical Dissolution of Reality' – are meant to respond to this question. According to Vattimo, when we think Being as the unchanging givenness of the object, we are not only removing every sense of freedom and novelty from existence but also ignoring those who are unsatisfied with the current order. Even though 'knowing that Being is not an object but an event does not set us free', Vattimo believes it will allow us to stand 'against those who reject difference, conflict, change – against those who forget and want to make us forget Being itself' (*OR*, 112).

The novelty of these lectures within Vattimo's vast philosophical oeuvre is that now 'weak thought' is not meant to facilitate only Being's recollection, but also its practical interpretation as an event that happens, in other words, as a 'historical process in which we ourselves are involved' (*OR*, 115). This involvement does not call for a practical or theoretical rejection of the 'real world', but rather for an ethical dissolution that 'appeals to our freedom', to 'reduce violence and the supremacy of entities that pretend to be true Being' (*OR*, 117).

See also **realism/new realism**.

GIOACCHINO DA FIORE (JOACHIM OF FIORE)

Francisco Arenas-Dolz

Vattimo finds affinities with his conception of postmodernity in Joachim of Fiore's thesis on the kingdom of the Spirit (*BI*, 48, 50). The recovery of Joachim of Fiore (1135–1202) is of an apparently paradoxical nature, for just at the time when the metanarratives, or rather the unitary, linear and progressive conception of time, are coming to an end, Vattimo takes up the Joachimite philosophy of history and its theological 'progressivism'. But Vattimo's interpretation of this theology of history is more prophetic than metaphysical; it is a reading of the 'signs of the times' that takes place within the process he prophesies (*B*, 77). The Calabrian abbot announces an event that in some way has already happened, and at the same time calls us to take part in it, for it is still in progress. Through the correlation between the idea of salvation as the spiritualisation of Christianity and his elaboration of the categories of weakening and secularisation, Vattimo interprets postmodernity as the coming of the kingdom of the Spirit.

For Vattimo, the category of spiritualisation has two meanings: one, theological, according to which spiritualisation would be the renunciation of the literal and authoritarian interpretation of the biblical message in favour of a spiritual interpretation capable of recognising it in its secularising, not strictly sacramental and ecclesiastical, sense, which would lead to charity as the only constraint to secularisation and the core of Christian proclamation; and another, ontological, which refers to spiritualisation as a weakening of being, since in postmodernity reality is no longer seen as the stable presence of things defined in themselves that the mind has to reflect, but as a play of interpretations. Postmodernity is, therefore, understood by Vattimo as a period of spiritualisation of the real in a sense that is reminiscent of Joachim of Fiore and that also serves to show the correlation between postmodernity and Christianity.

GIRARD, RENÉ

Pierpaolo Antonello

The reading of René Girard's theory of the sacred marked a decisive moment in Vattimo's philosophical trajectory, which also intersected with personal and existential issues in relation to his Catholic background. In *Belief*, Vattimo claims that his reading of Girard's *Things Hidden since the Foundation of the World* had a momentous impact on his 'nihilistic rediscovery of Christianity' (*B*, 34). Vattimo establishes a relationship between his 'weak thought' and Girard's reading of the Christian scriptures seen as the subversion of the violent matrix intrinsic to the archaic sacred, which Vattimo translates 'in terms of secularization and weakening, or rather of incarnation' (*B*, 27). Vattimo identifies the violent deity of the sacred with the God of metaphysics, the *ipsum esse subsistens* of the ontology of Being (*B*, 39), whose 'death' was finally and rightly proclaimed by Nietzsche (whom Girard claimed should be read theologically rather than philosophically – see Girard 1984: 816–18; see also Fornari 2013).

It is in the Incarnation, God's abasement to the level of humanity (the *kenosis* of which Paul speaks in the Letter to the Philippians), that Vattimo rediscovers the very vocation for weakening present in the Heideggerian philosophy. Vattimo thus inscribes the hermeneutic philosophical tradition (Nietzsche, Gadamer, Heidegger, Derrida and himself) into a 'history of revelation', by claiming that the interpretative freedom that we have acquired over the course of Western cultural history is itself a sign of the process of weakening of Being brought forward by the Christian revelation.

Modern secularisation appears therefore as the true fulfilment of Christianity. Secularisation shall no longer be conceived of as abandonment of religion, but as the paradoxical realisation of Being's religious vocation (*AC*, 24; *BI*, 42–57). It is an 'application, enrichment, and specification' of the Christian origins of our Western civilization (*AC*, 65). In Heideggerian terms, secularisation as the weakening of Being is similar to the desacralising work of the Paraclete proposed by Girard through the rejection of victimisation and scapegoating introduced by the Judaeo-Christian scriptures. In *Christianity, Truth, and Weakening Faith*, Vattimo further clarifies the communal theoretical ground he shares with Girard, but also the diverging implications, specifically in relation to any analysis of the role of religion in contemporary society. Girard deems the question of secularisation as the fulfilment of Christianity an 'excessive' consequence, because with the total renunciation of the transcendental dimension of Christianity, humanity loses an essential element to control the process of social undifferentiation (the unleashing of rivalrous mimeticism, resentment and envy) that would lead to collective forms of violence. Conversely, the integration of the Judaeo-Christian tradition and vocation into a post-metaphysical, anti-foundational philosophical perspective, Vattimo maintains, would actively and positively contribute to the process of deconstruction of all those (residual) metaphysical claims which still aim at defining in 'natural', fixed terms what humanity is, including all those 'scientific', ontological 'truths' that thinkers such as Girard still resort to (Vattimo and Girard 2010: 34–5). For Vattimo, these are contingent products of history and, above all, ideological superstructures that have been used as coercive impositions on the part of those who, over the course of history, have held economic, political or symbolic power.

GLOBALISATION

Cristina Basili

Vattimo's nihilistic and 'weak' version of hermeneutics must be intended as a philosophy of praxis related to a democratic and emancipatory project. The critique of metaphysics that he mostly draws from his reading of Heidegger and Nietzsche has not just a theoretical purpose, but aims to release power from its ideological foundations. Accordingly, Vattimo performs in his writings a deconstruction of the link between metaphysics and violence, while he pursues a philosophy that, no longer conceived as recognition and acceptance of a peremptory objective foundation, develops a new sense of responsibility towards the oppressed and the marginalised (*OR*, 151).

On this basis, Vattimo offers a severe criticism of the pervasive effects of globalisation, viewed as the Western project of global dominion responsible for the ongoing destruction of entire cultures and the increase of economic and social inequalities on a worldwide scale:

The 'globalization' of the economy from which thinkers and democratic politicians expect so much has ended up producing an intensification of control. The differences between the rich – ever less numerous – and the poor, always increasing in number and in poverty, have grown exponentially in those very years of the globalized economy. (*OR*, 111)

Therefore, the threat today is constituted 'by the neutralizing forces of globalization in which mastery is hidden under the mask of economic rationality and techno-science seen as the only hope for "progress" and for "peace"' (*OR*, 204).

Globalisation, acknowledged as the imperialistic homogenisation of the world under technical and scientific rationality, realises the dominion of metaphysics, accomplishing the reign of total administration. As Adorno and Horkheimer pointed out in *Dialectic of Enlightenment*, we assist in the reversion of social rationalisation into generalised oppression. This is the reason why Vattimo can define globalisation as 'purely electrification, to use Lenin's term, without the Soviet, without the involvement of the people affected, and without the participation of the citizens in the decision-making process; in other words, without the responsibility of the interpreters' (*BIS*, 71). From this point of view, Vattimo recognises globalisation as the pervasive reduction of the social and economic spheres to the economic only: 'the realm of economics, of survival, is no more than a violent battlefield, unless there is mediation at a different level, the level of the political' (*NE*, 121). Drawing from Arendtian categories, he states the need to restore the independence of the political sphere from the economic. The political form that can accomplish this mediation is, for him, socialism, intended 'as a program for setting politics free of the laws of economics, especially the laws of the globalized economy, which, as we now see on every side, bring with them growing limits to freedom, to recognition, to the conditions for a "good life"' (*NE*, 129).

Hermeneutics as a critique of globalisation leads Vattimo to purge Marxian theory of its metaphysical and scientific elements, and to account for a 'hermeneutic communism' (*HC*) that would restore a political project based on a democratic transformation of social structures and an egalitarian redistribution of wealth (Vattimo 2007b: 46).

See also **Enlightenment; hermeneutic communism; universalism.**

GOD (see DEATH OF GOD)

HABERMAS, JÜRGEN

Eduardo Mendieta

Jürgen Habermas (b. 1929) is the most important German philosopher of the last half-century, and along with Vattimo, one of the most important public intellectuals in Europe. He has published a series of paradigm-shifting works: *The Theory of Communicative Action* (1984–87), *The Structural Transformation of the Public Sphere* (1989), *Moral Consciousness and Communicative Action* (1990a), *The Philosophical Discourse of Modernity: Twelve Lectures* (1990b), *Postmetaphysical Thinking: Philosophical Essays* (1992), *Between Facts and Norms: Contributions to a Discourse Theory of*

Law and Democracy (1998), and more recently *Auch eine Geschichte der Philosophie* (2019), a massive study of the relationship between faith and reason since the Axial Age. Their works overlapped in terms of the way they relate to the inheritance and reception of phenomenology, hermeneutics and pragmatism, as well as through key figures, such as Kant, Hegel, Nietzsche, Heidegger, Gadamer and Rorty, who was a dear friend to both.

Vattimo came to Heidelberg in 1959 to study with Hans-Georg Gadamer and Karl Löwith, at the time that Habermas was beginning his first teaching job there. Vattimo notes in his biography that while he was in Heidelberg he 'couldn't understand' Habermas's pronunciation (*NBG*, 28). Vattimo has made numerous and intense critiques of Habermas over the last decades, dealing with hermeneutics, phenomenology, ethics, politics and aesthetics (see Zabala 2019: 700–1). With respect to hermeneutics, Vattimo has argued that Habermas, who also inherits the 'hermeneutic *koiné*', has attempted to escape the historicist consequences of hermeneutics either by retreating into the social sciences, as he does in *The Theory of Communicative Action*, or by returning to a form of Kantian transcendentalism that dehistoricises language use, interpretation and understanding (*AD*, 28–9; *EM*, 145–6; *TS*, 109). Vattimo criticises Habermas's idea that language can be considered either transparent or reducible to the context, transcending the ideal presuppositions implied in every speech-act (*BI*, 32–4). Vattimo sees merit in Habermas's appropriation of Edmund Husserl's concept of the 'lifeworld' as a way to evade some of the historicist and relativist consequences of hermeneutics. But he also notes that Habermas, in contrast to Husserl, does not acknowledge the Western roots of the concept of the lifeworld as a discursive and dialogic horizon that is putatively non-coercive, and further, that this 'normative' conception of the lifeworld privileges a scientistic orientation, that is, the lifeworld as the analogue of the open and transparent community of scientists (*BI*, 20). With respect to aesthetics, Vattimo is critical of Habermas's deference to Kant's tripartite structure of reason that results in the autonomy of the aesthetic realm, as well his deference to the 'modern' and 'modernity' and its 'untroubled acceptance of the independence of the aesthetic' (*TS*, 65). Finally, Vattimo, particularly over the last years, has intensified his critique of Habermas (and Apel's) discourse ethics, which he sees as being one of the possible ethical responses to the hermeneutic transformation of modern philosophy. The key objection is the attempt to linguistify Kant's ethics, which has meant a retreat into a no longer tenable transcendental position that dehistoricises what Vattimo calls the 'ineluctable vocation for communication' that is carried by every language (*BI*, 32–3). Further, Habermas's discourse ethics is prey to Kant's subjectivism and solipsism (*BI*, 33). In more recent works, Vattimo has also criticised Habermas's revival of a dehistoricised and ahistorical concept of human nature (thus aligning himself with conservative Catholicism) in order to counter the threat of the biotechnological manipulation of the human genome (*FT*, 25, 57).

While Vattimo and Habermas have shared similar political views, Habermas has not directly or in print expressed his views on the former. In 2007 at the 14th International Congress of Philosophy held in Mazatlán, Mexico, Vattimo and Habermas held a public conversation, as one of the plenaries of the Congress, on the status of modern philosophy. Vattimo immediately turned the conversation to the decisive influence of Heidegger, who could not be denied to have been a Nazi. Habermas was visibly uncomfortable and instead talked about Nietzsche. Vattimo's loyalty to the Heideggerian tradition might explain Habermas's silence on him, notwithstanding their political loyalties.

HEGEL, GEORG WILHELM FRIEDRICH

Jakob Helmut Deibl

In *Poesia e ontologia* (1967b: 12; *ACT*, 17), Vattimo speaks of two motifs that constitute the essence of Georg Friedrich Wilhelm Hegel's (1770–1831) philosophy: 1) dialectics and 2) totality. While Vattimo firmly rejects the claim of totality, the motif of dialectics plays an increasingly important role in his thought, at least subliminally.

At many points in Vattimo's work, Hegel functions as a cipher for a self-enclosed thinking of totality. This goes hand in hand with the idea of a necessary process that culminates in a final telos, an all-encompassing unity or the reconciliation of all opposites. It represents the return of the spirit to itself (Vattimo 1974: 165). Vattimo continues the Schelling-inspired critique of Hegel by his teacher Luigi Pareyson (Vattimo 2000a: 87–8; *AC*; *DN*), but repeatedly expresses doubts as to whether this actually does justice to Hegel. An example of these reservations can be found in a passage where Vattimo speaks of a system 'that wanted to be "closed" like Hegel's (assuming one thinks it was this)' (Vattimo 2007c: 9). In addition, Vattimo also develops elements of a broken-affirmative reference to Hegel in brief hints throughout his work, which, however, does not find any systematic elaboration.

In *Art's Claim to Truth*, Vattimo understands the dialectical process as ground-giving. Particular systems are integrated in ever more general totalities and find their ground in this process. With regard to aesthetics, this means that a work of art only unfolds its truth when it is incorporated into the conceptual framework of philosophy and replaced by reflection (*ACT*, 41, 55–6, 112, 137–8; see also **death of art**). However, a passage in which Vattimo speaks of the hermeneutic circle contrasts with this totalising understanding of dialectics: comprehension is never without pre-comprehension; this only receives its reality in the process of comprehension, in which it is nevertheless absorbed. Probably with regard to the Hegelian dialectic of positing and presupposing, Vattimo cautiously speaks of a 'certain "truth" of Hegelianism' (*ACT*, 64).

In *Il soggetto e la maschera* (1974: 165), Vattimo acknowledges that Hegel, analogous to Nietzsche's project of a genealogy of guiding concepts, gives a historical reconstruction of the categories of thought and thus opposes a philosophy of principles.

'Dialectic and Difference' (*AD*, 158–86) presents the dialogue of a thinking of difference (Heidegger) with one of dialectics (Hegel). As Vattimo argues, for Hegel, structures of knowledge are not timelessly given, but represent historical forms of consciousness knowing itself, and as such presuppose a process of (re-)memory. What is external to consciousness is internalised, however, in a process that is under the auspices of reappropriation and necessity. At this point, Vattimo distances himself from Hegel and emphasises with Heidegger's thinking of difference a rupture with the logic of foundation, whereby this rupture prevents the representation of Being (*Sein*) in the all-encompassing linking of beings (*Seiende*). However, this does not amount to a form of irrationality, but rather means the opening towards historically-linguistically structured horizons of thinking. In this way, Vattimo approaches Hegel's thinking of historicity again. This is why he does not speak of overcoming the thinking of dialectics through a thinking of difference, but of a 'dis-location with respect to Hegel' (*AD*, 168).

In the programmatic text 'Dialectics, Difference, Weak Thought' (*WT*, 39–52), Vattimo returns to the relationship between dialectics and difference and now defines it more precisely as *Verwindung*. Dialectics and difference are not obsolete forms of thought, but retain their topicality in the sense of Heidegger's *Gewesenem*. Today, they are the inevitable point of departure for thinking, and thus also for the *pensiero debole* (*WT*, 39; see **weak thought** [*pensiero debole*]). Within dialectics, the thinking of difference brings to light a dissolutive tendency that dissolves the phantasm that thinking is the perception of external necessity. The thinking of dialectics, on the other hand, reminds us of the reference to memory. Being opens up to us as tradition/transmission (*Überlieferung*), which means taking leave of it as presence. This could be expressed with the three meanings that Hegel gives to the verb *aufheben* (to bid farewell, to keep, to raise to a new level), if, on the one hand, one does not see an algorithm in it and, on the other, does not think of the moment of raising to a new level as part of a teleological development, but rather as an actualisation or correspondence to the contingency of history.

Vattimo explicitly expresses this understanding in 'After Kant, After Hegel' (*RP*, 47–51):

> If Hegel were not claiming an entirely determined and rational destiny for reason (and it isn't clear how far he pushed this claim), there would be nothing objectionable in the Hegelian vision of philosophy. It's a vision in which the only thing left to philosophy is a way of apprehending the historicity per se of all that comes to pass in human reality. (*RP*, 51)

If Kant stands emblematically for the search for supra-temporally valid conditions of truth, Hegel stands for the historicity of being (*NBG*, 34–5). In line with this, Vattimo finally also connects Hegel with his concept of the 'weakening of the real' (*NBG*, 156) – as long as he is not perceived as a thinker of an absolute position.

HEIDEGGER, MARTIN

David Webb

Along with Nietzsche, Heidegger is the most important influence on Vattimo's work and the philosopher with whom he maintains the most consistent dialogue. This engagement extends throughout his work but is most clearly seen in *Essere, storia e linguaggio in Heidegger* ([1963] 1989), *Introduzione a Heidegger* (1971), *The Adventure of Difference: Philosophy after Nietzsche and Heidegger*, *Beyond the Subject: Nietzsche, Heidegger, and Hermeneutics*, *The End of Modernity: Nihilism and Hermeneutics in Postmodern Culture* and *Beyond Interpretation: The Meaning of Hermeneutics for Philosophy*. Vattimo's Gifford Lectures (*OR*) also engage with Heidegger's work.

For Vattimo, Heidegger alone was 'capable of opening us authentically to the experience of late modernity without a persistent implicit reference to metaphysical canons and principles' (*TS*, 73). His work introduces the idea that Being is an event, not a thing or a fixed structure, and thereby calls us to an experience of Being that is non-metaphysical, that offers a profound reflection on technology, and that opens the way for Vattimo to develop a hermeneutic engagement with nihilism.

It is arguably Heidegger's middle and later periods of work that are most important for Vattimo, including his lectures on Nietzsche and the essays in *Off the Beaten Track*, *Vorträge und Aufsätze*, *Identity and Difference* and *Time and Being*, in which Heidegger elaborates his thinking about language, history, art, technology and the finitude of Being. However, Vattimo reads Heidegger's major work *Being and Time* as the compass that orients all that follows. For Heidegger, the history of metaphysics is a prolonged forgetting of the question of Being, as a result of which our understanding of the meaning of Being has narrowed to 'being-present'. Another way to say this is that metaphysics has failed to recognise the ontological difference between Being and beings. Metaphysics has tended to treat Being as if it were a thing that can be known, whereas Heidegger reminds us that it cannot be defined or conceived in this way. Being is disclosed historically and through language, and therefore to think ontologically is to think historically, to think historically is to think hermeneutically, and hermeneutics involves an interpretation not of meaning, but of the event by which Being is disclosed in the world.

This event is understood in line with Heidegger's conception of truth. Heidegger tells that before we can make judgements that are true or false according to their correspondence to the things about which they speak, those things must first have shown themselves to us in some way, and for Heidegger this initial disclosure is the primary notion of truth. Vattimo takes this to mean that from the point of view of hermeneutic ontology, our primary task is not to produce statements that correspond to things but to adopt a stance towards the world that corresponds to the way things show themselves to us in our own historical situation, for example via new forms of information and communication technology (see **media**).

Vattimo acknowledges that our historical situation is that of nihilism, encapsulated in Nietzsche's declaration that God is dead. For Heidegger, it is the history of metaphysics that has brought us to this point, but metaphysics is coming to an end, and this makes it possible once again to raise the question of Being. To engage with this question through a hermeneutic practice is to respond positively to nihilism, not by returning to lost principles but by taking seriously our own interpretative response to the disclosure of Being in our own time.

In Vattimo's return to Christianity in his later writing the Christian concept of *kenosis* becomes key to thinking the history of secularisation and the weakening of strong foundations. But Vattimo also notes a profound reflection on Christian experience running through Heidegger's work. For example, when Heidegger describes the temporal character of salvation in his 1920 lecture course *The Phenomenology of Religious Life*, Vattimo reads this as an anticipation of the account of the original temporality of Dasein in *Being and Time*.

In *Being and Time*, the focus of the analysis is on the individual Dasein and an attempt to recover the horizon for understanding the meaning of Being. Soon after its publication Heidegger's thinking moved away from fundamental ontology, undergoing a shift towards thinking Being through the event of its being given in language and art. For many commentators on Heidegger's work, this represents a decisive 'turn' or *Kehre* in his thinking, but there remains disagreement over its precise terms and significance. Vattimo sees in the *Kehre* Heidegger's recognition that his attempt in *Being and Time* to displace transcendental philosophy still allowed too central a role for the individual subject. If authenticity has to do with truth as a response to the opening of worlds, then it has to be articulated not in relation to the individual but historically and with regard to community. In this way Vattimo's interpretation of Heidegger dovetails with his reading of Marx, a conjunction he elaborated in the form of hermeneutic communism.

Vattimo takes seriously Heidegger's view that technology is the apotheosis of the tendency of metaphysics to rationalise the world not just in terms of cause and effect and instrumentality, but above all on the basis of a strong foundation or first principle. By carrying this to an extreme, technology allows us to see it more clearly, but it also reveals the extent to which humanism, understood as the project of knowing the world and organising it to meet human beings' needs and interests, is dependent on metaphysics. With the end of metaphysics must therefore come the end of humanism as well.

Vattimo is an optimistic thinker and sees in this an opportunity to begin a new venture in the interpretation of the world, but only if we take up an appropriate attitude towards the end of metaphysics. Heidegger underlines that our thinking today remains caught up in the ending or closure of metaphysics. While on the one hand we must avoid renewing an appeal to first principles of any kind, on the other we should resist the temptation of thinking that we can simply leave metaphysics behind us through a decisive overcoming (*Überwindung*). Instead, overcoming must involve an acceptance of metaphysics coming to an end, an attitude that Heidegger calls *Verwindung*, a convalescence and gentle twisting free from what nonetheless remains the horizon of our thinking. For Vattimo, *Verwindung* denotes a response to the 'interminable weakening of Being'. It is central to Vattimo's understanding of the hermeneutic relation of thinking to its metaphysical past (*EM*; Vattimo 1987c) and also characterises what Vattimo calls his 'left Heideggerianism' (*BI*, 13; Rorty 2007). As *Verwindung*, thinking becomes 'a recollection of the oblivion of Being' (*BI*, 13): not a making present of the past, but a long leave-taking from metaphysics as a historical possibility that we accept both as our own and as contingent and changeable.

Thinking (*Denken*) thereby becomes remembrance (*Andenken*) (*AD*), which situates itself within metaphysics in a spirit of quiet subversion. Therefore, if Heidegger calls our attention back to ontological difference, we cannot, Vattimo points out, simply return to a single determination of difference, metaphysical or otherwise. Not only is difference not given as such, withdrawing to leave us to trace its provenance, but insofar as it is historical, difference may not occur as it has occurred in the past. *Andenken*, Vattimo writes, 'thinks Being *as difference*, that is, as what differs in multiple senses' (*AD*, 138). Hermeneutical philosophy must therefore interpret the way Being as difference occurs in our time, which is to say how it has been handed down to us in language, knowing that there is no objective truth that interpretation can retrieve.

See also *Andenken* **(remembrance); being; convalescence (*Verwindung*); hermeneutic communism; hermeneutics;** *kenosis*; **media; Nietzsche, Friedrich; nihilism; truth.**

HERMENEUTIC COMMUNISM

Eduardo Mendieta

In Vattimo's work, the term 'hermeneutic communism' must be taken in at least four senses. First, it refers to the volume *Hermeneutic Communism*, which he co-authored with Santiago Zabala, a long-time collaborator and now director of the Vattimo Archives at the Pompeu Fabra University in Spain. Second, it refers to the way in which communism, and more concretely the promise and project of communism, must adopt the key insights of weak thought in order to remain relevant to our times. Third, and in a related way, it argues that the telos of hermeneutics is to provide tools that can have historical efficacy in terms of political projects. The claim is that hermeneutics is not simply exegetical, philological or interpretative, but that its effects of historicisation, and historicising in general, have a political relevance and efficacy. Hermeneutics is both critical and political insofar as interpreting better means aiding in the project of both enlightenment and social emancipation. A fourth sense of the term is that weak thought is not simply what we get from either ontological hermeneutics (Heidegger and Gadamer) or genealogical critique (Nietzsche and Foucault), but rather the very height of historicising thinking. This in turn means that all attempts at transcendental groundings have to be abjured; all we have of being that has been interpreted is the task of interpretation guided by the imperative of social emancipation. In the following, by focusing on the book, we aim to elucidate the other three meanings of the term.

Gianni Vattimo and Santiago Zabala's *Hermeneutic Communism* reads very much like a 'manifesto', or at the very least a 'proclamation'. Manifestos, like proclamations, have three distinct components. First, they offer a bird's-eye view of why we might find ourselves in a given historical situation. They don't offer reports but reconstructions and historical interpretations. That panoramic view, however, is neither innocent nor neutral. The way it paints the temporal horizon of our time is itself a partisan stand, an invested and interested way of constructing a story about how we got to be where we are. Second, manifestos aim to dissect historical reality in a very specific way, aiming to locate those social agents or forces that have been decisive in bringing us to the historical crossroads where we stand, and which have been either the primary beneficiaries or primary losers from the socio-economic system under analysis. Manifestos and proclamations are to political reality what scalpels are to surgery. Thirdly, manifestos and proclamations are rhetorical exercises that, once read, make it difficult not to want to get up, march and join the movement that the manifesto proclaims. Manifestos mobilise language so as to produce a certain affective response that has efficacy. They are the adrenaline and passion of the body politic.

The indisputable and inescapable point of reference for any and all manifestos is clearly Marx and Engels's 1848 *Manifesto of the Communist Party*. As Umberto Eco pointed out in a wonderful little essay, the *Communist Manifesto* is probably one of the most important political documents of the last two hundred years. It should rank up there with Luther's 95 theses that launched the Reformation, the French Declaration of Human Rights, and the American Declaration of Independence. The *Communist Manifesto* taught us to think in a historical-materialist way, without expressly arguing that this is what it sought to do. It is a great pedagogical tool precisely because its linguistic flourish aimed to give us concrete tools of social analysis. But these tools of analysis can't be dissociated from their rhetorical embodiment. After reading the *Communist Manifesto*, we find it almost impossible not to see history in the way Marx and Engels have articulated it.

Like the *Communist Manifesto*, *Hermeneutic Communism* is full of provocative readings that aim to provide grounds for their basic argument, namely that only weak thought, qua the realisation of hermeneutics, can prepare us for the advent of communism, which in turn is now conceived as a historical event. In a word, hermeneutic communism is communism purified of all metaphysics. The argument proceeds in this way. We live in the age of the end of metaphysics. All that remains after the demise of metaphysics is the imperative to interpret. Consequently, hermeneutics is all we have left, since all we have left is history, and our attempts to make sense of it, and thus all we have left is the history of interpretations. What remains of being, all *ontos*, is pure interpretation. Since there are neither transcendental grounds nor ontological groundings left that can offer theoretical foundations or rational warrants for our projects, all we have is the ceaseless task of historical interpretation. Hermeneutics is all the philosophy that is left and all that we need or could need, for in it we find both a politics and an ethics. The politics is that of a weakened communism, that is, a communism without metaphysical stilts, which offers itself simply as the clamouring of the oppressed and the call for economic justice of the victims of capitalism. The ethics implied by this hermeneutics that is all that is left to us is an ethics of interpretation in which all interpretations have a prima facie claim to be heard and countenanced.

If these are the key philosophical moves, then *Hermeneutic Communism* raises a series of questions. First, and most importantly, how did metaphysics come to an end? Sometimes our authors seem to write as though the end of metaphysics had happened qua the dispensation of being itself. So, like the God of Jewish mysticism and Schelling's onto-theology, being contracts and retracts to make space for the human will and human history. But the end of metaphysics has not come, at least not in the sense that Vattimo and Zabala seem to imply. On the one hand, what they call 'framed democracy', with its handmaiden, analytic philosophy and its metaphysics of descriptions and truth as objectivity, is still chained to a metaphysics of representation. Let's call this metaphysics of representation the metaphysics of representational equivalences. Evidently, this metaphysics is still operative, even if it seems to be anachronistic. How can something come to an end, and yet remain operative?

What remains relevant is not whether metaphysics has come to an end, which is not unlike Nietzsche's announcing the 'death of God', in order to reveal that we now live in a post-secular society (Habermas 2019), in which God has not died but in fact seems more alive than ever. What *Hermeneutic Communism* leaves us with is the concern with how the end of metaphysics might have come about and – to use Nietzsche's allegory of theocide – how we killed God, that is, how we abolished metaphysics, not as a final act, but as a project, an endeavour, the highest calling of the philosophical vocation. Metaphysics did not come to an end of its own accord, nor was it a gift that we have received or struggled to interpret from being, or some transmundane force. Metaphysics keeps being abolished by the work of philosophy, which is carried out by philosophers using different tools in different philosophical traditions.

There are many great phrases in *Hermeneutic Communism*, and one of them is the following: 'the task of philosophy is not to describe the world, but to interpret it productively' (*HC*, 5). This phrase is particularly relevant because it points out that the task of philosophy is not simply, and least of all, to attempt to describe the world, but to contribute to our transformation of the world by achieving 'better', more 'expansive', more ecumenical, more emancipatory understandings. Vattimo and Zabala mean 'productively' in this latter sense, namely that understanding has a practical intent. Hermeneutics is a praxis that transforms us, others, our worlds, our forms of life. It does this by the fusion of horizons of meaning, but it does this already at the lowest register of hermeneutics: when a new interpretation is put forth. But not all interpretations are equally close to God and not all interpretations interpret the world productively. When Vattimo and Zabala urge us to engage in a hermeneutics that interprets the world productively, they have already directed us to a major question: what counts as a more productive interpretation? This turns out to be the question of what are the criteria of evaluation of better or worse interpretations.

In *Hermeneutic Communism*, Vattimo and Zabala have made very persuasive arguments about the philosophical and practical consequences of weak thought, its radicalisation of hermeneutics into the kind of philosophical ethos that should replace dialectical and historical materialism, and the need to fuse communism with our contemporary horizon of interpretation. The many threads and suggestive arguments developed in the book have already generated a lively discussion covering the four senses (and more) of 'hermeneutic communism', which was explored in the volume edited by Silvia Mazzini and Owen Glyn-Williams, *Making Communism Hermeneutical: Reading Vattimo and Zabala* (2017).

HERMENEUTICS

Gaetano Chiurazzi

Philosophical hermeneutics is the cornerstone of Vattimo's philosophy. His hermeneutics differs from the other two main strands of twentieth-century hermeneutics, that is, the German one, whose most prominent representative is Hans-Georg Gadamer, and the French one, represented by Paul Ricoeur. This difference stems from the pre-eminent influence of Nietzsche, which characterises Vattimo's hermeneutics as having a 'nihilistic vocation', radically anti-metaphysical, secularised and aimed above all at highlighting the emancipatory implications of interpretation.

In the history of hermeneutics, four main stages can be distinguished: 1) the ancient world, 2) the era of the Protestant Reformation, 3) the Romantic era and 4) the contemporary era. In the ancient world, hermeneutics did not exist as a separate, methodologically self-aware discipline: what is identified as 'hermeneutics' is rather a series of studies and critical works covering various other disciplines, from grammar to rhetoric, from exegesis to philology. What these studies have in common, however, is the fact that they concern the production of meaning handed down in writing. In antiquity, hermeneutics is strictly confined to the literary sphere. Starting with the Reformation, the privileged focus of hermeneutics becomes the holy text of the Christian tradition, the Bible. The emergence of the new reformed Churches together with the process of 'democratisation' of Scripture thanks to its various translations into the new national languages raised especially urgent interpretative problems. It was in fact in this context that the problem of the relationship between interpretation and truth began to arise.

It is, however, with Romanticism that we witness a first universalisation of the task of hermeneutics. With Schleiermacher – an author to whom Vattimo devoted one of his earliest writings (Vattimo 1968) – every meaning formation, not only written texts but also verbal communications, becomes an object of hermeneutical concern. Hermeneutics, as the 'art of avoiding misunderstanding', is the discipline that deals with the elucidation of *loci obscuri*, that is, those misunderstandings, gaps, obscurities that can arise in human communication. It was between the end of the nineteenth century and the beginning of the twentieth, with Dilthey and Heidegger, that hermeneutics became a clearly delineated philosophical discipline. In fact, Dilthey makes it the main discipline of the human sciences, that is, a discipline aimed at understanding not nature but history (Dilthey 1996). Heidegger investigates the ontological foundation of this connection between understanding and history, locating it in the temporality of human existence. Thus, Heidegger paved the way for a philosophy that made hermeneutics the fundamental tool for a critique of traditional metaphysics and its emphasis on the present (Heidegger 2001). This, for Vattimo, brings to fruition a tendency implicit, in his opinion, in the history of hermeneutics, namely its 'nihilistic vocation', that is, its emancipation from strong, dogmatic, metaphysical and violent structures in favour of a more participatory, secularised and human vision of existence.

Some of the main traits that Vattimo attributes to philosophical hermeneutics can be summarised under the following headings: 1) philosophy of history, 2) ethics and 3) emancipation.

1) According to Vattimo, the history of hermeneutics shows a general tendency in the history of the West, and is therefore indicative of a specific philosophy of history. This tendency is what he calls the 'nihilistic vocation' of hermeneutics' (*BI*), that is, the tendency towards an ever-increasing reduction of strong metaphysical instances and structures,

culminating in the cultural-historical phenomenon that Nietzsche called the 'death of God'. The forceful introduction of Nietzsche into the history of hermeneutics – or the hybridisation of this history with Nietzschean philosophy – constitutes the distinctive feature of Vattimian hermeneutics. The history of hermeneutics is encapsulated in Nietzsche's aphorism 'How the "True World" Finally became a Fable' (Nietzsche 2003): a progressive loss of cogency and meaning of the distinction between the intelligible world and the sensible world, the true world and appearance, until the affirmation of a philosophy of the full acceptance of the finite condition of human life.

2) Vattimo combines in an original way the nihilistic element that he attributes to the history of hermeneutics with a spiritualistic element stemming from Joachim of Fiore's philosophy of history. The history of interpretation, typical of Western civilisation as a civilisation of Scripture, is also a history of salvation, marked according to the three moments of the age of the Father (the law), the age of the Son (grace) and the age of the Spirit (*AC*). This progression goes in the direction of an ever-increasing liberation of meaning from the letter, which on an ethical level corresponds to the shift of focus from law to charity. For Vattimo, philosophical hermeneutics has a profound ethical significance: not only in the sense, as Gadamerian ethics also shows, of a rehabilitation of Aristotle's practical philosophy as a form of rationality suited to the historical dimension of human existence, but above all in the sense of a specific ethical orientation that posits charity as the end of history in a process of progressive emancipation. Such an emancipation is achieved through participation in the communitarian and communicative dimension of the spirit, of which language is the expression on an intersubjective level.

3) Hermeneutics is therefore intrinsically emancipatory (*NE*): the interpretative operation of the texts of the tradition does not aim at the determination and preservation of their authentic or true content, but at the multiplication of differences, in accordance with the historico-ontological condition of the interpreter. This aim for Vattimo does not lead to mere relativism, because it is not a structural concept of the coexistence of multiple cultures, but rather expresses a sense of history that, as in Joachim of Fiore, also has a prophetic, that is, historico-destinal meaning.

Vattimo's hermeneutics therefore accomplishes an important conceptual shift from an epistemological problem (the relationship between truth and interpretation) to a fundamentally ethical problem (the problem of reducing violence), which is the core of his philosophical proposal also known as 'weak thought' (*WT*).

See also **Dilthey, Wilhelm; Gioacchino da Fiore; Schleiermacher, Friedrich**.

HISTORY/HISTORICITY

Thomas Winn

History and historicity are key terms that underlie the entirety of Vattimo's work. Their meaning emerges from the hermeneutic understanding of historical knowledge that developed at a time when Friedrich Nietzsche began to criticise the 'malady' of historical objectivism. Starting with Wilhelm Dilthey, hermeneutics began to see that historical knowledge has its own historical embeddedness, its own historicity. Vattimo took from this that history could not simply be an objective modelling of past events, determined as a 'fact' that subsists from a 'supreme or comprehensible viewpoint' around 'which events are gathered and ordered' (*TS*, 3). Rather, historical knowledge is bound to interpretation. What Vattimo calls history is only ever a product of the oscillating and discursive activity of the interpretative process, caught in the circularity of language and the historicity of the interpreter. This observation is coupled with an awareness that the collected fragments of the past are themselves figured and disfigured by the historicity of their transmission: the past is a product of the 'interpretative processes of others' (*HC*, 93).

Vattimo sets out to show that what this historicity really meant was not fully appreciated in hermeneutics until Martin Heidegger's acceptance of the 'universality of the interpretative structure of knowledge' (*AD*, 21). This move – following what Vattimo sees as Nietzsche's recognition that 'there are no facts, only interpretations' – shifted 'the ground from under knowledges' as it caused 'them to be seen as dependent on this historicity of Being' (*NBG*, 110). He argues that this radicalisation of the historicity of all knowledge was extended to Being itself, because if 'Being, that can be understood, is language' and 'language is the fundamental mode in which Being occurs' (*AD*, 24), then the circularity and historicity of our language inevitably constitutes a kind of 'third horizon' in which Being appears to us. As with historical knowledge, Vattimo understands that:

> Interpretation is not description on the part of a neutral observer, rather, it is a dialogic event in which the interlocutors are equally played out and from which their result changed in some way. They understand one another being situated within a third horizon, a horizon they do not have any control over but within which and by which they are placed. (*BS*, 86)

This third horizon is the historicity of Being itself. Our participation in the interpretative process of Being '"realises" or "sets into play" [*mette in opera*] and modifies at the same time this horizon' (*BS*, 86). History then is bound to the temporal aspect of interpretation's circularity and so history becomes that which constitutes the appearance of Being as it appears in language. This enables Vattimo to read Heidegger's *Being and Time* as 'Being *is* [or 'eventuates in'] Time' (*OR*, 44). Being appears to us as an event in existence. It appears now as flashes, as sudden illuminations. It appears as the historical horizon itself, foregrounding the phenomenon of the interpretative act in the interpreter's temporality, in their finitude. Vattimo shows that in witnessing the temporal aspect of this circularity we again realise that history is not constituted by a unitary and continuous succession of events that have happened, but that it happens in the present and so is linked 'to existence, and to the existence of mankind' (*NBG*, 20). Vattimo believes that this inevitable temporalisation of all knowledge, and so of Being itself, is what Nietzsche theorised as the advent of nihilism. The horizon of Being today has become a horizon in which Being itself is being degrounded and dissolved. The nihilistic horizon, then, forces us to encounter 'the experience of the nothing' (*OR*, 59), the experience of mortality.

Vattimo puts forward the argument that even in the degrounding consequences of nihilism, both history and historicity keep their emancipatory potential. In fact, he states that 'the authentic relationship with the past is opened up by the awareness of one's own mortality, a condition that assumes as only mortal even the traces and the models which have been handed down through history' (*BS*, 77). The mortality of the past, of the fact that history starts from existence and finishes within the circularity of interpretation, allows Vattimo to follow Nietzsche in claiming that history is now open to follow the freedom found in the world of symbols, in what Heidegger called remembrance (*Andenken*). History becomes effective as play as it remains open to a 'vision of history as the history of language and as open dialogue' (*AD*, 25) – what Hans-Georg Gadamer called 'effective history' (*Wirkungsgeschichte*). It becomes an ontological possibility as an ontology of actuality – one that theorises the past, present and future while remaining within the contradictions of existence and meaning, of doing and knowing; within the transmissions themselves. In 'knowing the groundlessness of these transmissions, we can play and forward ourselves (weakly) into history as interpretation' (*BS*, 78).

HÖLDERLIN, FRIEDRICH

Jakob Helmut Deibl

Single verses by the poet and philosopher Friedrich Hölderlin (1770–1843) accompany Vattimo's writing in much the same way as significant verses from the Bible: as motto, emblem, or summary of specific discourses. Vattimo's reference to Hölderlin has two directions: 1) the articulation of an ontology of language, and 2) a historical-philosophical determination of our epoch. Mostly, quotations from Hölderlin occur in connection with Vattimo's reading of Heidegger (see **Heidegger, Martin**).

1) Vattimo prefaces his first book on Heidegger (Vattimo 1963) with some verses by Hölderlin: 'humans can / Endure the fullness of the gods only at times. Therefore / Life itself becomes a dream about them' (*Brod und Wein*, vv. 114–15; *NBG*, 163).[8] In this way, he expresses that the identification with the event or the meaning ('fullness') can never be thought of as presently available, but must be remembered as one that has already diminished (*BS*, 82). He contrasts the notion of being as presence with a language-oriented understanding of being, which is given an emblem in the verses, 'Have called by their names many of those in Heaven / For we are a conversation / And able to hear from each other' (*Versöhnender der du nimmergeglaubt*, vv. 72–4; *BIS*, 30, 44; *NBG*, 108).[9] 'Conversation' (*Gespräch*) here has the meaning of dialogue with the living and the dead, as well as with works of lore. The copula 'are' (*sind*) is to be understood *strictu sensu*: We are only as conversation, being occurs linguistically-hermeneutically as dialogue. The fact that human action does not primarily take place technically on external objects but linguistically, and that the idea of rigid contours of reality dissolves in favour of an aesthetic or poetic understanding of reality and truth, is summarised by Vattimo in the verse: 'Full of acquirements, but poetically, man dwells on this earth' (*In lieblicher Bläue . . .*; *BIS*; *AC*, 54; *BI*, 99).[10] In all of this, the nihilistic calling of being emerges; the figure of the *Übermensch*, which Vattimo interprets as the 'man of the beyond', is ready to take this on. Vattimo sums this up in the verses: 'But where danger lies . . . there also grows / That which saves' (*Patmos*, vv. 3–4; Vattimo 2012: 211; *OR*; *DN*, 129, 182).[11]

---

8 'Nur zu Zeiten erträgt göttliche Fülle der Mensch. / Traum von ihnen ist drauf das Leben. [. . .]'
9 '[. . .] Der Himmlischen viele genannt, / Seit ein Gespräch wir sind / Und hören können voneinander.'
10 'Voll Verdienst, doch dichterisch, wohnet der Mensch auf dieser Erde.'
11 'Wo aber Gefahr ist, wächst / das Rettende auch.'

2) For Vattimo, reference to Hölderlin is connected with the historical-philosophical determination of our position in the time of the ending of metaphysics. According to him, Heidegger sees in Hölderlin's verses basic words of thought, which on the one hand enable us to ask the question about the character of our epoch, and on the other hand open ('found') its hermeneutic horizon. As an emblem for this, Vattimo uses two verses of Hölderlin often quoted by Heidegger: 'What use are poets in times of need?' (*Brod und Wein*, v. 122; *NBG*, 106)[12] and 'what remains is found by the poets' (*Andenken*, v. 59; *NB*, 199–205; *BIS*, 32, 211).[13] With Hölderlin, Heidegger seeks an exit from the experience of the world trapped in techno-ordained thinking – as a renewal of culture from the German tradition (Hölderlin, Nietzsche), but also as the possibility of a new experience of being in the technological age, illustrated in the above-mentioned words: 'But where danger is, grows / The saving power also' (*Patmos*, vv. 3–4; *NBG*, 114; *BIS*, 40).[14] Furthermore, the *Oldest System-Programme of German Idealism* is a foundational text for Vattimo's understanding of the inextricable link between art, religion and philosophy in the process of secularisation. In its wake, Hölderlin's poetry holds open a place of waiting between human beings and the escaped gods (*BI*, 58–74).

I

IDEOLOGY

Thomas Winn

Vattimo's direct consideration of the meaning of ideology and the scope of its critique is quite fragmented in his work, even if his project is directly engaged as an 'ethico-political' critique. Vattimo believes that interpretation, as the mode in which all thinking occurs, is both discursive and discontinuous, and so 'ideological, moral, or cultural biases' (*BIS*, 58) are commonplace. We look 'at things with interest' (*HC*, 92) as we are involved in political and social 'realities' that 'are nothing but the crystallization of prior existential decisions' (*OR*, 64). The force of these horizons, and their attempted overthrow, are always tainted by ideological

---

12 'Wozu Dichter in dürftiger Zeit?'
13 'Was bleibt aber, stiften [found] die Dichter.'
14 'Wo aber Gefahr ist, wächst / das Rettende auch.'

tendencies and violence because of the totalising effect of human thought, which presumes from the start that what is 'out there' is 'of reality'.

A critique of ideology then, as understood by Vattimo, ranging from efforts made by Marx to the Frankfurt School, has as its starting point the aim of revealing the intricacies of these horizons and the motivations behind them, showing the biases, power structures and mechanisms that sustain them. Since Martin Heidegger, the activity or task of hermeneutics has followed a similar footing. Hermeneutics has set out with the intention of revealing the 'untenability [*insostenibilità*] of what metaphysics has always ascribed to Being, namely its presence, its eternity, its "thingness" or *ousia*' (*WT*, 44). The metaphysical conception of Being has violently assumed that 'what there is' is truly understandable. Vattimo calls this assumption 'the main mystification of ideology ... what one might call the "Platonic fallacy" – the attribution of an eternal and stable character to Being' (*BS*, xxx). In response, the task of hermeneutics has been to deground this claim by showing how the historicity and finitude of interpretation makes a metaphysical conception of anything impossible. Vattimo believes that the Marxian perspective of the critique of ideology parallels this activity in one respect as it also assumes that 'the general traits that constitute the horizon within which beings become visible and the single experiences are made possible, are not eternal, but are qualified historically' (*BS*, 59). As such, Vattimo has claimed that what 'Marx and Marxism called the critique of ideology, Heidegger conceived and practiced as the critique of metaphysics, namely, the critique of the definitive claim to truth' (*OR*, 7).

It is here, however, that Vattimo sees two stumbling blocks which have prevented the critique of ideology from actualising its hermeneutical potential. The first is that the critique of ideology becomes limited to a kind of dialectical 'uncovering' when it believes that it can reveal those hidden and repressed truths in order to move towards a truer perspective on what there really is. Vattimo recognises that hermeneutics also involves this risk – the risk of 'being taken as an activity of deciphering, of retracing grounds and meanings that are hidden yet ultimately attainable' (*BS*, 59) – and so becoming a kind of 'hermeneutics of suspicion'. Vattimo argues that in 'thinking in terms of a truth that would refute ideologies and forms of false consciousness' (*OR*, 15) we return to a type of realism that forgets the ontological difference. The second stumbling block is what in 'Dialectics and Difference' (*WT*, 39) Vattimo sees as the more prevalent critique of ideology today, one which centres on the metaphysical assumption of 'totality and reappropriation'. This critique makes a different 'effort to reconstruct a non-partial point of view, one which would thus allow us to grasp totality as such' (*WT*, 40). However, Vattimo believes that, as with the first stumbling block, this modality of the critique of ideology falls back on to a perspective that avoids both the discursive and discontinuous character of interpretation and, ultimately, the freedom, historicity and open possibility of existence that can never be totalised into a new scheme or position.

Vattimo's 'alternative' to these risks is to follow the key task of weak thought, that is, to make the decision for 'the nexus grounding–degrounding (*fondazione-sfondamento*)' (*BS*, 60) and to think difference properly (*WT*, 43). This grounding–degrounding nexus is the play of putting into action the finitude of each horizon in the circularity of interpretation. Ideology cannot be overcome but weakened; in experiencing the historicity and finitude of being-there (*Dasein*) what is left is a 'nothing', on the other side of which the ideological frame itself becomes substantially non-affirmative. Vattimo claims specifically that 'if this nexus is misunderstood or forgotten' then 'the theory of interpretation loses its specific originality, falling back into philosophical horizons of a different nature' (*BS*, 60). As such, Vattimo can be followed as arguing that there are possibilities to be 'impurely ideological' (*OR*, 3). That is, possibilities for setting forth in the 'fusion of horizons', aiming not for direct and objectified outcomes, but for open possibilities such as charity or the reduction of violence – acts that do not need ideological justification, only *pietas* (see *pietas*).

INFORMATION TECHNOLOGY/*GESTELL*

Ashley Woodward

Vattimo develops an important original reading of Heidegger's meditation on the ontological meaning of technology, which twists it free of the technophobia that often seems to saturate it, and at the same time extends it to contemporary information technologies. This entry focuses on his interpretation of Heidegger's presentation of the essence of technology as *Gestell*, and how he connects it with information technologies (see **media**; **technology/cyberspace**).

For Heidegger, the essence of technology is nothing technological, but must be understood ontologically – that is, as a factor in how Being gives itself and reveals beings. Heidegger sees a correspondence between modern machine technologies and the epoch of modern metaphysics. The latter is characterised by the distinction between subject and object, and the project of domination and manipulation of the world of objects by the mastering subject. The essence of modern technology is, then, the 'enframing' (*Gestell*) of all beings as *Bestand* ('standing reserve' or resources), as objects to be stored, manipulated and controlled by the willing subject. For Heidegger, *Gestell* is the apogee of metaphysics and nihilism because the ontological difference is entirely eclipsed and Being itself falls into oblivion (see **ontological difference**).

Vattimo focuses on Heidegger's brief suggestion in *Identity and Difference* that in the *Gestell*, we see the first flashing of *Ereignis*: that is, the overcoming (or *Überwindung*) of metaphysics and the advent of a new epoch of Being. The essence of technology is, then, at one and the same time the culmination of the metaphysical forgetting of Being and the prelude to its remembrance (*AD*, 172; see *Andenken* [**remembrance**]). Vattimo's most detailed interpretation of *Gestell* is given in the essay 'Dialectics and Difference' (*AD*). Here, he focuses on the way that an attentive reading of the language Heidegger uses in describing *Gestell* shows that it isn't in fact a stable frame, but an oscillation (a shaking, a mobility or a transitivity) which works to undermine the modern metaphysical categories of subject and object, precisely at the point where they seem to have become most fixed. While the most dangerously metaphysical aspect of technology, its character as total planning, calculation and organisation, is usually what is emphasised, Vattimo underlines that in Heidegger's thought this is always subordinated to the more fundamental characteristic of *Gestell* as an urging and a challenging which produces a continuous dislocation (*AD*, 173). While what we are urged to is planning and calculation, it is this urging that produces the mobile and transitive character of the *Gestell*.

What allows the *Gestell* to become the prelude to *Ereignis* is that Being and human being lose their metaphysical characteristics – that is, the determination of beings as subject and object. And it is this aspect which allows Vattimo to specify – beyond Heidegger, though he had already pointed the way in his remarks on cybernetics – the special characteristic of information technologies as the highest development of *Gestell*, where the point of transformation begins to appear. As most philosophers have done, Vattimo links information with language, and he thus understands the transition from machine or motor technology to information technology as coinciding with the linguistic turn in philosophy. With information technologies, entities lose their object-like character as they become understood in terms of images and languages, as patterns of information that are fluid and transformable. In this way, information technologies index the material world of objects becoming more immaterial, mind-like and – most importantly for Vattimo – language-like, linking these technologies to his nihilistic hermeneutic ontology, in which Being *is* language. The subject, on the other hand, also loses its qualities by being dispersed in distributed informational networks, decentred in complex fabrics of competing interpretations, undermined in its role as a knowing and willing anchor point (see, for example, Vattimo 1988a).

For Vattimo, the society of generalised communication that information technologies have given rise to corresponds with the decline of Being and its weakening, because metaphysical foundations tend to dissolve in the fabric of multiple and conflicting messages. Human beings are no longer situated as grounded subjects within a homogeneous cultural horizon of meaning, but have become decentred interpreters. From this perspective, the society of mass media – and today, we might venture to add, of social media even more so – is not to be understood as alienating and controlling, but as displaying the hope of an emancipation in line with Vattimo's positive interpretation of nihilism (see, for example, 'Ethics of Communication or Ethics of Interpretation?' in *TS*). The originality and importance of his work on information technology and *Gestell* is in having found a positive, progressive ontological meaning for technology by adapting Heidegger's reflections, which have seemed to many to offer only a condemnation of technology and a nostalgia for rustic traditions.

INTERPRETATION

Gaetano Chiurazzi

Vattimo's conception of interpretation represents an original synthesis of Heideggerian and Nietzschean elements against the backdrop of a Christian philosophy of history. In his early writings on Heidegger, the problem of interpretation is seen in reference to the theme of the unsurpassable linguistic character of existence (Vattimo 1963). Every relation to the world is in fact mediated by language, by oral and written productions, and there is no relation that can be separated from this structure, that is, from meaning: perception, as both Heidegger and Gadamer observed, is also always a form of interpretation, because it consists in the individuation of the thingness of the entity, of its *Als-Struktur* (its 'as'), as founded in a pre-understanding that orients in advance every relation to the world (Heidegger 2001: §§31–2). Pre-understanding, moreover, is not a timeless structure (in the sense of a Kantian a priori), but is historical, that is, determined by interpretative forms deposited in tradition, which operate implicitly at the linguistic level. In other words, pre-understanding is constitutively rooted in *Geworfenheit*, that is, in the thrownness of the human being.

The insistence on the historical dimension of the pre-structure of interpretation is what leads Vattimo to see in it the key for a general theory of hermeneutics. Interpretation, in fact, is not only the act through which an understanding is articulated and which gives concreteness to a sense. Interpretation is also and above all the act through which every production of factual sense is remobilised, redynamised and therefore reconfigured. This means that interpretation has the function of reactualising, necessarily modifying and differentiating them, the productions of meaning deposited in tradition, thereby preventing their scleroticisation into consolidated and oppressive forms. Interpreting is therefore an intrinsically historical and temporal operation, it is the very essence of a human being's temporal existence.

Here lies the profoundly philosophical significance of interpretation, which is thus no longer a problem inherent in the linguistic nature of existence, but concerns the ontological dimension of human being as such. This ontologising of interpretation, already initiated by Heidegger, entails various implications, first of all with regard to the problem of truth and reality. In the history of hermeneutics, the problem of interpretation was posed as the problem of the relationship between truth and history, between the content of faith and its various actualisations. This way of setting up the problematic of hermeneutics betrayed a Platonic horizon, which tended to separate truth and history as belonging, respectively, to an ahistorical (intelligible) world and to a historical (sensible) world. Philosophical hermeneutics abandons this distinction, to the point of claiming that there is no experience of truth except as interpretation (*BI*).

In this way, interpretation, far from putting us in touch with a truer reality, performs for Vattimo a derealising function. This is where the 'Nietzsche effect', as Vattimo calls it, is added on to the 'Heidegger effect' (*OR*) as a further component of philosophical hermeneutics. Indeed, derealisation produces a 'fabulisation' of the world, that is, a nihilistic erosion of every principle of reality, the experience of a loss of objective and transcendent references and principles, summed up in the announcement of the 'death of God'. For Vattimo, the Nietzschean phrase that best expresses this condition of accomplished nihilism, towards which hermeneutics tends, is 'there are no facts, only interpretations' (Nietzsche 1968: §481). To this claim Vattimo always adds also the clause 'and this also is an interpretation'. From a formal point of view, this thesis can raise many objections, similar to the refutation that Plato addresses to Gorgias's sentence 'every discourse is false'. If everything is an interpretation, then so is this statement, which therefore cannot claim to be true. However, Vattimo emphasises not so much the gnoseological content of the phrase but rather its ethical-emancipatory implication, consisting in the dissolution of the very concept of truth, of its violent peremptoriness, and its resolution in interpretation. Interpreting means never being able to consider any fact as definitive: it means seeing facts as the result of interpretations that can in turn be interpreted once again, that is, they can be transformed. The interpretative relation can then be defined as a *Verwindung* (see **convalescence** [*Verwindung*]), a word that Vattimo derives from Heidegger and defines as a movement of 'distortion' (from the German *winden*, 'to twist'), as a 'deviant alteration' (*EM*). *Verwindung* designates the fact that every interpretative process produces at the same time a continuity (a permanence in the tradition) and a discontinuity (a differentiation), thus contributing to the constitution of a sense that supposes neither a substantial permanence nor a radical fracture.

Every interpretation is therefore historical. Yet the reflexivity of the phrase 'there are no facts, only interpretations; and this too is an interpretation' indicates, for Vattimo, not a logical vicious circle, but the reflexivity of the hermeneutic structure of existence. Being historical means not being able to place oneself outside one's own life context (as metaphysics claims), which can only be interpreted from within history.

Nietzsche's sentence should therefore not be understood as a metaphysical thesis, but rather as the expression of the self-awareness of our historical era: hermeneutics is not a metaphysical worldview, but the way to respond to the historical condition of the postmodern era, as the end of the strong and oppressive structures of modernity (*EM*).

The need not to let interpretation collapse into facts appears therefore as a consequence of both Heideggerian ontology and Nietzschean nihilism, but it is also animated by an ethical demand that for Vattimo is at the heart of the whole history of hermeneutics. If the history of hermeneutics is the history of liberation from dogma, as Dilthey wrote and Vattimo recalls in several places, this is because hermeneutics responds to the need to constantly point to a future, to an open horizon, that prevents the conversation from coming to a halt, in the name of the presumed peremptoriness of facts. Its purpose is the reduction of violence and the transformation of law into charity.

Vattimo's conception of interpretation, which combines Heideggerian existential ontology and his critique of the metaphysics of presence with Nietzschean nihilism, corroborates his general philosophy of the history of the West interpreted in light of the history of Christianity (*AC*). The fundamental event of Christianity is, for Vattimo, the Incarnation of Christ, which encompasses the manifold functions he attributes to the act of interpretation. The Incarnation is actually understood by St Paul as a *kenosis* (Philippians 2:7), that is to say, as an 'emptying' and weakening of God who becomes human, which for Vattimo indicates the loss of cogency, peremptoriness and transcendence of the Old Testament God and of the law, in favour of a more terrestrial, human and thus secularised vision of religious experience. In the *kenosis* Vattimo sees the link between the history of Christianity and the history of nihilism, that is, the fulcrum of the nihilistic vocation of hermeneutics: 'Nihilism is too much "like" *kenosis* for one to see this likeness as simply a coincidence, an association of ideas' (*BI*).

The history of salvation (Christianity), the history of metaphysics (Heidegger) and nihilism (Nietzsche) are therefore closely interrelated in Vattimo's philosophy. What holds them together is the concept of interpretation, which characterises Western civilisation as a civilisation of Scripture: the history of the interpretation of Scripture becomes the paradigm, not only of the history of salvation, but also of the whole history of the West. Salvation – that is, the goal of Christianity, nihilism and hermeneutics – consists in the reduction of dogmatic, authoritarian, 'metaphysical' elements in favour of a freer and more varied relationship with the very content of revelation, that is, with 'truth'.

See also **interpretative turn**.

INTERPRETATIVE TURN

Daniel Innerarity

The contemporary hermeneutics of which Vattimo is a particularly qualified representative has contributed decisively to freeing reason from the slavery of the scientific ideal of objectivity (*BI*). This is why the interpretative turn has also meant an extension of the scope of truth, restricted in modernity to the type of truth regulated by an abstract and exempt objectivity. From this new horizon of meaning it turns out that matters that had been confined to a subjective and publicly irrelevant discretion also appear to be susceptible of truth. Far from posing a threat to truth, Vattimo's hermeneutics implies an extension of the sphere in which the criteria of truth are relevant in the form of reasonableness, verisimilitude, taste, authenticity, correctness, agreement and meaning. The ethical conditions of knowledge also rightfully enter the realm of rationality, once the ideal of objectivity as neutrality has lost its validity. The ethical and political consequences of interpretation are not few, either, thanks to which practical issues are freed from axiomatic rigidity and opened up to the personalisation of style. Vattimo's entire practical philosophy is an attempt to draw the ethical and political consequences of this interpretative turn.

Interpretation is not one more act of reason among many, but the means by which the exercise of reason takes place. This is the great contribution of the interpretative turn that took place thanks to the impulse of Heidegger and Wittgenstein, who picked up a tradition initiated by Nietzsche, Dilthey and Schleiermacher, and whose echoes in more recent thought can be found in philosophers such as Vattimo, for whom interpretation is a fundamental vector of thought (*AD*). Far from leading to a new hegemony or the enthronement of an alternative lineage to replace the previous one, the peculiarity of the interpretative turn is its desire to be something more than a change in the distribution of the old hierarchies. It has designed a new scenario in which questions such as what is the first science, what differentiates a superficial approach from a deep one, or how to get things to be well founded become less and less relevant. That is why it makes little sense to proclaim that hermeneutics must be set up as the heir to an unsustainable metaphysics (Greisch 1998), as if we were properly facing an inheritance and a succession, when it is perhaps more accurate to say that something similar to a new distribution of goods has occurred. Such actions cannot be qualified by the records of truth and goodness (or their opposites), but by those of opportunity and meaning. This is precisely the decisive point: that with the interpretative turn the most interesting questions are asked from criteria such as opportunity, relevance, meaning, expressiveness or sense.

The key to Vattimo's interpretative turn lies in the fact that it lacks an ontological vocation. To say that there are not pure facts absolutely free of all conception and that we always have to deal with interpretations does not mean that 'there are' interpretations in a strongly ontological sense, that the interpretations assume the function of the facts and come to occupy their place in an inverted ontology towards the subject. The critical function of the interpretative turn also extends to the interpretations themselves. Many of the resistances to thinking in the context designed by this turn are explained by the difficulty of abandoning that 'ontological commitment' (Quine 1981) that inclines us to consider hermeneutics as the new ontology, that is, to think the change in terms that turn out to be inadequate to understanding it. From here come both the criticisms of relativism and its celebration; in both cases it is still thought from a fundamental ontology, which it would be necessary to continue supporting with a firm objectivity or whose transgression constitutes the only source of freedom in a world that does not leave space for the subject (*BS*).

An interpretative thought would be that which guides the participation of the subject in the corresponding vital contexts, without trying to ignore the finitude that results from this involvement. And this leads ultimately to a primacy of meaning – of common interstices, of incalculable references, of shared and sharable backgrounds – over subjectivism and objectivism. The interpretative turn does not imply maintaining the thesis that objects have no existence regardless of interpretation. This is usually an interested paraphrase, elaborated for interpretative purposes by a certain anti-relativism that seeks the weaker side of the opposite thesis by investing it in the assertion of a non-existence. The interpretative turn does not defend the thesis that the non-interpreted does not exist, it does not bear the burden of proof of the non-existence of something. The accent is rather on the fact that there is no way to explain the representation of objects independently of a categorising, identifying interpretation that places them in space and time. Saying this does not imply any denial of the existence of objects or events, nor does it make them mere products of our imagination.

See also **hermeneutics; interpretation**.

JOACHIM OF FIORE (see GIOACCHINO DA FIORE)

JUSTICE/LAW

Ana Messuti

Vattimo's most important text on law and justice is 'Doing the Law Justice' (*NE*, 133–51). A separation between law and justice can be derived from this phrase. If we can make law into justice, it follows that we can also refrain from doing so. Frequently enough, law is not made into justice.

Essential to Vattimo's analysis of the subject 'law and justice' is violence. Therefore, in order to know what the terms law, justice and – by implication – injustice mean to Vattimo, we have to start by ascertaining what the meaning of violence is for him and what violence he refers to. The one who is hungry and thirsty for justice believes always that there is a 'true' situation that has been disrupted and should be repaired, and that it is known to them. They pretend that this pure and simple assertion of self-interest should be treated as if it were a principle of just justice. However, these disrupted situations that upset the equilibrium are no more than an interpretation, an interpretation that is never devoid of interest. Vattimo refers to the original violence, origin's violence. What is the meaning of original violence? Law and justice, like most philosophical subjects, including philosophy itself, are linked to the 'problem of how to begin', that is, the issue of the primary foundations (*NE*, 134). The task of the jurist is always related to a rule, a statute or a decision that precedes the one he or she is about to make and that is the source of legal standing for the latter. But the first rule, statute or decision preceding all the rest has no other foundation than violence. Violence is apparent in the silencing of questions, in ruling out further questioning (*NE*, 179).

The only supreme principle, in Vattimo's conception of justice and law, is the reduction of violence. If we want to make law into justice, that is, make it just where it was violent, it is necessary to reduce the original violence. This would be a matter of resolving particular cases by progressively reducing the original violence. And reducing violence progressively involves a weakening (*NE*, 146–7).

From this interplay of law, justice and violence at the time of the end of metaphysics, interpretation emerges as a fundamental resource. Vattimo contends that, in order to progressively bring down original violence, one has to resort to interpretation. He proposes a way of interpreting justice that he calls 'proceduralism', and relates it to a form of secularisation (Vattimo 2002d: 459; *NE*, 152–62). Justice takes shape through successive interpretations upheld by judges, lawyers, jurists and other law operators, and thus the law's violence is gradually reduced. The connection with interpretation is to be seen in the interpretational element of judicial activity, whereby the need is stressed for justice to be just: the need for a just justice. However, this proposition implies that justice can be unjust. Not only can law be unjust and require some interpretative act that would reduce its original violence and make it just; the same would equally apply to justice.

> Interpretation confers justice on the law only to the extent that, perfectly arbitrarily but with close attention to the specific demands of the situation, it adapts the norms of the law to the unique set of interests and goals at which it aims in each case, producing consensus around a specific application of the law, like good rhetorical discourse. (*NE*, 141)

An ontological-hermeneutical conception of relations between law and justice leads to withdrawing from substantial justice, where an original condition has been altered or an objective equilibrium upset. The 'very idea of a "true" equilibrium . . . is a violent invention' (*NE*, 149; see **violence**).

The certainty of law, the stability of the legal system, lie in the network of interpretations that they have been the subject of through history. But the main element of law is its procedural nature. 'Justice' – Vattimo says – 'is a procedural system that exists in opposition to the potential chaos of individual choices' (2002d: 457).

'To apply justice to human affairs is basically to adjust things.' Human justice is always an adjustment, always linked to the acceptability of given situations. In order to reach this common acceptance, certain procedures are required. 'Equality before the law means that everyone is treated in the same way on the basis of the same behavioral norms' (Vattimo 2002d: 458). It is necessary to admit the essentially procedural nature of the law, rather than its accordance with natural laws.

In relation to the procedural nature of justice or of the search for justice under the law, Vattimo points to another term he considers suitable for the definition of justice: administration. There is a close connection between justice as administration and philosophy as hermeneutics, because both are lacking a metaphysical foundation. Just as democracy is no more than the application of a certain voting procedure, justice for Vattimo is the administration of, or the procedure for, the application of laws.

How shall we make law into justice? First of all, by depriving it of its sacral character, of its formalism; having it take into account the actuality of facts and the legitimacy of the rights asserted by new subjects; expediting its answer to new situations; and, principally, promoting a more humane consideration of laws and court sentences.

KENOSIS

Felice Cimatti

In the Letter to the Philippians, St Paul wrote that Christ 'emptied (ἐκένωσε) himself, taking the form of a slave, coming in human likeness; and found human in appearance, he humbled himself, becoming obedient to death, even death on a cross' (Philippians 2:7, 6–8). What is at stake is an operation whereby an entity endowed with absolute power voluntarily but somewhat joyfully renounces it. The theme of *kenosis* (κένωσις) is pivotal to understanding the whole philosophical and biographical trajectory of Gianni Vattimo. In the first trajectory, the entity that empties itself is the classical Western metaphysical subject who faces an external and passive object. It is such a subject who, at the end of metaphysics, internally deactivates its own power; therefore the whole dualism of subject and object collapses on itself.

According to Vattimo in *Il soggetto e la maschera* (1974), it is in this vein that the often misunderstood Nietzschean figure of the *Übermensch* must be interpreted: in fact, this is not 'an intensification of the human essence as it has been until now manifested nor, as Heidegger wants, the man as capable of "going over" into a direction that merely confirms and enhances the metaphysical structures upon which our world is based'; on the contrary, it is a form of 'humanity placed completely *beyond* the man [*l'uomo*] as he is today' (Vattimo [1974] 1994: 283). In this sense the *Übermensch* is not an enhanced human being (that is, it has nothing to do with transhumanism); rather it is a living entity who has internally deactivated its own will to power. The deep conceptual similarity between this human being to come, no longer subject to the will of will (Western metaphysics is nothing but such a will of desire), and the theological figure of *kenosis* as an autonomous process of self-emptying from any desire for power and dominance is apparent.

In this context the concept of *kenosis* can be considered as a theological analogue of the more mundane concept of 'interpretation', which simply means that 'there is no experience of truth that is not interpretative' (*ADG*, 28): that is, there is no such thing as an 'objective truth'. This does not mean that some truth cannot exist, nor that a scientific truth is merely an opinion. The point at stake is that there is no power position (not the state, nor science, nor the Church) that can impose *the* absolute truth. This position shares a similarity with the self-weakening Christ in respect of his own divine nature, that is, his own power. When the possibility of appealing to an absolute authority is no longer available, the space is definitely open for dialogue and conflict.

The political consequence of this philosophical stance is quite direct, in particular in Vattimo and Zabala's very peculiar *Hermeneutic Communism*. In fact, such a seemingly strange passage from hermeneutics to communism becomes much less strange if one takes into account what communism is for Vattimo: 'Communism's promise of a society "without classes" must be interpreted as "without dominion," that is, once again, without an imposed unique truth and compulsory orthodoxy' (*HC*, 116). Communism is what power becomes after a radical gesture of *kenosis*. Therefore, 'in a Nietzschean-Christian style, one could say: *Now that God is dead and the absolute truth is not credible anymore, love for the other is possible and necessary*' (*HC*, 110–11; see **death of God**). The notion of *kenosis* reveals itself as the key concept in Vattimo's philosophical and political stance. In particular, it is the concept that allows the definite overcoming of traditional Western metaphysics. To such a tradition Vattimo opposes a 'weak' 'ontological hermeneutics', which 'replaces the metaphysics of presence with a concept of Being that is essentially constituted by the feature of dissolution [...] Being is also oriented toward spiritualization and lightening, or, which is the same, toward *kenosis*' (*AC*, 48).

The concept of *kenosis* occupies the centre of Vattimo's philosophy, but it also represents the core of his own human experience: 'I am Christian. Because I am someone who thinks of the good in terms of withdrawal rather than of affirmation. God incarnates himself. Indeed he does . . . but he's a carpenter who winds up being crucified – in other words, he's not exactly the triumphant Messiah' (*NBG*, 149).

See also **kenotic sacrifice**.

KENOTIC SACRIFICE

Paolo Diego Bubbio

In the 1980s Vattimo began to see parallels between the Christian notion of *kenosis* and philosophical nihilism (*B*, 8), thanks to a reading of René Girard's book *Things Hidden Since the Foundation of the World*, which maintains that Christ's sacrifice is not the satisfaction of God's need for justice with regard to Adam's sin, but unmasks the violence of sacrificial religion (*B*, 36–7). The association between *kenosis* and nihilism is made explicit in *Beyond Interpretation* (*BI*, 52) and in *Belief*, where Vattimo construes incarnation in terms of a kenotic sacrifice. Kenotic sacrifice is charity considered in the light of *kenosis*, that is, the abandonment or relinquishing for the sake of the other. It also has an epistemological value, insofar as the openness to the viewpoint of the other is the premise of a genuine hermeneutic experience. Kenotic sacrifice also expresses the 'dissolution' or the 'weakening of strong structures' (*B*, 52); in this sense, 'there is a sacrificial-kenotic spirit in the Heidegger who aims at the overcoming of metaphysics' (Vattimo 2015b: 432). Jesus' sacrifice, 'as an event both salvific and hermeneutical', is 'an archetypical occurrence of secularization' (*AC*, 67); it is not inspired by 'victim-based logic', but 'demands to be understood as kenotic salvation' (*B*, 14; *AC*, 120). Christ did not incarnate and sacrifice himself on the Cross to realise the identification of 'the blessed life with the perfect knowledge of geometry' (*AC*, 104), but to bring a message of *caritas*. Examples of kenotic sacrifice as 'subtraction, withdrawal, free negation' are given to us 'when Christ speaks of gaining one's soul by losing it' or when the Letter to the Philippians expresses 'the privileging of the nothings and nobodies, the "least of these"' (Vattimo 2016: 148).

For Guarino (2009: 99–100), Vattimo's notion of kenotic sacrifice is best conceived 'not as an actual historical event' but 'as a metaphor or a theological "cipher"'. In fact, Vattimo warns against the danger of turning *kenosis* into a metaphysical theology (Vattimo and Dotolo 2009: 4). For D'Isanto (1999), kenotic sacrifice means that God has moved out of eternity and into time. For Sciglitano (2013), kenotic sacrifice is for Vattimo an 'event' in the history of the withdrawal of Being.

Vattimo's notion of kenotic sacrifice has been developed in various ways. Frascati-Lochhead (1998) argued that some feminist theologies, such as that of Rosemary Radford Ruether, have a kenotic quality that surrenders any claim to metaphysical foundations and is similar to Vattimo's understanding of nihilism. Guarino (2009: 21) has argued that theologically, the kenotic sacrifice is 'the outpouring and diffusion of the divine into the human'. Bubbio (2014) argued that post-Kantian philosophy, including its hermeneutic developments, is characterised by kenotic sacrifice. Vattimo agreed that the idea of kenotic sacrifice is 'functional in providing a coherent and productive point of view on contemporary thought', and that 'what is alive [. . .] in the philosophy of today' is represented by the two elements identified by Bubbio as constitutive of the Kantian legacy, that is 'perspectivist epistemology' and 'kenotic ethics' (Vattimo 2015b: 434).

See also *kenosis*.

LANGUAGE

Libera Pisano

Language, along with being and history, is one of the three fundamental axes of Vattimo's hermeneutics, which can be roughly characterised as an attempt to adequately describe the relationship between language and being beyond metaphysics. Even in his early works, language is the guiding thread that runs through Vattimo's reflections and his views on this issue remain fairly constant.

Vattimo's hermeneutics entails a profound revolution in ontology: philosophy must break away from the notion of being as an objectivity to which thought must conform. Therefore, 'being is neither objective or stable', but it 'manifests itself as an event with respect to which we are always engaged as interpreters somehow on the way' (*AC*, 22). In other words, being is understood through language, or rather through the historical languages of its transmission and reception. In this context, language is a disclosing event (*Ereignis*) that concerns us, involving us in a mutually enabling relationship (*BIS*, 30). This provenance from a common tradition brings together the linguistic, historical and political aspects of being.

Vattimo's emphasis on the intertwining of language and being is elucidated in the famous 'story of a comma' (*RP*, 56), that is, the translation into Italian of Gadamer's dictum: *Sein, das verstanden werden kann, ist Sprache*. To avoid the risk of misunderstanding, Vattimo decided to keep the commas in order to make it clear that 'Being in its most general sense has the character of being comprehensible, inasmuch as it is language. *Not*: only that being that can be understood is language [. . .] The supposition would be entailed that somewhere beyond all linguistic comprehension there might subsist a Being "in itself"' (*RP*, 57).

If language is the way in which being 'happens' – which 'eventuates in history, it eventuates in historical languages' (*NBG*, 42) – then human understanding does not take place outside the linguistic articulation of the world. Therefore, human understanding cannot be absolute, but is always limited and situated in a historical perspective. On the one hand, the heritage of words, traditions and culture forms the 'background of this preliminarily given world-totality' (*OR*, 104). On the other hand, there is a givenness of language that constitutes the very form of historical experience: 'we encounter the world already possessing forms, words, grammatical structures through which we give it order, otherwise to us the world would appear to be an indistinct mess' (*AC*, 7). In this context, poetry also plays a central role – quite in the sense of Heidegger – as the inaugural event of Being: 'It is in poetic language that Being originally happens. This means that one can never encounter the world except in language' (*BS*, 38).

The historical-natural languages in which everyone speaks allow the 'opening of truth' (*OR*, 54). Therefore, truth cannot be understood as an objective fact, but rather as a linguistic assertion that occurs through the sharing of a particular language and under the acceptance of its rules. For this reason, Vattimo rejects the distinction between the science of nature and the humanities, for both are forms of interpretation, each according to its own rules and special terminology. To avoid the danger of arbitrariness in interpretation (*BIS*, 186–7) – 'anything goes and anyone can say whatever they please' (*FT*, 68) – Vattimo leans on the late Wittgenstein, according to which every language, like a game, has its own rules and is a form of life (*RP*, 87; *BIS*, 21–7). The theory of language games as something we are thrown into from the beginning explains the anti-fundamental attitude of Vattimo's philosophy. Moreover, it is a way of describing the irreducible 'pluralism without a center' (*AC*, 16) and the Babel of the postmodern multiplication of truths, communities and sectorial discourses (*FT*, 41; *HC*, 101–7).

Despite the proliferation of specialised linguistic fields, Vattimo sees the task of hermeneutics after Gadamer as keeping the search for unity and continuity in collective and individual experience. This need for a 'hermeneutic koiné' (*OR*, 21), that is, the horizon of comprehension of different discourses, is also linked to his concrete commitment to politics. Indeed, in the last phase of his work, Vattimo emphasised concrete and 'collective language' as 'the event of being' (Zabala 2007: 30) and a radical idea of freedom (*BIS*, 30). Vattimo explicitly stated that

We possess a *Sprache*, a language and therefore a world only because, as the Hölderlin cited by Heidegger says, we are a *Gespräch*, a conversation. The hermeneutic dialogue, however, is given in the concrete historical dialogues as ideal norm and possibility to be realized, more than as an actual fact. (*BS*, 56)

Being is a continuous dialogue that happens but is not (*BIS*, 38: 'It is the *Ereignis* – the event – that *happens* without being there'). This radical notion of dialogue constituting being is at the heart of Vattimo's idea of community.

In this context, even charity – as 'metarule that obliges and pushes us to accept the different language games and their different rules' (*FR*, 72) – can be interpreted as a linguistic attitude. According to the 'profoundly different kind of philosophical militancy' of the late Vattimo (D'Agostini 2010a: 33), the chain of linguistic tradition is the continuity of the logos itself in a permanent conversation that constitutes being and shapes community: 'Even if there is no objective logos of the nature of reality, every time we agree on something, we actually give a sort of testimony, we realize a sort of continuity of the logos, which is the only criterion we actually have' (*FR*, 72).

LAW (see JUSTICE/LAW)

LIBERATION (see EMANCIPATION)

LITERATURE/NARRATION

Gabriel Serbu

While never part of the mainstream of Anglo-American academia, Vattimo's philosophy has nevertheless been recognised as a valuable theoretical asset in the study of literature since the heyday of postmodernism – see, for example, Linda Hutcheon's recourse to Vattimo's understanding of history and tradition in her seminal elaboration of a postmodern poetics (Hutcheon 1988). In more recent times, as critique itself has become an increasingly problematic concept and practice, to the extent of generating a so-called 'postcritical turn' in literary theory, Vattimo's use of a 'non-demythifying hermeneutics' has inspired modes of critique that probe beyond the reductive and often redundant methodologies of a hermeneutics of suspicion (see Felski 2015).

The notion of 'weakness', which is the hallmark of Vattimo's *pensiero debole* or weak thought, has drawn so much attention that *Modernism/modernity* (the journal of the Modernist Studies Association) dedicated a special issue to the topic of 'Weak Theory' as recently as 2019. While 'weak' is sometimes used as an umbrella term to refer to a wide range of trends in literary criticism, such as surface readings, thin description, new formalism, book history, etc., Vattimo's weakening of foundational metaphysics is generally acknowledged as one of the main sources of inspiration behind 'Weak Theory' (Saint-Amour 2018). Other contemporary commentators on literature have kept even more closely with the original intent of weak thought – which emerged mainly as an ethical project in response to the escalating political and ideological violence in Italy during the 1960s and 1970s (see Zabala 2007: esp. 11–20) – by focusing on the ethical potential of the literary to engender modes of thinking and arguing that elude the violent outcomes of an instrumental-rationalist mindset (see, for instance, Mason 2017; Woessner 2017).

To better grasp the implications of Vattimo's 'weak philosophy' for literary studies, it is necessary to stress the fundamental affinity between philosophical thinking – and by extension all critical disciplines, including literary criticism – and literature (see Vattimo 2017: 289). Philosophical discourse, although primarily concerned with persuasion, ultimately belongs to the category of narration; in his formulation of a 'weak aesthetics', Zawadzki (2013) draws precisely on this aspect of weak thought in order to connect it to literature. This is not to say, however, that for Vattimo philosophy should be assimilated to literature as a merely aesthetic activity (*RP*, 74–5). Rather, as the distinction between reflective/explanatory and productive/creative disciplines is weakened (*ACT*, 131), the practice of art, including literature, can no longer be seen as 'a disinterested activity beyond true and false, good and evil, and so on, or as an activity that could appear to be true only once unmasked, demythologized, and relativized by reflection' (*ACT*, 42).

This has crucial consequences for the understanding of both literature and literary criticism. Literature is bound to recover its 'ontological bearing' on reality and its consequent claim to truth, which implies a permeating of the aesthetic into the ethical and the epistemic. This does *not* mean that a work of literature possesses the capacity to reveal some previously hidden, objective aspect of the external world. What the work does, rather, is ground a world of its own during the process of reading or interpretation. The encounter with the work in its singularity thrusts the reader into a dialogic tension between recognition and defamiliarisation so that the already existing world of meanings – to which the reader belongs and which makes the encounter possible in the first place – is altered in unpredictable ways. Such is how Vattimo describes the 'aesthetic experience', which characterises, albeit to different extents, any event of understanding (see **aesthetics**; **art**).

As far as the practice of literary criticism is concerned, Vattimo's 'weakening project' is meant to work against the temptation to 'explain' literature according to predetermined methodologies based on psychological, sociological or formalist models of analysis. The point is not to reject such models as inadequate, but to stress the limited and non-exhaustive character of their scope. As essentially a narrative act, the purpose of criticism is to preserve the openness of the encounter with the work towards further interpretation, rather than 'resolve' the work by reducing it to a single master reading (see *ACT*, 110–16).

LOGIC

Franca D'Agostini

The notion of 'logic' plays an apparently marginal but in fact crucial role in Vattimo's thought. The term for him 'means the mode in which we think truth, and in which we engage in thought and discourse in whatever contingent circumstances, historical and linguistic, are given to us' (*RP*, 81). As the main concern of Vattimo's weak thought is to propose a new 'mode of thought' with philosophical as well as political impact, his project can be seen as the proposal of a new 'logic' (in the above specified meaning) for philosophy, politics and common thought in general (see especially *WT*, 40: weak thought 'has a logic, its development is hardly arbitrary').

Vattimo favours a broad notion of logic, in line with a conception that is typical of Continental philosophers (D'Agostini 1996; 2001). But his view only slightly differs from the notion that is currently active in the sector of studies nowadays called 'philosophical logic', which is dominated by analytic philosophers. In the analytical approach, 'logic' means (in general) the formal study of valid inference. As we see in Vattimo's definition, there is no reference to 'forms' but to the 'mode' (way, manner) in which we think and reason, and reflect about the truth or falsity of our beliefs. So even for Vattimo, logic is the science of inferring possibly true conclusions from possibly true premises. The shift is minimal, but significant.

Vattimo concedes that logic deals with 'forms', meaning the general structures of inferences, but he does not accept that these structures can be fixed once and for all by logic as 'a unique (supra-historical) description of (supra-historical) forms of thought' (*RP*, 87). In 'Logic in Philosophy' he specifies that if logic merely denotes the technique of mathematical forms, then this notion is incompatible with a hermeneutical, history-sensitive conception of thought. Formal logic as such has never been able (and it has never wanted) to capture the role of truth in the concrete use of the concept. Rather, once 'the strict connection between truth and the history of being' is admitted, we can see that logic regains its own ancient role of 'science of the *logos*, as reflection on the modes of thought available to us in the single historical apertures of Being' (*RP*, 81–2).

Logic as 'science of *logos*' is not 'formal', in the sense of 'formalised', and it is not practised by using the standard symbols and devices borrowed from the mathematical tradition (such as set theory and other languages of formal semantics). But the possibility of a dynamic and non-standard formalisation of the 'ontology of actuality' is not to be excluded in principle (*RP*, 83). Rather, 'non-binary, many-valued logics, non-Euclidean geometries' are of extreme interest 'for a hermeneutics focused on the history of Being' (*RP*, 82). The movements of non-classical, alternative, sub-classical logics are all conceivable as expressions of the general 'weakening' of the idea of rationality as it emerged in the twentieth century. And in the same idea of logical pluralism – defended by many logicians nowadays – Vattimo finds a confirmation also that 'the domain of formal, exact sciences is itself caught up in the history of Being' (*RP*, 83).

On the role of logic in philosophy, Vattimo states that evidently, in doing philosophy, we use some definite 'mode of reasoning', but once we acknowledge that our inferential styles evolve, that there is no suprahistorical description of inferential forms and no eternal logical norm, then the use of logic in philosophy is to be systematically oriented by self-criticism. We have thus the capital question: is there a specific 'logic' for philosophy? Can the critical and self-critical attitude of philosophy be captured by some form of special 'logic'? The answer given by the tradition of Hegelianism is that the logic of philosophy should be dialectical (see **Hegel, Georg Wilhelm Friedrich**). Poststructuralists have proposed 'a logic of difference' as a new logic for philosophy (see **difference; poststructuralism**). Vattimo's answer (see **weak thought** [*pensiero debole*]) is inspired by the combination of hermeneutics and nihilism that informs his original perspective. The logic emerging from a 'weakened Being' is ductile and pluralist; it follows the human modes of thought, listening to their destiny and normativity, without the abstractness of dialectical 'totality' and without the emphasis on affirmative differentialism. A logic philosophically (hermeneutically) oriented has 'a privileged relation with common discourse'; it comes from an analysis of ordinary language, but embraces the intrinsic pluralism and dynamism of the hermeneutical ontology, its preliminary nihilism, its rejection of 'the last word' (*RP*, 90).

LOVE

Giuseppe Iannantuono

Love in Vattimo's thought emerges as the ultimate sediment or fundamental value that arises at the end of the process of weakening of being, and that accompanies and sustains nihilism as a reduction of the destructive and violent force of the ontological categories in the metaphysical tradition. The Dasein gives itself and happens in an act of love, with a radical reversal that has its roots in the God of the Incarnation, in the God whose son renounces his own omnipotence to become a man, weak among the weak, thrown into the insecure waters of trust, friendship, respect and love. The experience of love, according to Vattimo, achieves openness to otherness, being conceived as an event, as something that is not initiated by the subject. As the very condition of opening to the other, love reveals itself to be the last act of weak thought. It exercises itself in the remaining space after the dissolution of reason. Love is capable of accounting at the same time for reality after the eclipse of the founding principles, of absolute values, of the necessary and ineluctable laws of history; it accounts for the human being who reads and interprets the world without arrogance and aggression, but rather with the lens of love, modesty and friendship.

Love, therefore, is the hard core that remains after the process of secularisation of the metaphysical structures of strong objectivities – in other words, weak thought. Given that the latter translates into the philosophical register the doctrine of *kenosis*, the Incarnation of God, his lowering and self-dissolution as an act of love, and the renunciation of an absolute transcendence, love then shapes the theoretical prologue of Vattimo's reflection. He interprets the implicit consequences of the secularising vocation of Christianity as an act of love, as openness to the other in terms of the reduction of the peremptoriness of being and the subject. Love, as the eventual giving of the metaphysical God, is the point of arrival of the conceptual work carried out by weak thought against dogmatism and authoritarianism of all kinds that feed violence, fear and social injustice. Weak thinking, attentive to everything that reason excludes, unifies and oppresses through its conceptual categories, becomes a source of non-violent emancipation, of listening to the event of being, of tolerance of difference, of respect for the infinite diversity of reality, lifestyles and ways of thinking. Christian thought, weakened in its metaphysical version, becomes a less dogmatic thought, more aesthetic, handed over to interpretation, more open, suited to the realisation of its constitutive and original values, such as brotherhood, charity, empathy, love, and more generally the bond between man and his neighbour.

However, Vattimo also includes in love its broader meaning of friendship, the decisive factor of weak truth, which prevents the thought of the end of metaphysics from falling into Nietzschean reactive nihilism. The other, in the act of love, regains a central role as a gift, which becomes a principle of truth after the farewell to the claims of objective and universal foundations, which have previously dispensed and guaranteed the meaning and order of the world and its essence. Love is the ultimate and first gesture of the human being who has abandoned the certainties of metaphysical objectivity and ontological categories, who has learned to live with themself at the end of all absoluteness, who turns their gaze no longer to what is transcendent but to their historical time by working to practise and uphold the ideals of pluralism and tolerance, by actively practising solidarity, charity, irony and love.

LUKÁCS, GYÖRGY

Giovanni Giorgio

Vattimo is very critical of the assessment that Lukács – almost everywhere in his philosophical aesthetics – gives of twentieth-century avant-garde art, 'rejecting any positive content from it and treating it at best as a "symptom" of a crisis situation and of the disintegration of the bourgeoisie' (Vattimo 1972a: 3). Lukács fails to see in it 'the rejection of the existing moral ideals, of the social order [. . .] in the name of an actually *possible* alternative' (Vattimo 1972a: 3), of which the artist becomes the first witness and announcer. Similarly, Lukács's critique of Nietzsche sees him simply as an exponent of irrationalist thought (Lukács 1954), failing to grasp how 'Nietzsche does indeed present the idea of the *Übermensch* primarily and explicitly as a proposal for the renewal of [. . .] individual and social dimensions of life, as the ideal of a new – radically new – mankind' (*DN*, 89).

On the other hand, the relationship that Vattimo has with the earlier Lukács (1923) is different, since in this work, the 'moment of the fundamental crisis [. . .] between the nineteenth and twentieth centuries' (Vattimo 1990c: 58) is shown as a moment that starts a contrast between the epistemology of the natural sciences and the dialectical method of the historical-social sciences. This work, in Vattimo's opinion, offers 'a great example of the theoretical horizon in which Western Marxism develops. In general, here and in other authors [. . .] we are witnessing an accentuation of the humanistic elements of Marxism' (Vattimo [1997b] 2002: 22), those same elements that will converge in Vattimo's thought, albeit reinterpreted in the light of Nietzsche and Heidegger.

Suffice it to say that Marxism, thanks to the dialectical method, materialistically understood, proposes an approach to reality that does not aim at mere knowledge. The latter method, typical of the natural sciences, would claim to describe reality as consisting of pure atomic facts, excluding any mediation of the subject. According to Lukács, this dismemberment of reality is characteristic of capitalism, as well as being the perception of it according to a metaphysical view, that is, as naturalistically given and immutable. In this way, individuals live alienated, since they are expropriated from any practical power over reality, and inserted, like small gears, into a foreign system – as it is 'given' – which functions according to its own, unchangeable laws. The dialectical method, for its part, manages to grasp the historical character of facts, freeing them both from their false metaphysical fixity and from their atomicity. Inserted into a historical process, which enjoys its own 'global rationality' (*OR*, 223), facts become products of human activity, giving back to the subjects – the revolutionary proletariat – the ability to be able to intervene in reality, and to be protagonists of a possible project of social transformation. The connection with Heidegger's planning is thus accomplished (Vattimo, 1972a: 30).

See also **art; being; emancipation; hermeneutic communism; history/historicity; metaphysics; overcoming** (*Überwindung*).

LYOTARD, JEAN-FRANÇOIS (see POSTMODERNISM/POSTMODERNITY)

MARX, KARL (see MARXISM/ITALIAN MARXISM)

MARXISM/ITALIAN MARXISM

Stefano Azzarà

A confrontation with Marxism is already present in *Essere, storia e linguaggio in Heidegger*, where 'what for Heidegger is the oblivion of being' and what Nietzsche 'calls nihilism' is assimilated to 'what for Marx is alienation' (Vattimo 1963: 49). Heidegger himself points out that this Hegelian concept 'sinks its roots in the being-without-home of the modern man' (Heidegger 1976a [1946]: 339) and therefore has to do not with a subtraction of the human essence due to the insertion of the subject into a social mechanism of expropriation of meanings, but with that arcane game of revealing and hiding by which being itself opens the various historical eras, exposing itself in innerworldly beings and at the same time subtracting itself. It is clear, then, that the overcoming of the 'discomfort of modernity' cannot be carried out through 'the implementation of certain scientific or political tools', because it 'does not have its roots mainly in a certain psychological condition or in certain political structures' but refers to 'an "alienation," which concerns the relationship of man with being' (Vattimo 1963: 49).

It follows that no 'orthodox' reading of Marxism can be, for Vattimo, productive, and that the main way to an integral revolution of the vision of the world and of the life forms of contemporary bourgeois society passes through a type of Marxism that binds to the subversive experience of the twentieth-century artistic avant-gardes. It is a need that is born from the 'current times', because it is first of all 'in the context of thought and revolutionary practice', as Vattimo in *Arte e utopia* says, that 'a vast criticism of the bureaucratic degeneration of communism is underway, together with an effort to find the "human" contents of the revolution' (1972a: 1). Unavoidable at this point is a confrontation with Bloch, who 'strove to keep alive in revolutionary Marxist thought a link with the aspirations of freedom, of authenticity, of profound renewal of man' – those instances that Soviet bureaucratism had denied, integrating in collectivism the traditional forms of familist and labourist bourgeois morality and creating a new form of 'repression' (Marcuse) – both renewing the Marxist reading of Hegelian dialectic (against Engels), and incorporating in a 'utopian thought' the 'revolutionary contents' proposed by the avant-gardes; a thought capable of grasping the world-of-life and imagining the future and a real 'new man', freeing human creativity from the schemes of a reason reduced to techno-scientific instrument (Vattimo 1972a).

Also following the experiences of the 1968 movement, Marxism ends up meeting, for Vattimo, with Nietzsche, as is evident in *Il soggetto e la maschera* (1974), where the proposal for a liberation of the Dionysian from the steel cage of the *ratio*, which stiffens the symbolic power of human beings in a single utilitarian configuration of the relationship with the world, binds with the need to 'live the great future of science and technology outside the dominating schemes, which block science and technology [. . .] in fetishistic and repetitive forms, however capable of producing only, as the capitalist (and also pseudo-socialist) organization of factory work, not liberation but new neurosis' (Vattimo 1974: 347); and therefore with the need to set an alternative development of the productive forces, that is at the same time the irruption of the possibility of giving life to new worlds and new stories.

The more the critique of the capitalist *ratio* slipped in Vattimo towards a critique of reason as such, the more, however, Marxism turned out to be intrinsically linked to a rationalistic attitude. It is no longer a question of integrating it with a supplement of existential reflection. Dialectics is a domination machine, in which the subordination relationship is simply upside down, so that it always produces new figures of the Master and is unable to think that 'difference' that transpires instead in Deleuze (Vattimo 1978). Furthermore, the Marxist claim of an overcoming of capitalist alienation towards a dimension of authenticity that restores a non-dejected human condition has become increasingly doubtful. Marxism shares the same metaphysical setting of all Western philosophy, and can only lead the plurality of phenomenal life to an alleged base of being, with a further *reductio ad unum* of the richness of reality. It is no coincidence that the parable of Marxism ends in state totalitarianism and terrorism, the necessary expressions of a violence implicitly present in the dialectics itself (Vattimo 1984; *BS*). In this sense Marxism, as it claims to be based on an objective idea of truth and to model world and history according to a plan, proves to have 'still too much nostalgia for metaphysics' and is not capable, despite its emphasis on the critique of ideology, of bringing 'really to its end the experience of the oblivion of being or of the "death of God"' (Vattimo and Rovatti 1983: 9). Marxism has entered an irreversible crisis, it is not reformable, and should be passed over together with all the 'definitive' worldviews with which it disputed hegemony in the field of cultural forces of modernity.

The failure of the perspectives of weak thought, that is, of the hope of a transparent society open to the game of free interpretation and experimentation of the real that had accompanied the end of the Cold War and the triumph of liberal democracies, brings Vattimo to a further rethinking (Vattimo 2007b). An uninterrupted series of wars of the rich world against the Third World; an increasingly evident 'proletarianisation of society' in the West: hence the need to renew the idea that any 'human emancipation project' can 'only be based on the search for equality, and for a political culture that corrects any "natural" inequality' (Vattimo 2007b: 37). It is the return of a sort of 'communism', which, having cut its bridges with dogmatism and Leninism, presents itself as an 'ideal', a 'liberal' or a 'libertarian communism' (Vattimo 2007b: 107). Marxism is now that of a '"weakened" Marx' (Vattimo 2007b: 41). It is a new synthesis that, by reconnecting the most advanced experience of Western Marxism (Gramsci), finally redefines communism as 'hermeneutical communism' (*HC*), that is, as a communism that coincides with a constant action of reimagining and renaming reality, and that takes place on the ground of 'hegemony' and culture – an idea that finds a more political formulation in the proposal for a radical democracy of Laclau and Mouffe (1985).

MASK

Robert T. Valgenti

The concept of the 'mask' is central to Vattimo's interpretation of Nietzsche in the 1970s and represents a more utopian reading of the history of metaphysics that precedes his concept of 'weak thought'. *Il soggetto e la maschera* (1974), a work Vattimo hoped would make him 'the ideologist for the radical libertarian Left' (Vattimo 2009d: 322), examines the subject's ability to 'unmask' the controlling metanarratives of history and to interpret its own existence in a manner that is fluid and transformative, but not relativistic (for an extended treatment, see Valgenti 2011; Azzarà 2011).

The mask is not a common concept or image in Nietzsche, but Vattimo utilises it to interpret the various forms of 'masking' that are characteristic of metaphysics. In this view, symbolic claims about 'natural' or 'essential' realities are an inevitable human reaction to the flux of history and the inevitability of death. Vattimo suggests that in Nietzsche's early works, the ancient age of tragedy is not a more originary alternative to the metaphysical masking tradition of Socratic *ratio*, but is itself a 'peculiar form of mask' (Vattimo 1974: 20) – a Dionysian, creative, plastic, life-empowering force and a freely political possibility that lives within the world of forms and remains free from the foundational thinking of metaphysics. Vattimo argues that Nietzsche eventually rejects the historicism of the second *Untimely Meditation* and cultivates a free relationship with the past – the nihilist, the free spirit, can play with those forms like masks, as they have no intrinsic order or necessity (*DN*, 81).

Nietzsche's key insight arrives in his middle period as a critique of the historicity of scientific reason from Socrates to Darwin: if the goal of science is to unmask the deceptions of appearance and the falsehoods of belief, Nietzsche now performs an 'unmasking in order to unmask the unmasking itself' (Vattimo 1974: 83; also *DN*, 81) and to show how reason and science also generate masks that dogmatically assert truth (*N*, 127). Science and its unmasking of reality are an 'event' of the very metaphysics it tries to overcome (Vattimo 1974: 91). Art also shares this metaphysical history, but it does not portray its truth as absolute or definitive (Vattimo 1974: 135). Art's 'good will to masking' allows it to resist the practical needs of scientific reasoning. The 'free spirit' tolerates error, lives with the 'good mask', and resists the will to truth and knowledge. Vattimo's interpretation is not simply a reduction to aestheticism; the free play of masks offers a conception of existence that requires no transcendent or external basis for meaning, and thus no logic of domination: 'Strength and weakness, health and sickness are the only criteria that Nietzsche has left after unmasking metaphysics' (*N*, 127).

Vattimo reads Nietzsche's later period – in particular, *Thus Spoke Zarathustra* and *Twilight of the Idols* – as an attempt to identify the subject who no longer depends on external values, foundations and origins, but embraces the moment of decision itself. This 'free spirit' offers more than a poetic covering for the violent reasoning of metaphysics, and instead constitutes reality through its own *hubris* and the very act of unmasking (*BS*, 10). The 'eternal recurrence of the same' and the 'death of God' thus mark the birth of 'becoming' and a true liberation of the symbolic (in both senses of the genitive) in the figure of the *Übermensch* – an interpretation that rejects this hermeneutic act as a 'will to domination' (*BS*, 14) and clarifies a hermeneutic ontology, suggested in the sketches for the *Will to Power*, that 'begins with the unmasking reconstruction' of the origin and objects of metaphysics and provides 'a theory of the conditions of possibility of a being which is given explicitly as the result of interpretative processes' (*BS*, 14). This reading also sheds light on Vattimo's frequent invocation from the *Twilight of the Idols*: 'How the "true world" finally became a fable'. Vattimo's primary contention is not that the 'fabling of the world' sets loose an unending conflict of interpretations, nor that it establishes a newer, truer fable that replaces an inadequate one; rather, the fabling liberates the Dionysian – the symbolic, the creative, form-giving aspect of masking – from the idea of a stable, unchanging, metaphysical reality that would provide its foundation. This markedly utopian interpretation of the fabling of the world, however, does not survive Vattimo's own encounter with violence in the late 1970s and, along with the theme of the mask, succumbs to the tendency of all fables to dissolve and weaken by their own hand.

MEDIA

Daniela Angelucci

Vattimo's thought on media is situated within his reflection on the end of modernity. Resuming the reflection on postmodernism initiated by Jean-François Lyotard in his 1979 text *The Postmodern Condition*, in various essays, but mainly in his book *The End of Modernity*, Vattimo describes the present age as a leave-taking from modernity and metaphysics, that is, an age that shuns both the logic of development and the thought of the foundation. In this situation, history loses its universality and unity, and becomes *post-histoire*, that is, a dimension in which the progressive vision and univocity of meaning gives way to difference, to multiple and relative senses. Through Nietzsche's announcement of the death of God and the Heideggerian conception of Being not as what it is but as what happens, Vattimo arrives at an 'ontology of decline', of weakening, and at a dismissal of the traditional concept of the subject. As is evident in the book edited by Vattimo and Pier Aldo Rovatti, *Weak Thought*, this 'weak nihilism' is not nostalgic for the old certainties, nor is it a search for new values; rather, it envisages in the contemporary situation a possibility, a chance (see **weak thought** [*pensiero debole*]). If absolute truth has produced only authoritarianism and intolerance, it is necessary to implement a *Verwindung*, or a distortion of metaphysics (see **convalescence** [*Verwindung*]). With this Heideggerian term Vattimo means that metaphysics cannot be deleted but should be twisted and weakened, therefore representing an opportunity to live without neurosis in a fluid and plural world. In this world, technology and information play a fundamental role according to Vattimo: the planet is configured as a place of continuous exchange of heterogeneous messages coming from different centres. The explosion of the media, which has produced a multiplication of information, but also a multiplication of the interpretations of facts, is the protagonist of the decline of a unitary history, which Vattimo welcomes.

In the 1989 text *The Transparent Society*, Vattimo deals with contemporary society, highlighting the decisive role played by mass media. Vattimo's diagnosis is that the multiplicity of information does not lead to greater transparency, but rather to complexity and chaos. The intensification of the possibilities of information renders the idea of a unitary reality inconceivable, whereby the principle of reality is missing, and gives way to a society characterised by oscillation, plurality and differences (see **difference**). Vattimo writes: 'the increase in possible information on the myriad forms of reality makes it increasingly difficult to conceive of a single reality. It may be that in the world of the mass media a "prophecy" of Nietzsche's is fulfilled: in the end the true world becomes a fable' (*TS*, 7). This loss of a unitary reality in favour of a world of multiple images and phantasmagorias is transformed, according to Vattimo, into an advantage. In fact, Vattimo claims: 1) that the mass media play a decisive role in the birth of a postmodern society; 2) that they do not make this postmodern society more 'transparent', but more complex, even chaotic; and finally 3) that it is in precisely this relative 'chaos' that our hopes for emancipation lie (*TS*, 4). In opposition to the position of Theodor Adorno and the Frankfurt School, which saw in the mass media only an instrument of homologisation, according to Vattimo the chaotic nature of information induces a disorientation that is precisely that of the liberation of differences, of the highlighting of plurality. It is in this chaos, Vattimo claims with some emphasis, that our hope lies. This position is not meant to hide the difficulty of pluralism, which requires continuous dialogue and interpretation, but Vattimo nevertheless argues against the recovery of a unitary reality, which is far more threatening, and against the neurotic attitude of nostalgia for the past. Compared to a world that gravitates around stable and univocal truths, reassuring but authoritative, the plurality of information allows the growth of tolerance, dialogue and emancipation, and the liberation of local and minoritarian rationalities. In the same way, the omnipresence of mass media can lead to a decentralisation of control structures and the emergence of new communication channels can contribute to a proliferation of points of view. Therefore, even if the possible liberating effect of this complex and plural society, in which communication through newspapers, radio and television (and cyberspace) is increasing every day, is not guaranteed, it must be recognised and supported. In fact, according to Vattimo, the contemporary society dominated by the mass media, so-called transparent society, which is actually chaotic and disorientating, can produce new visions of the world and 'a new way of being (finally, perhaps) human' (*TS*, 11).

METAPHYSICS

Elena Ficara

Vattimo's use of 'metaphysics' is substantially consistent with the Heideggerian use after the *Kehre*. Metaphysics is seen as the bearer of a wrong/reductive attitude towards being, and the terms 'metaphysics' and 'metaphysical' have, just as in the late Heidegger, a negative connotation.

Besides the negative use, weak thought as the original perspective delineated by Vattimo and Rovatti (*WT*) is characterised by Vattimo, especially in the seminal essay 'Dialectics, Difference, Weak Thought' (*WT*, 40–52), in association with a new meaning of metaphysics as either 'ultrametaphysics' or ontology – whereby ontology is also thought of in contrapositive terms with respect to metaphysics, in an interpretation that is, again, drawn from the late Heidegger (see **ontological difference**). In its negative connotation 'metaphysics' is the basic trait of modernity as opposed to postmodernity and has different meanings: it qualifies a modality of thought; a conception of being; a conception of the thinking subject; an approach to truth.

Metaphysical thought is hard/strong; it is associated with deductive thinking and with reasoning proceeding from first principles (see *EM*). Metaphysical in another but still negative connotation is dialectical thought: not metaphysical as proceeding from first principles or based on a solid foundation, but as having a 'providential' and teleological nature. Moreover, dialectical thought as it is developed and practised in the tradition of Hegelianism (by authors such as Sartre, Adorno, Benjamin and Bloch) postulates notions (such as 'totality' and 'reappropriation') that are 'yet to be critiqued' and 'metaphysical' (*WT*, 43). In this interpretation, 'metaphysical' is an assumption that is not subjected to critique.

As a view of being and reality, metaphysics conceives being as stable, ordered according to rules, objective, ontic, simply present. In so doing, it obscures the account of being as event, dialogue, interpretation, and is guilty of *Seinsvergessenheit*. Thus conceived, the metaphysical image of the world is, for Vattimo just as for Nietzsche, a 'dream' and a 'myth' – though a reassuring one (see *TS* and *EM*).

As a specific account of the thinking subject, metaphysics aims at the full disclosure of the subject to itself (as in the Cartesian *cogito*) or the complete self-transparency of society (as in Apel's society of communication). The metaphysical subject is seen, accordingly, as a *fundamentum inconcussum*, and truthfulness is conceived in conformity with the ideal of a perfectly transparent subject (see *TS*; **truth**).

The positive interpretation emerges in association with Vattimo's notion of *Verwindung* (see **convalescence [*Verwindung*]**). Importantly, Vattimo (*WT*, 44) writes that the question of a new thought is not solvable in terms of overcoming a wrong metaphysical way of thinking by substituting one notion of being with another. Rather, following Heidegger's approach, Vattimo aims to unify the critique of metaphysics with the radical recovery of the problem of being. Metaphysics is thus not simply overcome by weak thought, but rather *verwunden*, that is, declined into weak thought (in 'Dialectics, Difference, Weak Thought' Vattimo translates the Heideggerian *Verwindung* into Italian as *declinazione/declination* of something into something – see *WT*, 39–52). More specifically, dialectics is declined (*verwunden*) into difference, and difference is declined into weak thought, which means that the metaphysical heritage of dialectics is in some sense maintained within weak thought. Weak thought is thus also called 'ultrametaphysical thought', insofar as it consists in working with the old metaphysical categories, 'distorting' them but also 'entrusting' oneself to them. In this perspective, weak thought involves rethinking metaphysics, entrusting oneself to its historical heritage (following Heidegger's colossal attempt to rethink and retrieve the philosophical tradition, as well as Gadamer's account of philosophy as hermeneutics). From this point of view, weak thought goes hand in hand with a Kantian and early Heideggerian (but also Aristotelian) approach according to which 'metaphysics' turns into 'meta-metaphysics', that is, an inquiry about metaphysics and its conditions of possibility/impossibility.

MODERNITY (END OF)

Thomas Winn

The development of Vattimo's work on the question of modernity has been central to his philosophical project ever since his first 'explicit "distortion" of the Heideggerian interpretation of Nietzsche' (*EM*, 176) in *The Adventure of Difference: Philosophy after Nietzsche and Heidegger* and *Beyond the Subject: Nietzsche, Heidegger and Hermeneutics*. These two books closely followed his theorisation of 'weak thought' in 1979 and were presented as a collection of essays on the contemporary issues of both difference and subjectivity. They should be understood as laying out for the first time not only the radical implications of the 'Nietzsche–Heidegger paradigm' (and how they are basically saying the 'same thing' with respect to nihilism) but how in reading this paradigm, Vattimo himself was destined to comment on the 'epochal meaning' of their work in light of the growing significance of the question of modernity's end.

In both books Vattimo recognises the problematic of the relationship between Heidegger's analysis of the end of metaphysics and its possible overcoming. This problematic was heightened by Vattimo's need to take Nietzsche's declaration of the death of God seriously. The problem lies in that if we are to theorise a potential end to metaphysics, we are at risk of providing a new ground from which we can establish this end. In saying that something has ended we are (potentially) prescribing a new vision of 'the way things are'. The same problematic was seen by Vattimo as being bound to the desire to progress beyond the demands of nihilism itself. In saying that nihilism can be overcome, we fall back into a 'reaffirmation' of presence and hence truth. Metaphysics and nihilism as such are bound to each other in this way. Both constitute an impasse in thinking, in which the terms of metaphysics and the demands of nihilism maintain a dichotomy between either a kind of deflated metaphysical hyperrationality or its very own destitution and hence impossibility in coming across its own 'ultimate *unfoundedness*' (*BS*, 5). In other words, if we are caught in the age of the *Gestell* as Heidegger said, where the rationality of modern science and the technological world is founded upon metaphysical ends (*OR*, 78), then, in being unfounded because of a (nihilistic) ontological difference, we will always be directed or destined back to the deadlock of nihilism.

Only a few years later in *The End of Modernity: Nihilism and Hermeneutics in Post-Modern Culture*, Vattimo began to show how the notion of modernity was also bound to the same problematic of overcoming its failure to ground itself. The history of metaphysics read as a decline towards the problematic of nihilism shows how modernity itself is tied directly to the 'deeply rooted process' of nihilism, which is 'in motion with our culture' (*BS*, 69). Vattimo argues that modernity's 'own constitutive tendencies' (*EM*, 166) have revealed that 'the notion of truth no longer exists, and foundation no longer functions . . .' and so also that 'there can be no way out of modernity through a critical overcoming, for the latter is part of modernity itself' (*EM*, 167). As with metaphysics, modernity accentuates its own violent and dominant desire to progress in the (dialectical) overcoming of falsity towards truth, as a kind of progression that in the end progresses for progression's sake. Vattimo states that in being 'defined as the era of overcoming and of the new which rapidly grows old and is immediately replaced by something newer' (*EM*, 166), modernity hastens its own decline.

This self-induced decline is drawn upon in the essay 'The Death (or Decline) of Art' in the second section of *The End of Modernity*. Here Vattimo follows an idea set forth in a crucial essay, 'The Will to Power as Art', stating that we should take art to be 'the locus of the decline of the subject, of the dissolution of form, unity and hierarchies' (*AD*, 4) and so also the decline of modernity. In modernity, art is recognised as the space in which the very newness (and so finitude) of the work today matches the progressive newness brought about by 'the impact of technology' (*EM*, 54). As with newness, and as with Being, art 'is not that which remains, but rather that which is born and dies' (*EM*, 60). In establishing the death or finitude of art we are confronted with the death of the ideal form of art, and so the death of modernity's claim to truth (see **death of art**). And so, in being overwhelmed with the new, we are brought towards the 'moment of the birth of post-modernity in philosophy' (*EM*, 167), which for Vattimo corresponds to the rebirth of the Heideggerian categories of convalescence (*Verwindung*) and remembrance (*Andenken*).

See also *Andenken* (**remembrance**); **convalescence** (*Verwindung*).

NIETZSCHE, FRIEDRICH

Stefano G. Azzarà

Vattimo approached Nietzsche's thought at the end of the 1950s, on the advice of Pareyson. In *Essere, storia e linguaggio in Heidegger* (1963) Vattimo reconstructs the Heideggerian reading, according to which

Nietzsche inaugurates the culminating moment in the history of being; that is, of that 'destiny' of Western self-awareness that puts in the foreground the being of the *Seiende* (being of beings) conceived as 'simple presence', but ends up hiding the 'self-giving' of being itself (Heidegger 1961). Nietzsche represents the fulfilment of metaphysics, in which it is possible to grasp the specific configuration of the relationship between the ontic meanings and the unveiling of truth that characterises the horizon of understanding of our age, and in which its overcoming is also prefigured. The being of the *Seiende* is now *Wille zur macht*, a 'will to power' that is an incessant production of ever new evaluations; in this nihilistic process, the supreme values are devalued and replaced by others. This concept gathers that 'experience of change of metaphysical perspectives and philosophical conceptions' (Vattimo 1963: 28) that at every epochal turn has redefined the meaning of being and the essence of truth, transposed into a different historical world; and thus summarises 'all the main lines of development [. . .] in the history of metaphysics' (1963: 32), expressed in turn 'in the history of modifications affecting the meaning of some fundamental concepts' (1963: 34). The *physis* of early Greek philosophy, still close to the experience of 'unveiling', becomes *energeia* and *ousia*, then *eidos* and *idea*, turning into the Christian *actualitas* and finally into the Cartesian *subiectum*. *Aletheia* redefines itself as *orthotes*, conformity, and as 'correctness of judgement', to then reappear as *Vorstellung* and finally, with Leibniz, as 'will'. If in Hegel the latter is first of all will of self-consciousness, in Nietzsche it finally becomes 'will of will', beyond which there is nothing else and which only wants itself as an eternal return. The conservation of power is nothing but the initiation of its growth and requires a subject that goes beyond the human being as it has been given until now: the *Übermensch* therefore represents the 'triumph of Cartesian subjectivism' (Vattimo 1963: 42). In this reduction of the *Seiende* in its totality to the will, any residual memory of being has vanished, because the very difference between being and *Seiende* has been removed, leading to the exhaustion of the ultimate possibilities of metaphysics.

Here the need for further investigation emerges: nihilism is not for Nietzsche 'a historical discourse that leads to historical, sociological or political outcomes'; however, 'a careful reinterpretation' of his thought is now necessary (Vattimo 1963: 50). Precisely this rereading is at the heart of *Ipotesi su Nietzsche* (Vattimo 1967a), a text that dialogues with the already underway Nietzsche renaissance (Deleuze 1966) and provides a massive rethinking of Nietzsche's thought in a context marked by the persistent influence of Lukácsian reading (Lukács 1954), proposing a depoliticisation which is also a first shift to the left. According to Vattimo, Nietzsche's problem is always nihilism, seen here, however, as a 'historical disease', that is, as the prevalence of that Hegelian attitude whereby every problem is understood in a historicist key, so as to be the consequence of a causal chain. If the past crushes the present under the weight of the '*es war*' and inhibits the future, making any production of the *Novum* impossible and making action superfluous, it becomes urgent for Nietzsche to rethink the very meaning of temporality and to replace any linear vision with a conception that frees human action. It is the sense of the 'eternal return', symbolised by the bite of the shepherd which severs the snake's head in the *Zarathustra*. What eternally returns is the present, the decisive moment in which time is established by decision and the escape routes for the future are arranged.

This move enhances human freedom as infinite freedom, but at the same time it brings out the responsibility that this freedom entails, according to an existentialist interpretation of Nietzsche's thought that reflects the formation of Vattimo. However, a further meaning of the 'eternalizing decision' emerges in this text, which transcends individual choice and alludes to the overcoming of a historical era and the possible opening of a new world of meaning. This innovative reading takes shape when Vattimo inserts Nietzsche into a theoretically original and now mature philosophical proposal. In *Il soggetto e la maschera* (1974), Nietzsche is repoliticised with the traits of an anarchist and libertarian author, prophet of a 'liberation' destined to intertwine with the revolutionary process inspired by Marxism. Vattimo met the 1968 protest movement, and reinterprets Nietzsche starting from the intellectual turmoil of that phase. Metaphysics, that is, nihilism, takes the forms of the *ratio*, a rigid and schematic configuration of the relationship between humankind and the world. In a situation of scarcity of resources and generalised insecurity, this configuration blocks the symbolic order by linking it to the centrality of *logos*, according to a causal chain that refers to an ultimate foundation, and that brings the multiformity and tragic process of reality back to a one-dimensional unity. The *ratio* categorises the world through language and morals, and subdues it with the institutional power of the state, after having split the community according to class hierarchies, and finally presents itself in late capitalism as a repressive apparatus that sets out the complete administration of the Earth. At the end of the millennium, however, as a consequence of scientific and technological development, the expansion of the productive forces is so intense as to make any domination superfluous and allow for a generalised liberation (see **science**; **technology/cyberspace**).

The Dionysian therefore emerges at the centre of this reinterpretation of Nietzsche, understood as a hermeneutic power and creative ability to always reconfigure meanings and horizons of sense, escaping the sclerosis of consolidated perspectives and giving life to new worlds and stories. It is not a question of favouring a liberation 'from the Dionysian' but 'of the Dionysian' (Vattimo 1974: 39), by combining the revolutionary process on the political and social ground with a philosophical and cultural revolution, which, freeing the human being from the necessity of every consolidated order, makes it a 'beyond-man'. If the aristocratic mindset of Nietzsche himself and the even more serious Hegelian, labourist and moralist limitations of the workers' movement had prevented this convergence at the end of the nineteenth century, Vattimo aims to reach a fusion between a workers' movement of a new type (the so-called 'mass-worker') and a new nomadic intellectuality that rediscovers the spirit of the aesthetic avant-gardes through Nietzsche (Vattimo 1972a).

However, this reading quickly falls into crisis. Vattimo understands that it is not possible to combine Nietzsche with perspectives of a dialectical nature (Vattimo 1983b). Marx is linked to Hegel, and even historical materialism, persisting in the search for an ultimate foundation, remains stuck in metaphysics. In the collapse of any reconstructive reading, Nietzsche is led back to the 'Enlightenment' as a critical philosopher, who does not indicate any authentic structure of being and does not wish for any transformation, but deconstructs the certainties of the systematic spirit (Vattimo 1979). His philosophy is now above all a deposition of every foundation and absolute truth, but also an experimentation with new possibilities of thought. The Nietzschean 'liberation' now becomes liberation from any metaphysical dogmas: an operation of breaking through the absolutes, of destroying consolidated notions and structures (above all the 'subject'), and a recognition of the differential fabric of the real. Nietzsche's thought therefore assumes an eminently hermeneutic meaning: 'there are no facts but only interpretations' (Nietzsche 1974: aph. 11315; *AD*; *BS*; *EM*). The Dionysian is freedom to exercise on the given world, on the actual reality with its social systems and institutions, a 'game of interpretation' (Vattimo 1981a: 15; *BS*): an 'interpretative work that does not refer to an ultimate meaning, which knows indeed that it cannot reach this ultimate meaning because it simply does not exist' (Vattimo 1978: 10).

It is a 'liberal' Nietzsche which first of all recognises the plurality of being, and which in the 1980s constitutes the presupposition of Vattimo's 'weak thought' (Vattimo and Rovatti 1983). With an extreme hermeneutical surprise, however, once the Cold War ended and the technocratic domination of the Earth expanded in the neoliberal era, Nietzsche (Vattimo 2007b) inspired again Vattimo's return to an original conception of politics as 'hermeneutic communism' (*HC*).

NIHILISM

Ashley Woodward

One of the most central and striking claims in Vattimo's thought is the positive revaluation of nihilism. The term is typically a deeply critical one; it derives from the Latin *nihil*, meaning nothing, and is deployed to refer to the negation of anything that the critic deems valuable. Vattimo's understanding of this term emerges from the dialogue between Nietzsche and Heidegger that he stages in his own thought. Both thinkers use the term to critique modernity, and present nihilism as a problem to be overcome. Vattimo's originality is in developing a conception of nihilism which, he argues, is itself the only viable solution to the very problems Nietzsche and Heidegger identify. He argues that what he sometimes calls 'positive' or 'optimistic' nihilism is our only chance for emancipation today.

In general, Vattimo uses the term 'metaphysics' to indicate the problems that he understands both Nietzsche and Heidegger to critically diagnose, and the term 'nihilism' as a solution to those problems. Simply put, metaphysics for Vattimo indicates a conjunction in philosophy between a 'strong' conception of truth, that is, correspondence, and a 'strong' conception of reality, that is, an objective and unchanging stable structure or enduring presence. For Nietzsche and Heidegger these metaphysical conceptions are problematic because they have undermined themselves in modernity: developments in knowledge, science and technology have not only undermined mythical, religious and other traditional structures of belief which previously gave human life meaning, but also belief in truth and reality themselves. Modern nihilism is summed up in Nietzsche's famous proclamation, 'God is dead' (see **death of God**).

According to many 'orthodox' ways of reading Nietzsche and Heidegger, the nihilism of modernity must be overcome through some kind of return to or reinvention of pre-modern forms of thought, exemplified in Heidegger's (in)famous statement, 'Only a God can save us'. Vattimo argues against this interpretation, citing the dangers of reinstituting the same problems of metaphysics in a different form, and also critiquing the idea of a definitive overcoming as the very logic of modernity. Instead, Vattimo develops ideas from Nietzsche and Heidegger which posit a positive conception of nihilism as a post-foundational way of thinking and being, and as the only viable solution.

Vattimo associates epistemological nihilism with Nietzsche's critique of truth and the famous declaration that 'there are no facts, only interpretations'. In Heidegger, this corresponds with a 'weaker' version of truth as ontological disclosure (*aletheia*) rather than correspondence. In Nietzsche there is an ontological version of nihilism in the critique of the idea of the 'true world', and this ontological dimension is emphasised by Heidegger's understanding of the history of Being. For Heidegger, Being is not a stable structure, but a historical process of different epochs in which beings are disclosed differently. Heidegger argues that there has been a decline or oblivion of Being because its disclosure has been increasingly obfuscated by metaphysical thinking. Today there is very little of Being left, and this is the condition Heidegger calls nihilism. Vattimo interprets this to mean that there is very little of Being left in the metaphysical sense, that is, as stable structure, or belief in a true world (see 'Nihilism and the Postmodern in Philosophy' in *EM*, and Vattimo 1986b). For Vattimo, nihilism means that there can be no strong truth-claims since there is no real world to which they might correspond, and this leads him to identify nihilism with a perspectival, relativist hermeneutics involving the irreducibility of heterogeneous interpretations. However, this is not a complete relativism, since nihilism itself is thought to act as a guiding thread (the metaphysically 'weaker', more nihilistic interpretation should always be privileged).

Vattimo links these readings of Nietzsche and Heidegger with his understanding of the postmodern cultural situation, where nihilism is evident in the generalisation of exchange in both globalised capitalism and communication technologies (see **postmodernism/postmodernity**). These developments have undermined the closed horizons which allow Being to disclose itself in a foundational way, in terms of a coherent worldview with consistent meanings and values, and have opened up a culture of multiple interpretations consistent with the decline of Being and a nihilistic hermeneutic ontology (see 'An Apology for Nihilism' in *EM*). Ethically and politically, Vattimo associates metaphysical thought with violence (strong beliefs motivate strong actions, and silence dissenters), and fears that attempts at overcoming nihilism through the return to pre-modern modes of belief or the reinforcement of metaphysical beliefs would be associated with totalitarian forms of community. Nihilism, in contrast, seems to him to offer a chance of emancipation through the reduction of violence in all its forms (see *NE*; Vattimo 2009b). In his writings on religion, Vattimo associates nihilism, understood as the death of God and the decline of Being, with the kenotic interpretation of Christ, and thus links nihilism not only with political emancipation, but with a (weakened) form of spiritual salvation (see *B*; *kenosis*; **kenotic sacrifice**).

ONTO-THEOLOGY (SEE METAPHYSICS)

ONTOLOGICAL DIFFERENCE

Francesco Tomatis

Throughout his theoretical journey, the philosophy of Vattimo has been oriented by the question of the (ontological) difference and of differences. Through his own interpretation of Heidegger, Vattimo declines the question of 'ontological difference' – that is, the issue of the difference between Being and beings, as the historical 'self-giving' of Being (as sending, eventuation, event, *Ereignis*), different from the beings in which it 'gives itself', 'there is', 'happens' – avoiding both the Hegelian reduction of the essence to historical appearance, and metaphysical objectivism, which separates Being from the sensitive world to make it a stable foundation, imperishable but not practicable, outside the world. Both concepts are violent, as homologising historical, existent and existential differences to purely rational univocal models. This perspective – present in books such as *Essere, storia e linguaggio in Heidegger* (1963), *Introduzione a Heidegger* (1971), *The Adventure of Difference*, *The End of Modernity*, *Beyond Interpretation* and *Being and its Surroundings* – allows the understanding of beings in their multiplicity and variety, in their differences, as significant in their own peculiarities, though not on the basis of an absolute relativism, potentially conflictual, but thanks precisely to the conception of Being as different from beings, not identifiable with any of them, and therefore 'historico-destinal giving' (*Geschick*: sending), a 'disclosure' of truth or 'opening' of meaning, only in the multiplicity of existential differences interpretable and livable.

It is therefore necessary to keep in mind the interpretation that Vattimo gives to the Heideggerian 'ontological difference' in historico-destinal and linguistic-interpretative terms, to also understand his reading of Nietzsche, in works such as *Il soggetto e la maschera* (1974), *Beyond the Subject*, *Introduzione a Nietzsche* ([1985a] 2002) and *Dialogue with Nietzsche*. For Vattimo, Nietzsche elaborates a symbolic and interpretative conception of truth, not in the sense of an absolutisation of perspective relativism, but rather as an interpretation itself, a symbolic experiment, an expression of human potentiality.

Vattimo interprets Nietzsche's *Übermensch* not as 'super-man' but as 'beyond-man' (*overman*), a man capable of understanding his own limitations and going beyond them; yet not in the sense of empowering them, by overcoming them in an infinite evolution or empowerment, but going beyond modern subjectivity itself, through moderation, weakness, self-irony and interpretative listening. According to the interpretation given by Vattimo, Nietzsche then opens up a philosophy of differences, which are nevertheless not absolutised, not made into a new foundational paradigm, as in many contemporary visions. For Vattimo this is possible – similarly to Heidegger – thanks to an alternative position both towards classical metaphysics and its objective and stable Being, and towards contemporary relativism, which absolutises the finite by making it a new ground of violence and ideological and political conflicts. This alternative conception understands truth or Being 'weakly', without a strong cogency, yet as a significant dimension for a humanity that, in the act of listening, makes itself interpreter of the smallest differences, even the most minimal and marginal.

The hermeneutics of Vattimo therefore remains ontological, but his conception of Being always passes through the historicity of the multiple, different interpretations of it. His book *A Farewell to Truth* is a farewell to the metaphysical conception of truth as an objective reflection of a 'given', as *adaequatio rei et intellectus*, an adjustment between object and subject separately understood, to give way to the perspective of truth as horizon, of Being as event. The 'ontological difference' of truth with respect to interpretation is not objectivistic, metaphysical, but eventual, which allows both a critique of the ontological foundational positions, and of the subjectivist, relativistic, just as absolutely foundational and ultimately fundamentalist and violent positions. His philosophy of interpretation, differentialist but not relativist, veritative in the sense of a conception of Being as a 'historico-destinal' event to be listened to and interpreted existentially in history, is therefore also an effective critique against the current ideological, religious, political and economic systems of power, and is potentially emancipatory (cf. *NE*; Vattimo 2007b).

In this sense, Vattimo also reinterprets the Christian tradition, particularly in volumes such as *Schleiermacher filosofo dell'interpretazione* (1968), *Belief* and *After Christianity*. His reinterpretation is focused on the Christian idea of *kenosis*, of the Incarnation of God in history as emptying, weakening and consequently proclaiming a Word that relies on personal interpretation, on the freedom of the individual and on existential listening, whose essential message is love, *caritas*, according to the Augustinian principle: *Dilige, et quod vis fac* (Augustine, *In epistulam Johannis ad Parthos*, VII 8). The Incarnation of God in history occurs through the man

Jesus Christ, *kenosis* of God the Father in history – according to a secularisation intrinsic to the Christian God, which in its uniqueness is freedom, up to the 'kenotic' creation and love towards humanity – and he himself freely operating a *kenosis* of his own humanity and divinity, to break the victimising mechanism present in human history, propagator of violence through causal logic and retributive justice (see also **kenotic sacrifice**). The *kenosis*, the secularised presence of God in history, is therefore an appeal to human freedom, because the message of Christian love passes through the interpretation of human beings who interpret this Incarnation in as many existences made of 'kenotic' love.

In the volume *Of Reality*, Vattimo stresses that the ethical commitment of dialogue between people and different perspectives, heir to the Christian ideal of charity, is made possible precisely by a 'weak' conception of Being. Only with the disappearance of absolutes, of foundational faiths, theories or ideologies, including the technological illusion and its idea of lightening the world in reducing it to an image, can a fruitful dialogue between differences occur – on the condition, however, that this dialogue is based on a perspective that recognises Being as an event, a historical opening of truth always to be listened to and interpreted in its difference with respect to every present reality. Without this hermeneutic perspective, only a banal realism remains – currently prevailing with deaf violence – of acceptance of the existing order.

See also **difference**.

ONTOLOGY OF ACTUALITY

Rogi Thomas

Vattimo's 'ontology of actuality' is derived from his Christian background and his untiring awareness of social and political questions. He says,

> My thought is a reflection of events: in some cases, I have simply echoed issues and problems that were part of the general environment around me, part of the air I was breathing every day . . . and my reflections were a response to the characteristic political, cultural, and religious situations of the epoch. (Vattimo 2009d: 311–50)

It is a constantly readjusted response to the historical and political situation of a specific epoch, and a retrospective vision of his own philosophical reflection. His philosophical journey, with its culmination in 'weak thought', 'secularisation' and *kenosis* through the process of dissolution and *Verwindung* (see **convalescence [*Verwindung*]**), is not an arbitrary event. He argues that the 'ontology of actuality' is the resultant outcome of his own 'weak thought'. When metaphysics is 'overcome' and we have 'emancipated ourselves from an eternal conception of being', our own 'philosophical precepts' will not be able to claim eternal validity; accordingly, philosophy can only become an 'ontology of actuality'. This is clearer when understood in the sense of Foucault, from whom Vattimo draws it, who set this as a historical way of philosophising against what he called the 'the analytic of truth'. He attempts in 'philosophical and historico-social actuality to go beyond phenomenology toward an ontology of actuality' (*FT*, 23). Hence, the ontology of actuality is interpreted as 'a thought whose mission is to define the conditions of and the content of, a truth not subject to the mutation of historical tradition . . . but was always taken to be a critical instance that reason could advance against history' (*FT*, 22). However, Vattimo observes that ontology of actuality is a difficult and vague phrase, though it has some generality and a touch of the sharp outline of terms such as modernity, postmodernity and so on (*FT*, 23). He uses it in a Heideggerian way of 'thought of Being in both senses, subjective and objective, of the genitive' (*FT*, 23).

Fundamentally, for Vattimo, the ontology of actuality is a response to the question, *che cosa ne è dell'essere?* ('Just how do matters stand with Being?' or 'What is going on with Being?') (*FT*, 28). Thus, the ontology of actuality makes possible the transformation of Being, which determines the epochal nature of postmodernity and technology. Understood in its most literal sense, the ontology of actuality does not represent 'a philosophy oriented primarily towards the consideration of existence and its historicity' (in Foucault's sense), but rather towards epistemology and logic, that is, towards an analytic of truth. It is a discourse that attempts to clarify what Being signifies in the present situation; that is, an 'ontological significance' (*NE*, 3–4; *FT*, 23).

Vattimo sees twentieth-century Western philosophy as taking the form of a 'sociological impressionism' or more concretely of 'the ontology of actuality', especially in the oeuvre of Heidegger; and he speaks specifically of 'the epochal essence of Being'. The epochal essence of Being gives an idea of how philosophy can speak about actuality, about modernity, postmodernity and above all about the situation now (*NE*, 4–5). The principal aim of the ontology of actuality accordingly is conceiving itself (epochality of Being) as an effort to grasp the meaning that Being has today, and to connect 'this meaning' with destiny as *Geschick*. For Vattimo, it is Heidegger who offers a comprehensive interpretation of 'the slide of philosophy toward sociology' through the binary senses given to the genitive in the ontology of actuality: 1) the ontology for which we are searching is a theory that speaks of actuality (the objective genitive), and 2) 'it' belongs to actuality (the subjective genitive). It is because there is no way to understand Being as something stable apart from its event that a theory of present existence is one that has no other source of information or legitimation apart from the present condition itself (*NE*, 7–8). The existential nuance of the ontology of actuality is that we must clearly see what the very fact of the 'slide' of philosophy into sociology signifies, which is not solely philosophy's disciplinary development. Phenomena such as the nineteenth-century debate about the relative status of the natural sciences and the humanities and social sciences are also linked to this 'slide'. For Vattimo, the 'slide' or 'sociologism' or the 'ontology of actuality' happened in response 'to the menace of the "total organization" of society that was beginning to take shape in the early twentieth century; resulting in the loss of unitary significance to existence, and diffusing into the multiple social roles that everyone finds themselves occupying' (*NE*, 8–9).

ORNAMENT (see DEATH OF ART/END OF ART)

OVERCOMING (*ÜBERWINDUNG*)

Ian Alexander Moore

Vattimo follows the later Heidegger (for example, 1977: 39; 1988: 313, 376 n.6) in contrasting an impossible 'overcoming' (*Überwindung*) of the hegemony of metaphysics with a possible *Verwindung* of it (see **convalescence [*Verwindung*]**). Unlike *Verwindung*, which suggests both distortion (cf. *winden*, 'to twist') and, on Vattimo's reading, a convalescence that does not erase the traces of illness (*FT*, 127–8), *Überwindung* suggests both prevailing over (*über*) something and getting beyond (*über*) it altogether. '*Over*powering' and '*over*coming', as well as the Latinate terms '*sur*mounting', '*sur*passing' and '*ex*ceeding', all bear aspects of the German *Überwindung*, as does Vattimo's Italian rendering of the latter as '*supera*mento' (in, for example, *EM*).

Like Nietzsche's description of the shadow of God still cast upon the world centuries after God has died, the effort to overcome metaphysics, like the effort to get beyond God, cannot – despite, or rather because of, itself – escape the metaphysical traits it purports to abandon (*NE*, 160). For, overcoming remains dependent on that from which it seeks to liberate itself (*NE*, 2), whether this be modern society or its metaphysical underpinnings. With Nietzsche (1995a), Vattimo sees the very idea of overcoming as inextricably modern, for it remains caught up in modernity's relentless logic of the ever-new: 'Modernity is defined as the era of overcoming and of the new which rapidly grows old and is immediately replaced by something still newer, in an unstoppable movement that discourages all creativity even as it demands creativity and defines the latter as the sole possible form of life' (*EM*, 166). In lieu of another historical stage, Vattimo proposes both an end to unitary history and its dispersal into countless histories (*EM*, 4, 9, 121). Such dispersal would also afflict not only efforts at dialectical sublation, which try to overcome through cooptation and purification, but also the temptation (felt by Heidegger and, on Vattimo's reading, by Heidegger's great commentator Reiner Schürmann) to come to a hidden source of Being over and beyond its metaphysical barriers (*EM*, 164, 171; *DN*, 188).

A violent impulse drives the desire for overcoming, as seen in countless campaigns for revolution and conversion, and as seen, Vattimo contends, even in Nietzsche's call for a revaluation of all values (*FT*, 128). Vattimo does not abandon the language of revolution and conversion, but he does endeavour to weaken it:

> A philosopher must convert in the sense that he cannot do otherwise than attempt to be in practical contact with all the phenomena of practical deconstruction of the still metaphysical order of his and our society. The latter cannot be radically overcome (no revolution of the world proletariat would have any chance of success within the real relations of power), but it can certainly be '*verwunden*-distorted' by the multiple anarchic initiatives of resistance springing up here and there within the *Gestell*, even without any (metaphysical) hope of constructing a new global order (another *ausgeträumt* dream of traditional philosophy). (*FT*, 130; see also *OR*, 152)

The approach of overcoming, in contrast, might try to speak a completely different language from that of realist metaphysics. But inasmuch as it aims at a truer, more real account of the nature of things, it ends up where it started: precisely with realist metaphysics (*OR*, 95). In the name of truth, truth cannot be overcome. One can, however, engage in *Verwindung*, a 'twisting or weakening' of truth 'in a productive manner' (Vattimo and Zabala in Mazzini and Glyn-Williams 2017: 31–2).

Vattimo proposes various alternative models to *Überwindung*. One is, as we have seen, Heideggerian *Verwindung*. Others include Nietzsche's eternal return, which disrupts the modern insistence on the new (*EM*, 168), Heidegger's Hölderlin-inspired *Andenken* (remembrance), the proclamation of the death of God, truth as fable, and Nietzsche's philosophy of morning. See especially *The End of Modernity* for these various alternatives.

See also *Andenken* (remembrance); death of God; realism/new realism.

OVERMAN (*ÜBERMENSCH*) (see NIETZSCHE, FRIEDRICH)

P

PAREYSON, LUIGI

Robert T. Valgenti

Luigi Pareyson (1918–92) was one of the most important Italian philosophers of the twentieth century, known for his work on aesthetics, hermeneutics and religious ontology, and on figures as diverse as Jaspers, Dostoevsky and Fichte. He was Vattimo's dissertation director, mentor and close friend at the University of Turin, encouraging his student to write a dissertation on the concept of 'making' (or 'doing': *fare*) in Aristotle – a project undoubtedly influenced by Pareyson's theory of 'formativity' and extensive theoretical work on the process of artistic creation. He encouraged Vattimo to study with Gadamer in Heidelberg, and later helped to secure him a position as a young professor of aesthetics at the University of Turin. Pareyson's philosophical influence is evident in the themes of ontology, truth, interpretation and aesthetics that pervade all of Vattimo's work. But despite this strong general influence, Pareyson receives only brief mention in Vattimo's corpus – typically with reference to three key ideas.

The first indicates Vattimo's indebtedness to the hermeneutic theory of Pareyson, which he purposefully places alongside the more recognisable names of Hans-Georg Gadamer and Paul Ricoeur (Vattimo [1967b] 2008: 5; *AD*, 18; *EM*, 130; *BI*, 1; *AC*, 98). In Vattimo's eyes, it was Pareyson alone who fully understood what interpretation was and how it revealed truth (*ACT*, 78; *NBG*,103).

The second idea can be found in Vattimo's frequent reference to Pareyson's 'tragic thought', which for Vattimo is indicative of 'the last great metaphysical misunderstanding of Christian thought' because it retains 'a radical separation between the history of salvation and secular history', granting the former a meaning that is 'exclusively apocalyptic' (*B*, 81). Tragic thought links the inexhaustibility of Being to lived reality; Being is no longer an absolute necessity or foundation, but rather the being of a reality that bears the indelible trace of an originary conflict through which existence triumphed over non-being. This connection to an originary conflict is, for Vattimo, a remnant of metaphysical thinking; nonetheless, he retains Pareyson's notions of conflict and risk as central to the unending process of interpretation. Moreover, Pareyson's hermeneutics of religious experience provides Vattimo with a method for reading the history of the West that grasps 'the internal rule of the process, as if it were like the meaning of an itinerary in which we are implicated' (*B*, 68). Despite this influence, Vattimo breaks with Pareyson by insisting upon a dissolution of the divine into the secular – an interpretation of Christianity that reflects Vattimo's formulations of 'weak thought' and hermeneutic nihilism. The Christ-event is no longer, as it was for Pareyson, a universal signifier for a still transcendent and necessary divine being that makes all other myths and manifestations of the divine possible through its presence; for Vattimo, Christ is emblematic of a larger metaphysical history of the West which unfolds through its own weakening, secularisation and dissolution into cultural forms.

The third idea is Pareyson's 'ontology of the inexhaustible' which, as outlined in *Truth and Interpretation* (Pareyson 2013: 37–8, 40–2), characterises the hermeneutic revelation of truth and shapes interpretation in all aspects of human activity. But it is Pareyson's aesthetics of 'formativity' (Pareyson 1960 [1954]) that provides the key to understanding the centrality of hermeneutic ontology in contemporary philosophy – a theme which Vattimo explores in his most extensive treatment of Pareyson, the 1993 essay 'Pareyson from Aesthetics to Ontology' (*ACT*, 77–89). Vattimo argues that Pareyson's existential trajectory (tragic thought) and aesthetic trajectory (ontology of the inexhaustible) are deeply connected and highlight a never-ending process of interpretation that remains without resolution. The key elements in this model are person and form, both of which refer to finitude, as they are outcomes of a formative process that generates a finality (definiteness) – its limiting conditions and the extent of its possibilities (*ACT*, 80). In contrast to Gadamer and Dilthey, the infinity of the process is not connected to the different natures of the two sides of the interpretation, which could lead to infinity understood as relativism. For Pareyson, person and form are 'finalities that bear in themselves, as the trace of their formative process, an infinity that opens onto interpretation' (*ACT*, 81). For Vattimo, these formulations from Pareyson provide the key to understanding why interpretation is not a relativistic 'anything goes'. The process of interpretation is infinite, but nonetheless has limits and guides, setbacks and inherent risks.

Pareyson's works in English include *Truth and Interpretation* (2013) and selected writings in *Existence, Interpretation, Freedom* (2009), both of which include biographical and critical introductions by the translators. Critical essays on his work have been collected in Benso and Schroeder (2018).

See also **aesthetics; phenomenology**.

PAUL, ST (see *KENOSIS*; INTERPRETATION)

PHENOMENOLOGY

Mike Grimshaw

Vattimo's phenomenology is understood through a European heritage of thought that takes its contemporary expression in modern hermeneutic philosophy, 'because here [in Europe] there is a religion of the book that focuses attention on phenomenological interpretation' (*BI*, 28). Because the secular turn can only arise out of that religious tradition and culture, Vattimo, via Girard, developed a phenomenology of secularisation as 'the complete application of the sacred tradition to given human phenomena' (Vattimo and Girard 2010: 28). Phenomenology therefore occurs out of interiority, which for Vattimo – via Dilthey (1989 [1883]) – arises from the interiority introduced by Christianity. This interiority is the ground of hermeneutics, for we exist in the world that is given and so 'subjective' images alone do not exist.

Twentieth-century cultural anthropology rethought neo-Kantian phenomenology and questions of truth. Phenomenology, responding to the reordering and 'decisive meaning of the sciences' (*BI*, 23) in modernity, that is, as 'a response to the world of incipient total organization shaped by the success and technologies they made possible' (*BI*, 23), became determined by science and technology. Because the central phenomenological event of modernity became 'the impact of the technical-scientific rationalization of society' (*NE*, 8), the phenomenological turn became that 'of "spiritual" liberty that could not be scientifically described'; and phenomenology was repositioned as that which 'could not fall under the sway of technology' (*NE*, 8).

Poetics is the artist's way of responding to and seeking meaning phenomenologically (*ACT*, 35). Drawing on Payreson's *Aesthetics* (1960 [1954]), 'phenomenological aesthetics' (*ACT*, 94) that is not 'a phenomenological description of the "fact" of art' (*ACT*, 94) occurs when the 'law of the work [of art] is both invented and discovered, created and found' (*ACT*, 106).

The phenomenological problem of Husserl's thought is that, as a type of radicalising of the Kantian programme, it was 'deprived of any metaphysical openness [and was] reduced only to the problem of the foundation for knowledge's validity' (*ACT*, 19). This means that to 'the extent that it opens itself to metaphysical developments, phenomenology manifests its vocation to take the foundation [the question of knowledge] as a way of locating the rational vocation of man in the midst of a nature that has become synonymous with being' (*ACT*, 20).

However, 'the Being of things (the ontic reality) is inseparable from the being-there of the human being' (*FR*, 45). For Vattimo, drawing heavily on Heidegger, this means that '[t]hings appear to us in the world only because we are in their midst and always already oriented toward seeking a specific meaning for them' (*FR*, 44); that is, more generally, '[i]t is not Being that is for man rather man is available for Being' (*ACT*, 105). Phenomenology is therefore an interpretative undertaking that is to be distinguished from the Kantian-derived sciences of phenomena; this hermeneutic phenomenology arises from the noumenal questions that 'break the paradigm'; these being 'values, ethics, ways of organizing social life, the general meaning of life' (*OR*, 90). Therefore we cannot turn noumenal questions into – or deal with them as – truths of fact, and we cannot find 'their solution with the methods of science' (*OR*, 90).

This hermeneutical distinction is why Vattimo's phenomenology always circles back to Husserl and Heidegger's disagreement arising out of Husserl's *Encyclopedia Britannica* entry on phenomenology in 1927. Because Husserl came 'to philosophy through mathematics; [and] Heidegger on the other hand, from Catholic theology' (*OR*, 37), phenomenology is a choice between 'a scientific-mathematical mind versus an intensely religious spirit' (*OR*, 96). Rejecting 'Husserl the mathematician' and the 'transcendental grounding of regional ontologies that arises' (*FT*, 27), which 'leaves out the being formulating it' (*FT*, 28), Vattimo's weak phenomenology is, via Heidegger, the posing of 'the question of the meaning of Being from the point of view of the being asking the question' (*OR*, 97).

It is Nietzsche's emphasis on 'the phenomenon of interpretation' (*DN*, 73) that gives rise to the ontological hermeneutic of weak thought. Being occurs as a phenomenological event, while phenomenology occurs 'as resistance to the accomplishment of nihilism' (*EM*, 23), as well as expressing the 'need to go beyond exchange-value, in the direction of a kind of use-value that can be kept free of the logic of permutability' (*EM*, 22). The phenomenological question is how to attempt a non-idealistic 'relationship between thought and perception, the body and the emotions' (*EM*, 34). Because Husserl's phenomenological theory is one of the 'most successful definitions of truth' (*HC*, 19), weak thought undoes such definitions by proposing 'a path running from phenomenology to the ontology of actuality' (*FT*, 22); that actuality being 'the common condition of our life at present' (*FT*, 23; see **ontology of actuality**). Otherwise phenomenology loses both the Marxist capacity and demand to change the world and the Heideggerian expectation that we need 'to think, to exercise our capacity to heed Being and not let ourselves be confused by calculating reason' (*FT*, 103).

PIETAS

Andrzej Zawadzki

In Vattimo's terminology, *pietas*, together with *Verwindung* (see **convalescence [*Verwindung*]**) and *Andenken* (see *Andenken* [**remembrance**]) form a conceptual trio, which characterises the most important aspects of post-metaphysical thinking, as well as of weak thought itself. As compared with the other two terms, *pietas* appears relatively rarely in Vattimo's writings (the broadest definition can be found in his seminal essay 'Dialectics, Difference, Weak Thought', in *WT*, 39–52). Unlike the other terms, it is not borrowed from Heidegger's vocabulary, but from the Christian tradition. This fact seems to be important, as it heralds the later religious turn in Vattimo's thought (*B*; *AC*; see **religion**). *Pietas* in Latin means, among other things, love in accordance with duty, piety, attachment, friendship, family feelings, fidelity and patriotism. It can be associated, first, with the well-known iconographical motif of the *Pietà* as mourning, and, secondly, with pietism, a seventeenth- and eighteenth-century German religious movement, which accentuated personal contact with God and love for one's fellow human creatures ('neighbours' in the biblical sense of the term).

The abovementioned Christian contexts play a subtle but important, even if not immediately recognisable, role in the way in which Vattimo interprets *pietas*. Basically, two meanings of *pietas* emerge. The first refers to death, remembering (much in the sense of *Andenken*) and mourning: '*Pietas* suggests primarily mortality, finitude, and passing away' (*WT*, 47).

As such, it is strictly associated with a rich metaphoric field of 'weakness', especially 'weak' ontology, and 'ending', especially the end of metaphysics, the end of modernity, the end of art (see also **being; death of art**).

The second meaning of *pietas* is an ethical one. In this sense, piety is an attitude which arises out of the collapse of traditional metaphysics, based on concepts such as essence, substance, objectivity, 'sameness' and 'the proper'. Understood as such, *pietas* is love for everything that lives, and for the traces, both those inherited from the past as our own tradition (Latin *traditio*, that which is *tra-ditum*, trans-mitted), an idea that is closer to a Gadamerian version of hermeneutics, and those left over by 'others', contemporaries to us and belonging also to other traditions, an idea that is closer to the more radical version of hermeneutics (Vattimo 1981a: 7; *BS*; see also *EM*, 155–6; **ethics; Gadamer, Hans-Georg; interpretation**). In its ethical sense, *pietas* is strictly associated with a set of concepts such as trace (*Spur*), transmission (*Überlieferung, Schickung*) and tradition (*Geschick*). They are all rooted in Heidegger's notion of Being. It is also worth noting that concepts of trace and transmission (*envoi*) appear widely in some of Derrida's writings from the 1980s and 1990s (Derrida 1987b: 63; 2007: 110).

POIESIS/POESIS

Ivelise Perniola

In Vattimo's aesthetics, both the term *poiesis*, which indicates the productive moment of artistic achievement through the working of tangible materials, and the term *poesis*, which indicates the productive moment of artistic achievement through an intangible material which is language, are articulated within a reflection which, ever since *Poesia e ontologia* (1967b; *ACT*), identifies these two expressions through the theoretical and hermeneutical lines provided by the aesthetics of Nietzsche, Heidegger, Pareyson and Gadamer. Vattimo addresses the evolution of artistic doing from a historical perspective, above all in his writings that are more clearly marked by a didactic approach to Western aesthetics (*Introduzione all'estetica* [1977b] 2010), while at the same time creating an original theoretical path aimed at moving out of a metaphysical, historicising or purely aesthetic contemplative dimension of artistic production in order to attain an ontological foundation for the latter.

Poiesis, that is, the production of the work of art, is connected with the technical knowledge implicit in doing/making. On the basis of the reflections of Pareyson, who interprets artistic doing as a continuous and unresolved process, Vattimo elaborates an idea of *poiesis* which can be expressed as such 'a doing that, in doing, invents a new way of doing' (*ACT*, 95–6), where in Latin the verb *invenire* also means 'to find'. Artists, while manipulating the materials by means of which they give shape to the work, invent their own rule, that is, the law that underlies the work and which is unknown, first and foremost, to the artists themselves. The artist therefore ontologically creates a historically connoted world, potentially more directed towards the future than the past, into which the viewer, after perceiving the shock (*Stoss*) of Heideggerian memory, is welcomed, perceiving the previous world as substantially distant and alien. The foundation of this new world produced by the work of art, by its material expression, is new for the artist, for the viewer and for the interpreter, who, endowed with previous knowledge, adapts his or her own knowledge to the new stimuli produced by the new work-world. The *poieo* (doing the work) is therefore the highest expression of a rationality which is an alternative to metaphysical rationality. Vattimo problematises Aristotle's interpretation of *poiesis* (Vattimo 1961). Aristotle believed that *poiesis* was a characteristic action of the practical arts, in which the action presupposed a material as well as a cathartic end; activities with a single end, such as the exercise of virtue, cannot be considered *poiesis*. In his aesthetic thought, Vattimo recovers the modelling value of the arts, of intervention in the real world, through the creation of a possibility of an alternative world in their doing and in their making over the course of time.

Poesis, artistic doing through language, is viewed as the highest expression of *poiesis*, starting with Heidegger, and Vattimo recovers this centrality. In fact, the term 'poetry' is connected at its root to artistic doing (to *poieo*) in a much more evident way than its synonym 'lyric', in which the production of affective moments prevails at the ontological level. Poetry is an event of being, which uses language as expressive material. From Heidegger, Vattimo also takes the concept of the work of art, of which poetry is a crowning point, as the enactment of truth, that is, as the place where truth originally occurs. *Poesis*, or poetic doing, possesses, more than any other artistic doing, the potential capacity to establish and found the world, insofar as it establishes a privileged channel between the artist and the viewer, which is that of language, since 'things come to being inasmuch as they come to language' (*ACT*, 66).

The passage that completes the overcoming of the metaphysics of the work of art, begun by Nietzsche and completed by Heidegger, is enhanced in Vattimo's thought by the interpretative, hermeneutic moment, integrated in the latter's aesthetic reflection through Gadamer's teaching (Vattimo [1972b] 1983). Doing poetry seems to be in a more intimate and profound relationship with interpreting than is philosophising; or rather, the inexhaustible ambiguity of poetic language seems to be able to constitute a real determination of being better than interpreting reflection can. Interpretation can never be resolved into complete self-transparency: while scientific doing claims to objectify experience to such an extent that it forgets its own historicity, hermeneutics is always aware of itself as something historically other than its object. Nevertheless, this self-awareness can never be resolved into completely open and deployed knowledge, because the clarification of the situation we find ourselves in is a never-ending task. In Gadamer, and in the theorisation that Vattimo makes his own, there is a transfer of knowledge beyond philosophy, not in the direction of science, but towards poetry and art. The creator of the work of art is the first to acquire knowledge, at the moment in which the form on which he or she is working undergoes a transformation, revealing itself to be something totally new and unexpected and therefore true. The unsuccessful work of art is not therefore that which is ugly, but that which is not open to any interpretation.

See also **art**; **interpretation**.

POLITICS

Cristina Basili

The political nature of hermeneutics is at the core of Vattimo's philosophy. His stance on the historical and eventual character of Being cannot be separated from the ethico-political aim of his thought. The anti-metaphysical and anti-dogmatic conception of philosophy that he develops in his writings is explicitly commanded by an anti-authoritarian political purpose. Philosophy as such should contribute to the emancipation and liberation of humanity. This entanglement between philosophy and politics is what he calls the responsibility of the philosopher, something that he or she should assume as their inherent 'duty': 'a tool of the trade that can't be given up, like the surgeon's ability to use a scalpel' (Flores D'Arcais 2007: 250).

Vattimo displays, throughout his work, the fundamentally political vocation of hermeneutics:

If you forget the political interest that spurred you, the religious interest, the emancipatory interest in general [. . .] theory can't (in the best of cases) be anything more than a simple literary exercise, or artistic-philosophical experimentation, or (more commonly), an exercise in individualism for its own sake, serving private interests and power. Philosophy, project, historicity, theory, emancipation – for me they all mean the same thing. (*RP*, 108)

Accordingly, he understands hermeneutics not just as a theoretical exercise, but as a philosophy of praxis, *the* philosophy of praxis in contemporary times (*OR*, 147). His proposal of a nihilistic hermeneutics is, in fact, intended as an 'antimetaphysical radicalization of Marxism' (*OR*, 147; see **Marxism/Italian Marxism**). Rereading Marx's eleventh thesis on Feuerbach, Vattimo affirms that, '[c]ontrary to the letter of Marx's famous phrase about philosophers who only interpreted the world while trying to change it, it is precisely by interpreting the world – and by not pretending to describe it in its given "objectivity" – that one contributes to its transformations' (*OR*, 102). This is the political task that he draws from his understanding of philosophy as hermeneutics and of hermeneutics as a radically democratic, egalitarian and emancipatory project. Insofar as philosophy affirms the end of metaphysics and, therefore, of the traditional conception of truth, it contributes to the deconstruction of any foundation for violence and domination, since 'violence always acts on the basis of absolute affirmations: whether in the many forms of private violence it takes its own desire, advantage, or preference as absolute; or whether a historical authority can justify much greater violence in the name of claimed absolute values' (*OR*, 116). Consequently, 'a politics grounded in "truth" can only be a politics of authority' (*OR*, 149).

In exchange, nihilistic hermeneutics, assuming the historical character of Being and the interpretative nature of truth, opens the theoretical space for thinking about an ethico-political project based on non-violence. To this end Vattimo appeals to the Christian principle of *caritas*:

Precisely because truth is 'liquidated', transvalued like all the highest values, one can finally practice charity, the Christian love of one's fellow human. Absolute truth is therefore exchanged for the agreement with others reached through the process of negotiation, whether in the private sphere or in the field of politics. (*OR*, 116–17)

This perspective implies that dialogue, 'the conversation between humans in which, solely, Being happens', demands the listening to the silence 'of that Being that metaphysics and the society of domination have always hidden and silenced', that is, the voice of the excluded, of history's defeated. Therefore, philosophy intended as the ability to listen to the other, especially the marginalised and the oppressed, should lead to a hermeneutic humanism that 'cannot in the end be anything but a revolutionary humanism' (*OR*, 152).

According to Vattimo, it is not a coincidence that the end of metaphysics coincided with the advent of democracy: 'The event (of Being) to which thinking had the task of corresponding in the age of democracy is the way in which Being is configured one step at a time in collective experience' (*OR*, 159). Philosophers, 'no longer sovereigns or the advisors of sovereigns' (*OR*, 159–69), must practise philosophy in the form of an 'ontology of actuality'. The 'ontology of actuality', an expression retrieved by the late Foucault, responds to the question of what becomes of the philosophy–politics relation in a world in which, in consequence of the end of metaphysics and the spread of democracy, politics can no longer be thought in terms of truth (*FT*, 41). In this situation, philosophy cannot supply politics with the guidance derived from its knowledge, but instead 'becomes intrinsically political thought' as it is conceived as 'an interpretation that naturally strives to be persuasive but that acknowledges its own contingency, liberty, riskiness' (*FT*, 43). This post-foundational understanding of philosophy focuses on a conception of the world as a conflict of interpretations, assuming the challenges imposed by current pluralistic democratic societies. In this respect, Vattimo's post-metaphysical stance coincides with the hermeneutical political project that he pursued both in his philosophical and political commitment: 'Working for revolution without falling back into metaphysics is the task of hermeneutics as the philosophy of praxis and the way for any emancipation here in the world of the end of metaphysics and of accomplished nihilism' (*OR*, 152; see **nihilism**).

POSTMODERN ART/AESTHETICS

Christine Ross

Vattimo's original contribution to the conceptualisation of postmodernity lies in the central role he gives to aesthetics in the postmodern elaboration of a post-metaphysical experience of truth. *The End of Modernity* establishes that centrality by positing that 'the post-modern – in Heideggerian terms, post-metaphysical – experience of truth is an aesthetic and rhetorical experience', and that the aesthetic experience is therefore the 'model of the experience of truth' at the basis of the postmodern, concluding:

> From architecture to the novel to poetry to the figurative arts, the post-modern displays, as its most common and most imposing trait, an effort to free itself from the logic of overcoming, development, and innovation. From this point of view, the post-modern corresponds to Heidegger's attempt to prepare a post-

metaphysical kind of thought which would not be an *Überwindung* but rather a *Verwindung* of metaphysics [. . .] the post-modern experience of art appears as the way in which art occurs in the era of the end of metaphysics. This holds good not only for what we call 'post-modern' figurative art, literature, and architecture, but also for the dissolutive tendencies already apparent in the great early twentieth-century avant-garde movements [. . .] (*EM*, 12, 13, 105–6)

Why is aesthetics so significant to postmodernity? To answer this question, it is useful to keep in mind the methodological perspective and theoretical premise that the philosopher's main publications discussing postmodern art and aesthetics (*EM*, *ACT* and *TS*) make manifest. First, although Vattimo's investigation of aesthetics never loses sight of art (from the early twentieth-century avant-garde movements to 1990s' visual arts, literature, music and cinema), he does not analyse artworks; his approach is predominantly aesthetic. His interest focuses on the European philosophical tradition of aesthetics (from Kant to Gadamer) and what he calls 'the experience of art'. For Vattimo-inspired analyses of postmodern artworks, one must go elsewhere (Silverman 2001; Zabala 2017). Secondly, postmodern art and aesthetics are understood not as a break with but as a critique of modernity, a dynamic that Vattimo explains by mobilising two Heideggerian concepts: *Überwindung* and *Verwindung*. Postmodernity, aesthetically understood, is not an overcoming (*Überwindung*) of modernity, insofar as modernity can never be dissolved by a process of rupture that is itself fundamentally modern (the value of the new, the cult of the *tabula rasa*), but a 'healing of . . . and a resignation to' metaphysics, as well as a distorting (*Verwindung*) of it – so that tradition might be remembered, to better orient its dissolution and renewal (*EM*, 52; see also Zabala 2007: 14).

The importance of aesthetics to postmodernity comes from Vattimo's view that existence, 'or in Heidegger's terms the "meaning of being" in our epoch', occurs 'first and most clearly in aesthetic experience' (*EM*, 45). Put differently, the aesthetic experience is one that brings to the fore a form of truth that troubles the problematic metaphysical reduction of Being to a being (metaphysics' denial of the concealing–unconcealing dynamic of the unfolding of Being); it is set into play in the work of art whose meaning is never fixed once and for all (hermeneutically speaking, art requires interpretation and reinterpretation), especially when it combines the 'founding and ungrounding' processes of the Heideggerian 'setting-into-work of truth' (*EM*, 126). Vattimo speaks from within the framework of the end of metaphysics, the end of modernity and what he calls 'the death of art' – a death that results from the avant-garde's undoing of the institutional autonomy of art, but also from the transformation of art by technological reproduction and art's 'silence', as rejection of the kitsch of mass culture. These endings are events that cannot be replaced by new fundamentals (such an overcoming would reinstate modernity). The perspicacity of postmodern art lies in its *Verwindung* relation to modernity – it survives, albeit weakly, the end of art. The death of art is therefore more of a decline than an end. '[T]he fact that in spite of everything else', Vattimo writes,

vital works of 'art' still are produced today probably depends upon [*Verwindung*]. For these products are the place in which – in a complex system of relations – the three different aspects of the death of art (as utopia, as *Kitsch*, and as silence) are brought into play and come into contact with each other. (*EM*, 58)

This is to say that postmodern art, deprived of the emancipatory and transformative power dreamed of by early avant-garde movements, still has a weak emancipatory sway enabled by its *Verwindung* activity: it ungrounds metaphysics by disclosing the loss of the main metaphysical attributes of modern art and aesthetics – the creative genius, authenticity, originality, beauty, formal harmony and unity; it sets truth to work by prolonging these attributes so as to twist them, by 'putting art directly in question, thereby raising the question of its limits, its tools, and its position in society' – as Alfredo Jaar's *The Rwanda Project* (1994–98), for example, does (*ACT*, 163). Such is postmodernity.

This being said, however, there is no understanding of the significance of aesthetics to postmodernity without a consideration of Vattimo's claim – formulated in *The Transparent Society* – that the meaning of the postmodern 'is linked to the fact that the society in which we live is a society of generalized communication. It is the society of the mass media' (*TS*, 1). The recent history of visual arts and poetry, in particular, has 'meaning only if placed in relation to the world of images of the mass media or the language of this same world' (*EM*, 58). Visual arts have not only increasingly integrated mass media images and technologies into the artwork, they have redefined art and, more importantly, have responded to mass culture, which has itself become 'a generalized aestheticization of life' (*EM*, 55; see **media**).

The question thus becomes: has aesthetics gone wrong? Vattimo's answer is: not necessarily. And this is why. The society of mass media and generalised communication, understood as emblematic of postmodernity, generates 'a general explosion and proliferation of [. . .] world views', as exemplified in the US, where minorities and subcultures increasingly express themselves through means of mass media (*TS*, 5). 'For us', he writes, 'reality is [. . .] the result of the intersection and "contamination" [. . .] of a multiplicity of images, interpretations and reconstructions circulated by the media in competition with one another and without any "central" coordination' (*TS*, 7). Mass media is a new aesthetic realm because of its capacity to create worlds in which we recognise ourselves as 'belonging to a group', following a reoriented Kantian aesthetics (*EM*, 56). This proliferation of worldviews produces plurality, fragmentation, oscillation, a certain loss of belonging and the 'erosion of very "principle of reality"' (*TS*, 7, 10–11, 53–4).

Key here is Vattimo's understanding that such a postmodern multiplicity can be conducive to a chaotic society, but that it likewise offers a possibility of emancipation; hence the *Verwindung* imperative to respond aesthetically to mass-media aestheticisation. He supports this postmodern ideal, seeing in mass media the possibility of weakening metaphysical universals, but he is also looking for a counter-force to the problematic flipside of the society of generalised communication – the drastic sense of dislocation effects, mass media's increased tendency to support the phantasmagoria of 'the world of objects measured and manipulated by technoscience', and their incapacity to guarantee our awareness of the relativity, historicity and finiteness of our own different worlds (*TS*, 8–10). The pluralistic world of postmodernity is an invitation to experience a new form of freedom as 'a continual oscillation between belonging and disorientation'; yet we are faced with the challenge of discovering how to take that postmodern experience 'as an opportunity for a new way of being (finally, perhaps) human' (*TS*, 10–11).

Interestingly, Vattimo goes back to the aesthetic work of Nietzsche, Benjamin and Heidegger to tease out the benefits of the identification between mass culture, aesthetics and postmodernity. As brilliantly observed by philosopher Matthew Edward Harris, Vattimo is searching for traces of being from past traditions 'by which we can – and must – orient ourselves' in the midst of the postmodern fragmentation of experience intensified by the society of mass media:

> What Vattimo considers to be potentially liberating – our 'sole opportunity' [. . .] – is how we approach, consider, and reuse the traces of Being from past traditions. This process involves the Heideggerian concept *Verwindung*. *Verwindung* has multiple meanings for Vattimo, such as being resigned to tradition, yet also distorting or 'twisting' it [. . .] (Harris 2013)

The Transparent Society dedicates two chapters ('Art and Oscillation' and 'From Utopia to Heterotopia') to explaining how postmodern aesthetics carries traces of Being that can be twisted productively. To show how the disorienting effects of mass media can be a source not of chaos but of emancipation, Vattimo mobilises Walter Benjamin's theorisation of the aesthetics of shock resulting from the avant-garde montage effects of reproductive media (film and photography) and Martin Heidegger's notion of *Stoss* or the 'blow' of the artwork (the experience of anxiety as one is confronted with an artwork that suspends the familiarity of our universe). These aesthetic investigations are not beyond supporting mass culture's dizzying effects: they support an aesthetic experience '*directed towards keeping this disorientation alive*' while showing its emancipatory potential (*TS*, 51–3).

By reinstating the tradition of aesthetics, whether the Kantian tradition or more progressively Benjamin's and Heidegger's, Vattimo is in fact inviting us, postmodern beings, to ensure a sense of continuity with past traditions and (re)twist their aesthetic ideals of harmony, stability and unity so that shock might finally 'take the form of creativity and freedom' (*TS*, 60; see **aesthetics**; **art**).

POSTMODERNISM/POSTMODERNITY

David Rose

Vattimo has a justified claim to being one of the first thinkers, alongside Lyotard (1979) and Jameson (1984), to articulate the concept of postmodernity. His understanding remains consistent and is developed in his more philosophical works, in *The Transparent Society* and *The End of Modernity* especially; yet even in the texts after *Beyond Interpretation*, the understanding acts as a refrain throughout his thought. The overtly diagnostic work of *The Transparent Society* and *The End of Modernity* would become an affirmative ethical historicisation of truth and tradition by the time of *Nihilism and Emancipation*, developing the idea of hermeneutics as the *koiné* of late modernity.

Lyotard's thought identified two overarching, progressive, legitimating metanarratives of modernity, empowerment and emancipation, relying on the monist idea of one unified explanation. The postmodern rupture occurs, for Lyotard, when truth transitions into the performativity of a system, producing the results required to restabilise a discrete system and not the whole. For Jameson, use-value, the material base of society which grounds the value of objects in that society, has, due to technological production processes, merged with and been replaced by exchange-value. Both Lyotard and Jameson see the rise of the digitisation of knowledge statements, and the reduction from meaning to information, as driving a crisis in modern self-understanding. Vattimo shares the social reasons for the emergence of a postmodern consciousness, that is, the rise in cultural pluralism and the multiplication of worldviews and voices thorough the rise of mass media. Modernity could not survive the fall of colonialism that led to the emergence of lost and different cultures, and the revelation that the Western point of view is merely another point of view; the society of generalised communication leads to an explosion of differing discourses and voices. And these social pressures cast light on the theoretical commitments of the modern project, revealing intellectual reasons to understand our own relation to history as Heidegger's end of metaphysics, as best expressed by the last of the metaphysicians, Nietzsche, and the other schools of suspicion, Marxism and Freudianism (*NE*, chs 1–2).

Vattimo agrees with the technocratic characterisation of society, but sees this as a symptom of deeper theoretical crises brought about by the rejection of the West's putative moral and intellectual superiority. Unlike the empirical societal bases of transformation one finds in both Lyotard and Jameson, Vattimo's understanding of the postmodern develops from a purely theoretical understanding of the history of thought. His 'transparent society' is characterised as the actualisation of the end of metaphysics and the emergence of pluralism. The validation of metanarratives or the obligation towards growth and free exchange both rest on the idea of progress or the completion of knowledge and overcoming of superstition. However, the idea of progress must be grounded in putative presuppositions about the end of history and its vantage point, and the unitary nature of development. Modern critical reason revealed its own presuppositions as ideological preferences and not metaphysical foundations. Vattimo recognises that in the twentieth century, such trust in first principles has been undermined and they become subject to justified intellectual and cultural suspicion.

The incommensurability between localised, fragmented discourses of meaning and historical progressive grounds is a symptom, for Vattimo, of emerging postmodern pluralism. Where, perhaps, Vattimo most differs from Lyotard and Jameson is in the meaning of the 'post' of postmodernity. Where the other two thinkers see this as a historical rupture or overcoming, for Vattimo it is a reflection back upon modernity once history itself is brought into question; not a break but more a distancing from the confident and hubristic flavour of the Enlightenment. The Lyotardian thesis of the performativity of statements expresses, for Vattimo, the digital and communication revolution whereby information replaces knowledge and the private individual slowly disappears. The feeling is that Vattimo saw in Lyotard, especially, the expression of deeper theoretical changes making possible the digitisation of society that was an expression of the weak nihilism and horizontal dialectic he wished to offer as an alternative to the inherent progressive social dialectic of Hegel and

Marx (*EM*, ch. 10). The rejection of progress leads to the end of history, but not in the Hegelian sense of completion, but rather failure. And this failure requires a healing or a turning back upon what went before; what Vattimo captures in the German word *Verwindung* (*TS*, ch. 6; see **convalescence** [*Verwindung*]). Vattimo's philosophical understanding of the technological transformations of modern society emerged from Heidegger's understanding of technology, itself understood as an expression of weak nihilism. Modernity was the last metaphysical age but also the age that broke metaphysics. Modernity sought the objectivity of the one true language to describe reality, whereas postmodernity wishes to heal the damage done to free thinking by this ideological commitment through the celebration of pluralism.

Vattimo's philosophical position oscillates between Heidegger and Nietzsche and he sees postmodern society as an expression of the world as the production of plural interpretations. From Nietzsche, the response to the rejection of all values as mere ideological masks is an affirmative nihilism, that is, a new postmodern form of emancipation via the demasking and demystification of power–knowledge constructs. From Heidegger, Vattimo develops hermeneutics into the *koiné* of postmodernity because no other philosophical position can express the pluralism of a fragmented and informational society; the perspectives which make possible our apprehension of reality are not transcendent but 'always qualified' and tied to 'historical-cultural, linguistic, categorical horizons' (*WT*; *BI* appendix 2). With the loss of metaphysics as a ground, or any overarching narrative that would bring the fragmentary discourse of postmodernity together into one cohesive whole, weak thought is the most appropriate, the right manner to do philosophy, when one understands nihilism as the plurality of possible interpretations, which are necessarily incomplete. The ground of one's judgements can no longer be a metaphysical position; instead, one always speaks from social pluralism. The humble pluralism of postmodernity overcomes and distorts (*Verwindung*) the metaphysical commitments of modernity, which led to the coercion and oppression of difference through the commitment to one truth and one right description (*EM*). Other postmodern theories responded to this, as with the critique of the subject, with pure negation, the arbitrariness of strong nihilism. Vattimo refuses the 'anything goes' of such theorists, instead proposing a nihilistic ontology, fragmented and with no centre, but given as an irreducible plurality of perspectives. Postmodernity is these social and cultural conditions when the proper comportment of a society and individuals is one of reflexive interpretation of one's place and history.

POSTSTRUCTURALISM

Clayton Crockett

Poststructuralism refers to the work of the generation of French thinkers who worked through and critiqued the limits of structuralism, including Jacques Derrida, Michel Foucault, Jean-François Lyotard and Gilles Deleuze. Vattimo does not use the specific word poststructuralism, and he is critical of the French philosophers who are characterised by this term. Vattimo shares certain affinities with many of these philosophers, but he argues that they remain too essentialist and metaphysical even when they appear anti-metaphysical. He uses the term postmodern, which represents an interpretative and historical turn that twists free from the Western metaphysics of being. Here Vattimo is influenced strongly by Nietzsche and Heidegger, who are also crucial influences on the poststructuralists.

Vattimo interprets Nietzsche and Heidegger via Hans-Georg Gadamer and Luigi Pareyson rather than through Merleau-Ponty, Deleuze and Derrida. In an interview Vattimo asks: 'And then what is the place of history in Lévinas? Here he resembles Derrida, another thinker who has no conception of history' (Vattimo 2009d: 339). The reason Vattimo asserts that Derrida and Levinas have no conception of history is because their anti-essentialism is expressed in essentialist terms, whereby concepts such as *différance* (Derrida) and the Other (Levinas) retain a certain transcendental and transhistorical status. Despite their criticisms of the ontological tradition as a metaphysics of presence that denigrates and denies alterity and difference, their opposition is viewed by Vattimo as too ahistorical and therefore too 'strongly' ontological. The overcoming of metaphysics is itself therefore too marked by metaphysics.

As Reiner Schürmann explains in 'Deconstruction is Not Enough', Vattimo is 'attempting to work through metaphysics rather than overcome it' in the tradition of Freud and Heidegger. This 'working through' is the task of weakening metaphysical being for the sake of a 'postmetaphysical "layout" of the relation between philosophy and society' (Schürmann 2007 [1984]: 118). The criticism here is that the deconstruction of Derrida as well as the affirmations of difference or otherness by other poststructuralists are not sufficiently post-metaphysical. And similarly, Vattimo charges that 'Derrida's deconstructionism cannot dispense with a renewed spirit of sovereignty' despite his efforts to deconstruct sovereignty, because deconstruction wants to deliver philosophy 'from the error of what Derrida calls metaphysical logocentrism' (*NE*, 27).

Of course, Deleuze remains the French poststructuralist philosopher who is most wedded to the term 'metaphysics', which he associates with philosophy in a positive sense. Vattimo argues that Deleuze's 'glorification of simulacra' represents an anti-Platonism that constitutes a reversal but not a liberation from the traps of metaphysical being. In constrast, Vattimo affirms a 'world of hermeneutic ontology' that expresses 'an active nihilism, where Being has an opportunity to re-occur in an authentic form only through its own impoverishment' (*EM*, 161). Deleuze, Levinas, Derrida and Lyotard are not nihilistic enough because they attempt to rejuvenate philosophy along quasi-metaphysical lines.

The poststructuralist thinker that Vattimo most appreciates is probably Foucault, whose genealogical approach is the most historical of these French philosophers. Foucault, like Vattimo, is deeply influenced by Nietzsche, but here the more actively nihilist, weakening philosophical work of Nietzsche rather than the more explicitly metaphysical Nietzsche of the will to power. Vattimo uses Foucault's phrase the 'ontology of actuality' in much of his work, including at the beginning of *Nihilism and Emancipation*, where he states that 'we can only speak intelligently about postmodernity . . . from a perspective that starts with Heidegger's teaching and goes on to elaborate what might be called, using a term from Foucault's late period, an "ontology of actuality"' (*NE*, 3). In his later work, Foucault turns to what he calls 'technologies of the self' as a way to think about our present historical existence, and the phrase 'ontology of actuality' gives Vattimo a way to describe those occurrences that lead us to constitute and recognise ourselves as the subjects of what we are doing, thinking and saying. In general, Vattimo appreciates the poststructuralists' critique of Western metaphysics. But he ultimately concludes that these French philosophers remain too ahistorical and enthralled by metaphysical presumptions (see **postmodernism/postmodernity; subject/weak subject**).

PRAGMATISM (see RORTY, RICHARD)

R

REALISM/NEW REALISM

William Egginton

Vattimo often frames his thought as a critique of philosophical realism, the presumption that reality exists independently of our interpretations of it. This critique is not merely epistemological but is also ethical. Its principal claim is that philosophical realism is de facto a defence of the status quo and hence can only ever be a thought in the service of those who hold power. Vattimo's 'weak thought' (*pensiero debole*) is a thought of the weak and for the weak, because it aims to reveal the power dynamics implicitly at work in philosophical and political discourses that dissimulate their own subservience to power.

As Vattimo writes (with Zabala), 'These metaphysically framed political systems hold that society must direct itself according to truth (the existing paradigm), that is, in favor of the strong against the weak. Only the strong determine truth, because they are the only ones that have the tools to know, practice, and impose it' (*HC*, 12). One political guise that such dominion has donned in the modern industrialised world is liberal democracy. The elites who benefit from the economic and political status quo ensure that real, existing democratic forms function to support the privileges that have accrued to them. Hence the Western democracies that host the majority of the world's multinational corporations have developed into lightly disguised oligarchies whose political systems entrench and support a class defined by its outlandish and ever-increasing wealth. For Vattimo, discourses such as realism that purport to know in advance what reality is and who has access to it hold hostage actual democratic practices, which are interpretative and contestatory. The unexamined nature of liberal democracy's own framing of truth-claims is thus a threat to unframed democracy.

By masking over power dynamics that are in fact never neutral, never truly objective, commonsensical understandings of objective reality stand in the way of discourses that strive to improve the world and its social relations rather than simply support them in their present form. In contrast, Vattimo's consistent adherence to Nietzsche's dictum that 'There are no facts, only interpretations; and this too is an interpretation' (*OR*, 21) requires that we renounce the crutch of objective reality when justifying our arguments and political positions and instead examine the place of the enunciation of our and our opponents' positions.

It is important to note that in attacking realism, Vattimo's thought is in no way anti-empiricist or anti-scientific. Indeed, empiricism and the scientific method, at least as practised if not always as theorised, are exemplary of weak thought. Just as reality-talk is strikingly useless for the politics of liberation and is instead a useful tool only for those seeking to slow or stop such politics, reality-talk has no conceivable utility for science, the interests of which lie in advancing knowledge, not defending something called reality. In fact, the very notion of reality gets in the way of scientists' drive to solve problems and answer long-standing mysteries.

Far from being a defender of 'anything goes' relativism, Vattimo has specifically criticised the condition of our current times according to which everyone is entitled to his or her own reality, his or her own conception of truth. The proliferation of realities we see today in fact relies on a flattened and flattening hermeneutic *koiné* that Vattimo calls 'the lack of emergency'. As Vattimo points out, it's not that we lack events. Indeed, 24-hour news cycles cultivate a heightened vigilance concerning the next event, the next crisis, the next emergency. But this very stream of information promotes a 'resignation . . . one that remains undisturbed even when there is an economic crisis like the one that we are experiencing' (*OR*, 108).

While the fragmentation of worldviews by the media and the diminution of any sense of common ground have been widely associated with post-hermeneutic philosophical schools of thought often mischaracterised and misunderstood as 'postmodern', for Vattimo this fragmentation emerges logically from realism. In such a media environment, individual positions are always justified as being grounded in a reality to which others are blinded by propaganda. Hence today's post-truth world is really an extension of realism's belief in a fundamental underlying reality independent of interpretation, just one in which multiple parties claim that they have access to the real reality. The response to this is obviously not more realism, more reality-talk. Rather, it is hermeneutics (see **hermeneutics**).

Hermeneutics, as Vattimo writes (with Zabala), is the essence of politics, which 'relies on a plurality of individual developments, that is, active interpretations'. Furthermore, such a philosophy 'must avoid not only any metaphysical claims to universal values, which would restrict personal developments, but also that passive conservative nature that characterizes descriptive philosophies in favor of action' (*HC*, 77). Hermeneutics names the circulation and exchange of active interpretations that occurs prior to and outside the metaphysical framing that claims access to an ultimate reality. It is in this way that, far from a symptom of the current proliferation of realities, Vattimo's thought becomes a tool to combat it in favour of a politics of liberation rather than quietism and stagnation.

RELATIVISM

Martin G. Weiss

From early on Vattimo has been accused of relativism both in relation to his hermeneutical theory of interpretation and his ethics (cf. Viano 1985; Antiseri 1995). For his critics, Vattimo, allegedly like many other prominent postmodern thinkers, advocates Feyerabend's motto 'Anything goes!' (Feyerabend 1975) regarding the concept of 'truth' as well as the concept of 'good'. Although this critique is too simplistic, it unintentionally points to the connection there is in Vattimo's philosophy between ethics and epistemology.

Vattimo stresses that the assumption of allegedly unquestionable objective facts always includes an element of violence, in so far as the invocation of these indubitable truths ends all further conversation. There cannot be a discussion on facts. In *Belief* Vattimo states: 'The only possible philosophical definition of violence seems to be the silencing of all questioning by the authoritative peremptoriness of the first principle' (*B*, 65).

The poststructuralist and hermeneutical insight into the relativity, that is, the historical and cultural contingency, of every experience destabilises the very concept of eternal truths and reveals them as what they are: naturalised interpretations, that is, the results of past conversations, whose historicity we have forgotten, so that they now appear as ahistorical facts. A good example of this kind of naturalised, substantialised interpretation is the traditional understanding of gender, which represents a form of materialised interpretation, as Judith Butler explains with explicit reference to Vattimo (cf. Butler 1993: 27).

Like Butler, Vattimo is also aware of the fact that these naturalised interpretations, aka 'facts', are not arbitrarily changeable, although we know that they are contingent, that is, relative. To know that, for example, the notion of gender is not an objective fact but the result of history does not deprive it of its effectiveness, that is, reality. In the same way that knowing that the language we are speaking is contingent and only one of many possible languages does not free us from its boundaries, so knowing about the historicity of the facts that surround us does not make them less real. At a closer glance, facts reveal themselves as being nothing more than naturalised preconceptions, but this does not mean we can modify them at will.

Vattimo claims that there is no first uninterpreted object underlying the interpretation, as all allegedly objective starting points are nothing but prior interpretations themselves. The object of interpretation is always already an interpretation. Thus, quoting Nietzsche, Vattimo stresses that there are no facts, only interpretations. But some of these interpretations that constitute our world are more stable than others. These naturalised interpretations are what we are accustomed to call facts; albeit weak facts. In *Il soggetto e la maschera* Vattimo states: '"Facts" are not interpretations only in the sense that we, when we recognize them, cannot desist from our preconceptions. "Facts" constitute themselves as "facts" only in a symbolic world, they are interpretations in the most radical sense' (Vattimo 1974: 310). With this concept of weak facts which invokes Foucault's 'historic a priori', Vattimo can address the problem of the limits of interpretation thematised also by Umberto Eco (1994 [1990]), without falling back into a metaphysical objectivism that states the existence of objective facts that our minds have only to mirror correctly to recognise the truth (cf. Rorty 1979).

Thus Vattimo's theory of interpretation may rightly be labelled relativistic historicism in so far as it rejects the notion of unquestionable facts that we must align to. But this hermeneutical understanding of reality, according to Vattimo, has deep ethical implication, as it makes it impossible to justify violence by invoking indubitable truths. Asked if violence is always based on the notion of objective truth, Vattimo responded:

Yes, as long as we stay in the realm of reasoning. In relation to justified violence in general absolute justifications are not given to minimize violence in a specific situation, but to force one's own opinion upon others [. . .] Therefore, it seems right to identify the need for justification with the need to impose an authority [. . .] If we look at history, we see that Popes and Emperors always gave 'good' reasons to justify their wars [. . .] In a nutshell: I know of a lot of massacres perpetrated by human beings who thought to be in possession of the truth, but I have never heard of massacres perpetrated by fanatic relativists. (Vattimo and Weiss 2012 [2003]: 177)

See also **violence**.

RELIGION

Martin G. Weiss

Vattimo's work on religion is based on a phenomenological and a hermeneutical premise. The phenomenological premise consists in Vattimo's conviction that the interpretation of religion and religiosity must be based on a personal, factual experience. Vattimo explicitly shares this conviction with Martin Heidegger (1976b) who criticised Karl Jaspers for analysing (in his case psychological) phenomena from an allegedly objective perspective, that is, from outside the factual situation, failing to consider that the interpreter is always already positioned and part of an ongoing historical and cultural discourse (cf. *R*). This brings us to the second, hermeneutical premise of Vattimo's philosophy of religion: philosophers born and raised in (post-)Christian Western societies, are, even if they proclaim to be atheists, entrenched, permeated by Christianity. Thus, according to Vattimo, many of us cannot not be Christians.

These two premises are the reason why Vattimo in his books on religion does not speak about religion in general, but mainly of Christianity, which is the only religious experience he, as a devout (albeit critical) Catholic, knows and which therefore is the only one he can speak about if he wants to remain loyal to his phenomenological and hermeneutic premises. Even in the rare instances where he speaks of religion in general he does so in relation to Christianity; for example, when he stresses that Christianity, characterised by the message of charity and the concept of a divine *kenosis* – that is, the radical disempowerment of the first principle expressed by the doctrine of the Incarnation, which Vattimo interprets as a weakening of the metaphysical idea of any unquestionable objectivity, be it truth or the good (cf. *BI*) – is the overcoming of the more primitive religiosity of natural religions (under which he seems also to subsume Judaism) that are based on the violent concepts of sacrifice and scapegoats, as Vattimo claims based on the studies of René Girard (1977):

[W]hat seems decisive in Girard's thesis [. . .] is the idea of the incarnation as the dissolution of the sacred as violence [. . .] To move closer to the nihilistic [i.e. anti-metaphysical] recovery of Christianity, it is sufficient to go just a bit beyond Girard by acknowledging that the natural sacred is violent not only insofar as the victim-based mechanism presupposes a divinity thirsty for vengeance, but also insofar as it attributes to such a divinity all the predicates of omnipotence, absoluteness, eternity and 'transcendence' with respect to humanity that are precisely the attributes given to God by natural theologies, even by those which think of themselves as the prolegomena to the Christian faith [. . .] By contrast, the incarnation, that is, God's abasement to the level of humanity, what the New Testament calls God's kenosis, will be interpreted as the sign that the non-violent and non-absolute God of the post-metaphysical epoch has as its distinctive trait the very vocation for weakening of which Heideggerian philosophy speaks. (*B*, 38–9)

Thus the relation between Christianity and Vattimo's post-metaphysical, that is anti-objectivistic, 'weak thinking' (see **weak thought**) is twofold insofar as, on the one hand, post-metaphysics is the consistent result of the Christian message that there is no given indubitable truth beyond our historically and culturally contingent interpretations, and on the other hand, insofar as post-metaphysics, that is, the dissolution of the notion of unquestionable objectivity (which includes the allegedly objective truth of science), provides new room for the recognition of the religious experience as a possible access to 'truth'. Therefore, according to Vattimo, the return of religions, not only of Christianity, at the end of the twentieth century is a consequence of post-metaphysics, which itself is part of the Christian history of salvation.

This link between Christianity and post-metaphysics, maintained by Vattimo, is of special importance as it points to the centrality of historicity, that is eventuality, in the understanding of the essential relationship between philosophy, or more precisely ontology, and religious experience. According to Vattimo, what his (Heideggerian) ontology and religion have in common is their reliance on the 'event' (*Ereignis*). Thus, Being, for Vattimo, is nothing else than the history of being, that is, the history of the different historical interpretations of what we mean by Being (for example *physis* in ancient Greek philosophy, creation in the Middle Ages, or technical resource in modernity), in the same way that God is nothing other than the history of the discourses on God. However, it is important to emphasise that Vattimo does not advocate the thesis that the history of Being and the history of salvation are the mere product of human subjectivity. On the contrary, Vattimo, like Heidegger, stresses that history is heavily affected by 'events' that are not dependent on human will or action, but on radical ruptures and the intrusion of the 'Other' into the alleged continuity of history. As this irruption of the 'Other', be it Being or God, is perhaps the fundamental meaning that religion has for Vattimo, his weak thinking may well be described as a form of secularisation of religious experience.

RESPONSIBILITY

David Rose

The issue of responsibility is generally characterised in terms of a relation, that is, to whom or to what am I responsible, or for what am I responsible. Modern thought has overtly realigned the question to a whom and the question of action, to the agents and person to whom I am responsible, both in terms of subordination and also accountability, and those actions which I have freely performed. Vattimo returns the question of responsibility and accountability to the obscured and forgotten question of to what am I responsible. Even in Kant, where one is responsible to others, the very accountability is grounded in a prior responsibility to oneself or reason itself, fundamentally a 'who'. But colloquially, one can be responsible for things (guardianship, custody) and also to things (my interpretation of *Hamlet* is responsible to the text). Vattimo turns the modern question of what conditions must be met for the agent to be responsible into the postmodern question concerning the propriety of one's interpretation to the place and time one inhabits. Above all, it is the responsibility or vocation of the philosopher to the appropriate interpretation of the situation, beyond the simple reduction to quantifiable scientific facts and one-dimensional opinion pieces, that best encapsulates his view of responsibility (*RP*).

Beginning with the modern ethical understanding of responsibility, Vattimo proposes a very postmodern relationship to oneself of situated authenticity. Modern ethics is problematic because ethical questions, we are told explicitly, embody an expectation, the expectation of a first principle from which one can derive specific duties, but the first principles must be incontrovertible (*NE*, ch. 3). And so, the freedom of the will necessary for modern responsibility is nothing but an ideological mask. Responsibility is living one's life authentically and that means taking a step back from those prescriptions that immediately impinge on us. And such a weaker relationship to metaphysical commitments is only possible in a postmodern, plural society. There are traces of many traditions to which we must orient ourselves and our sole opportunity for responsibility is in the interpretation of our pasts and presents as multiple. Our authenticity requires our tradition, and our tradition, the *koiné* of our situatedness, is hermeneutics.

To be responsible to oneself (a who) is to be responsible, as custodian, to one's situation or the postmodern tradition (a what) and to do so through hermeneutics and the avowal of pluralism, and thus make one responsible *for* the proper interpretation (responsible to or for). The vocation or responsibility of the philosopher is to turn thought away from simple objective and orthodox truth to a historicisation of understanding (*BI*, ch. 1). The characteristics of this interpretative relationship are the recognition and negation of the contextual, embedded nature of the self, that is, the recognition that those values which impinge on the agent's practical reason in a concrete situation must be put into question in order to ensure both their validity and relevance to the matter in hand (*NE*, ch. 3). This involves a step back to disentangle the responsible self from the particular, demoting the given to an enfeebled status and not an immediately binding one. The situation of the speaker – the voice and its tradition – is impossible to negate and yet cannot be immediately binding. Thus, one must express respect and this respect is grounded in an anti-metaphysical claim: truth is plural. And it is the philosopher who has a responsibility to express this complexity, in contrast to the scientist, opinion writer or rhetorician who seek simple, quantifiable truths (*TS*, ch. 8; *NE*, ch. 3). Weak thought is a form of affirmative nihilism: one realises that one's values and beliefs are grounded in an interpretation of reality; however, an interpretation is not mere fiction nor inconsequential, but one truth among many.

Vattimo talks explicitly of a responsible interpretation of one's own social and moral fabric with all its inherent values and the recognition that such values derive from a worldview and not from an incontrovertible, absolute truth. And the values which are to be preferred are those which – although derived from a particular tradition – are judged by the criteria of tolerance, the reduction of violence and consensus. Embracing these norms allows for a responsible interpretation of one's existence.

RICOEUR, PAUL

Alberto Martinengo

Paul Ricoeur (1913–2005) was the undisputed founder of French philosophical hermeneutics. In 1960, in the same year as Hans-Georg Gadamer's *Truth and Method* – and a few years after the publication of Luigi Pareyson's *Estetica. Teoria della formatività* (1954) – Ricoeur's *The Symbolism of Evil* (1967) was published. This is the work in which the author denounces the shortcomings of phenomenology in the thematisation of finiteness.

The hermeneutics to which Ricoeur refers in fact ranges from Schleiermacher to Heidegger, with two key roles attributed to Dilthey and Nietzsche. With regard to Nietzsche, Ricoeur should be credited with the success of the category of masters of suspicion, which associates Nietzsche with Marx (see **Marxism/Italian Marxism**) and Freud. Each of them contributes to demystifying some of the fundamental notions of Western metaphysics, in particular that of the Cartesian self. In this anti-Cartesian vein, Ricoeur encounters the existentialism of Heidegger's *Being and Time*. The Ricoeurian notion of suspicion is also central to Vattimo's hermeneutics, precisely because of the central role that Nietzsche plays for both authors (see *BS*): the destruction of the subject was the focus of Vattimo's thinking in the 1960s and 1970s and the premise of the subsequent shift towards weak thought. In a certain sense, one could say that – before focusing on history as a whole – Vattimo views metaphysics first and foremost as an epoch linked to modern philosophy and thus to the Cartesian *ego cogito*. He therefore regards the three masters of suspicion as essential references for thinking about the end of metaphysics.

In contrast to Nietzsche, Dilthey's role highlights significant differences between Ricoeur and Vattimo. For the former, Dilthey's idea of a foundation for the *Geistwissenschaften* based on the notion of understanding remains relevant. In fact, in the so-called conflict of interpretations (see Ricoeur 1974), hermeneutics explicitly assumes the role of a philosophy of understanding: on the one hand, philosophies of suspicion dismantle metaphysical illusions; on the other, the hermeneutics of understanding allows for the reconstruction – in a post-metaphysical sense – of notions from which anti-Cartesian criticism has ultimately subtracted substantial value. For Vattimo, contrary to Ricoeur's position, hermeneutics more clearly assumes the form of a philosophy of interpretation, setting aside the central role of understanding in Heidegger (2010a). While Ricoeur considers Dilthey's alternative between explanation and understanding to be fundamental, Vattimo views Nietzsche's alternative between facts and interpretations as key (see Nietzsche 1968). Indeed, interpretation is the principle that allows Vattimo (see *WP*, *FT* and Vattimo 1989a) to weaken the notion of truth which, following Nietzsche's perspectivism, he considers theoretically untenable (see **relativism**) and ethically violent (see **violence**).

Moreover, the shift in discourse from the hermeneutics of suspicion – the successor to Nietzsche's critique of culture – to the hermeneutics of interpretation becomes crucial in Vattimo's thinking from the 1980s onwards, in which he adopts more distinctly nihilistic positions, including in an ontological sense. While Ricoeur reflects on narration as a device for the construction of subjectivity (see Ricoeur 1984–88), Vattimo emphasises the fabulising function of interpretation (see **literature/narration**) as a means of deconstructing the very notion of reality (see *OR*).

RORTY, RICHARD

Martin Woessner

In addition to being a fellow public intellectual and personal friend of Vattimo, the American philosopher Richard Rorty (1931–2007) was also one of his most consistent philosophical allies in North America. Typically associated with the philosophical tradition known as pragmatism – or neo-pragmatism, given all the alterations he made to it – Rorty's ecumenical and pluralistic approach did much to de-provincialise American thought in the last decades of the twentieth century, putting the works of John Dewey and William James, for example, in fruitful conversation with post-metaphysical thinkers such as Martin Heidegger, Ludwig Wittgenstein, Jacques Derrida, Jürgen Habermas and 'the distinguished contemporary Italian philosopher Gianni Vattimo' (Rorty 2003: 40).

The admiration was mutual – and formative. In his philosophical memoir, *Not Being God*, Vattimo cites Rorty's early interest in his work as a much-needed vote of confidence when he was developing his signature idea of 'weak thought'. The two thinkers first met at an academic conference in, of all places, Milwaukee, Wisconsin, where Rorty gave Vattimo a copy of his recently published *Philosophy and the Mirror of Nature* (1979). Vattimo read it with 'enormous enthusiasm' shortly thereafter, while on holiday on Santorini. He was happy to discover that he and his new American friend 'were each saying more or less the same thing'. For the first time in his career, Vattimo felt like he was not 'just some little Italian linked only to the Italian situation', but rather someone 'who cast a shadow internationally' (*NBG*, 98–9).

For over two and half decades, Vattimo and Rorty worked in concert with each other in the international arena. Though they emerged from different philosophical traditions and often spoke to different audiences, they shared commitments to leftist politics, philosophical hermeneutics and what Rorty often described as 'commonsense Heideggerianism' (*NE*, ix–xx; Rorty 2007: 149). As critics of positivism and Platonism in all their various forms, Vattimo and Rorty dismissed notions of transcendental truth and objective reality in both the classroom and the public sphere. In the former, they argued that philosophy was best understood as a cultural, even aesthetic, practice, not a 'rigorous science' (Vattimo 2010a: 2). In the latter, they suggested that progressive, anti-authoritarian causes were better served by the pursuit of wider, freer conversations rather than the fruitless search for philosophical final answers (Vattimo 2010c). Their ongoing philosophical conversation was symbiotic, with Rorty happily embracing Vattimo's Nietzschean and Heideggerian nihilism, folding it into the notion of truth as 'intersubjective agreement' he found in the works of James and Dewey (Rorty 2003: 41–2), and Vattimo consistently praising Rorty's substitution of solidarity for objectivity, tirelessly recommending the 'many beautiful pages' of *Philosophy and the Mirror of Nature* as a tonic for anyone tempted by the false allures of fundamentalism, scientism or what sometimes gets called 'the new realism' today (*FT*, 133–4; *OR*, 91, 101).

Where Rorty and Vattimo most famously disagreed was on the proper place of religion in modern, democratic societies. A lifelong non-believer, Rorty often described religion – when invoked in public discourses, at least – as a 'conversation-stopper' (Rorty 1999). He thought it best relegated to the private sphere. But Vattimo, a Catholic, has touted the public value of belief, albeit in a thoroughly secularised, post-metaphysical, emancipatory form (*B*; *AC*). Indeed, Vattimo sometimes chided Rorty for 'his subtle historicist faith in the linearity and irreversibility of progress', which led him to dismiss religion as a vestigial element of an otherwise modern, secular culture (Vattimo 2003a: 30). Though he never abandoned his anti-clericalism, Rorty, through engaging with Vattimo's 'very sympathetic reading of Christianity' (Rorty 2010: 25), eventually came to take a softer tone when speaking about religion. In fact, he came around to seeing 'Vattimo's way of weaving together Heidegger, Christianity, and social democratic ideals' in a thoroughly positive light (Rorty 2007: 157). In a talk given on the occasion of his receipt of the Meister Eckhart Prize in December 2001, Rorty suggested that the only difference between his outlook and Vattimo's was a matter of temporal orientation: Vattimo's 'unjustifiable gratitude' for a secularising Christian *kenosis* was backwards-looking, and thus nostalgic, but his own 'unjustifiable hope' in a better future for humanity, though forward-looking, was admittedly utopian (Rorty 2003: 45).

Rorty and Vattimo continued discussing these ideas at a 2001 conference on 'Religion after Onto-Theology' in Sundance, Utah, and again in a stimulating 2002 conversation with the philosopher Santiago Zabala in Paris. They came to the conclusion that their shared commitments to hermeneutics in intellectual life and democracy in political life were no more than 'alternative appropriations' – as Rorty put it – 'of the Christian message that love is the only law' (*FR*, 74; see **love**; **justice/law**). Introducing Rorty to an audience in Turin in 2005, Vattimo summed it up this way: 'in the twentieth century, philosophy advanced from the idea of truth to the idea of charity' (Vattimo 2010c: 4).

S

SALVATION (see **GIOACCHINO DA FIORE; RELIGION**)

SARTRE, JEAN PAUL (see **EXISTENTIALISM**)

SCHLEIERMACHER, FRIEDRICH

Francisco Arenas-Dolz

Vattimo was the first to speak of hermeneutics as a new *koiné*, that is, as a shared language or philosophical style of our time, also pointing out the risks associated with this process. By becoming *koiné*, hermeneutics has expanded its boundaries to such an extent that it has lost its philosophical connotations. In addition to drawing attention to the philosophical assumptions of hermeneutics, Vattimo posed the problem of the truth of multiple interpretations. If there is no experience of truth except as an act of interpretation, if every experience of truth takes place through an interpretative experience, a thesis shared by those who refer to hermeneutics as *koiné*, Vattimo wonders about the ontological implications raised or even presupposed by the generalisation of the notion of interpretation. His response is a philosophical elaboration of hermeneutics and its nihilistic ontological significance (*BI*, ch. 1; Zabala 2007: 15–16).

The intention to develop the ontological implications of hermeneutics motivated Vattimo from his earliest works, in particular his work on Friedrich Schleiermacher (1768–1834). Vattimo reconstructs the thought of the German philosopher, taking as a leitmotif the ontological implications of hermeneutics, converted from a particular problem, focused on the technical interpretation of texts, into a general problem, concerning human existence as a whole. Vattimo notes the tendency of hermeneutics, already announced in its religious origins, to expand, to become a general problem, as evidenced by one of its basic notions: the hermeneutic circle. However, for Vattimo, the meaning of this circularity is diluted and constrained by many contemporary hermeneutical theories which, although inspired by Heideggerian ontology, tend to interpret its meaning in the context of the relationship that humankind has with itself or with history. In this context, the value of Schleiermacher's reflection lies in his having considered unsatisfactory the ideal of knowledge as a foundation or explanation which, through the insertion of the particular in a totality, leads us to highlight only the characteristics that the individual has in common with the rest and leaves out everything that is unique to the individual concerned. Schleiermacher sets out from this ideal, but in developing his reflection on the methods of interpretation and its meaning, he highlights the impossibility of comprehension as the insertion of the particular in a system that founds and explains it. Schleiermacher highlights the very impossibility of a definitive method of interpretation since the practices developed to explain the particular through its relation with a totality (language, epoch, personality of the author) are insufficient and provisional, thus questioning the confidence in the explanation-foundation as the ultimate guarantee of truth (Dotolo 1999: 323–41; Giorgio 2006: 76–92; Frank 2007: 171–8). With his interpretation, Vattimo places Schleiermacher on a different path from Dilthey, much closer to Heidegger and Nietzsche and their rejection of historicism and the notion of history as a totality in which everything is explained and resolved by dissolving.

See also **hermeneutics**.

SCHÜRMANN, REINER

Alberto Martinengo

A comparison with Reiner Schürmann (1941–93) sheds particular light on Vattimo's understanding of the Heideggerian notions of metaphysics and convalescence (*Verwindung*). In *Weak Thought*, Vattimo refers to the end of metaphysics as a break in the Western tradition. However, the possibility of going one step further must be distinguished both from dialectics (see **Hegel, Georg Wilhelm Friedrich**) and from deconstruction (see **Derrida, Jacques**). Tradition cannot be transcended through a kind of Hegelian synthesis that subsumes metaphysics into a different form of thought. Nor can it be abandoned, as suggested in some versions of French poststructuralism. Rather, it should be subjected to a form of weakening – hence the title of the book (see **weak thought**). For Vattimo, weakening metaphysics means demonstrating the historicity of being, in other words the transitory nature of values and the very notion of truth.

Here weak thought encounters Schürmann's thinking on anarchy, understood as the possibility of putting an end to the metaphysical regime of the *archai* ('principles' in ancient Greek). Vattimo and Schürmann share a reference to Martin Heidegger and the emancipatory reading of his critique of Western tradition (see **emancipation**). One thing in particular unites weak thought and Schürmann's anarchist ontology: the idea that the metaphysical regime is a kind of illness from which one can recover – a convalescence, as the English translation terms the Heideggerian notion of *Verwindung* (see **convalescence** [*Verwindung*]). Yet, as Schürmann (1987) explains, this is not true healing, but a process of endless recovery, similar to psychoanalytic translaboration.

Their interpretation of the post-metaphysical shift is therefore comparable and clearly distinguished from positions that insist on absolute discontinuity with tradition (see **modernity [end of]**). However, compared to Vattimo's weakening, which is presented as an ironic distortion of strong thinking, Schürmann emphasises another element: the practical dimension of convalescence. Freeing oneself from the metaphysical *arche* means above all overturning the Aristotelian structure of first philosophy and second philosophies, summarised by Thomas Aquinas in the formula: 'Action follows being'. Schürmann's anarchy gives *praxis* precedence over *theoria*: the concrete dimension of existence – language, ethical *habitus*, political action – is the principle for deconstructing foundation thinking.

At the same time, the precedence of action over thought traces a continuous thread between the end of metaphysics and a specific moment of Western theological thinking: Meister Eckhart's mysticism. Indeed, according to Schürmann (1978), Eckhart's heterodox theology in turn challenges Thomistic metaphysics through a complex anti-substantialist strategy centred around 'acting without why'. This explains Heidegger's late interest in mysticism of both Christian and – in other respects – oriental origin. It is therefore a very different kind of Christianity from the one that Vattimo has in mind, particularly in *Belief* and *After Chistianity*. Vattimo highlights other moments of Heidegger's 'religious' discourse, in particular those that refer to his early works. In this context, rather than in Eckhart's mysticism, Vattimo finds the key to support the anti-metaphysical value of religious experience, which is encapsulated in the notion of *kenosis*.

See also **anarchy**; *kenosis*.

SCIENCE

Martin G. Weiss

The hermeneutic tradition that Vattimo follows commonly opposes the allegedly scientific model of truth, which hermeneutics mostly identifies with the adequation theory of truth, for which truth consists in the *adequa-*

tio intellectus et rei, that is, the alignment of intellect and thing, as Thomas Aquinas famously put it in *Questiones disputate de veritate*. Different hermeneutic philosophers have stressed that this objectivistic notion of truth is dependent on a prior 'givenness' or 'appearance' of things. Thus Martin Heidegger in *Being and Time* speaks of the 'hermeneutic as' (the preliminary appearing of something before its explicit determination) as the condition of the possibility of the 'apophantic as' expressed in a proposition. The concept of a hermeneutical, non-propositional 'truth' as condition of (scientific) propositions has been thematised by a series of philosophers, using different terms to mark these two forms of truth: Wilhelm Dilthey (1981) contrasts scientific 'explaining' with hermeneutical 'understanding', Edmund Husserl (1989) opposes the mathematically constructed object of science to the phenomena of the everyday *Lebenswelt* (lifeworld), Martin Heidegger (2002b) distinguishes between science and thinking, Richard Rorty (1979) speaks about the difference between epistemology and hermeneutics, and Hans-Georg Gadamer (1989) stresses the dependence of scientific knowledge and methodology on language (*logos*), which is the subject of the humanities. This emphasis on the hermeneutic horizon that transcends the findings of science is necessary because, as Hannah Arendt puts it:

The modern astrophysical world view, which began with Galileo, and its challenge to the adequacy of the senses to reveal reality, have left us a universe of whose qualities we know no more than the way they affect our measuring instruments, and – in the words of Eddington – 'the former have as much resemblance to the latter as a telephone number has to a subscriber'. (Arendt 1958: 261)

In this perspective, science is a desperate and doomed to fail metaphysical endeavour to reduce the uncertainty, or 'unavailability' (*Unverfügbarkeit*) as Heidegger calls it, of the lifeworld to unchangeable disposable resources for human subjectivity:

Nietzsche showed the [scientific] image of reality as a well-founded rational order (the perennial metaphysical image of the world) to be only the 'reassuring' myth of a still primitive and barbaric humanity. Metaphysics is a violent response to a situation that is itself fraught with danger and violence. It seeks to master reality at a stroke, grasping (or so it thinks) the first principle on which all things depend (and thus giving itself an empty guarantee of power over events). Following Nietzsche in this respect, Heidegger showed that to think of being as foundation, and reality as a rational system of causes and effects, is simply to extend the model of 'scientific' objectivity to the totality of being. All things are reduced to the level of pure presences that can be mastered, manipulated, replaced, and therefore easily dominated and organized – and in the end man, his interiority and historicity are all reduced to the same level. (*TS*, 7–8)

Against this critical position towards science, which characterises the mainstream of hermeneutics, Vattimo advocates that if one wants to overcome a metaphysical, that is, an objectivistic and reifying, conception of truth and reality (because of its ethical implication, which for Vattimo consist in the intrinsic violence of the very notion of unquestionable truth), modern sciences are not an adversary but an ally: 'It is modern science, heir and completion of metaphysics, that turn the world into a place where there are no (longer) facts, only interpretations' (*BI*, 26).

Actually, modern science largely does not speak about 'facts' that are true or false, but about statistics, probability and falsifiability (Popper 1959). This is true not only for quantum physics but also for evidence-based medicine. The conviction that it is better to get vaccinated than not to get the jab is not based on 'objective facts', but is the result of interpretations and valuations regarding the comparison between the statistical probabilities of getting seriously ill from catching a certain virus and the likelihood of being affected by the side effects of the vaccine. Even if the ratio between these two probabilities is one to several thousand, the empirical data must be interpreted and evaluated in relation to the specific situation to become meaningful. Mere data are meaningless; the meaning of scientific data is the product of interpretation.

Modern science does not produce unquestionable truth but starting points for interpretations, which to be scientific must by definition be falsifiable. A scientific interpretation of natural phenomena is scientific only if it is possible to formulate the conditions under which the interpretation would no longer be convincing. In this sense, science is no adversary of post-metaphysical hermeneutics but one of its manifestations along with media and technology (cf. Weiss 2010).

SECULARISATION

Paolo Diego Bubbio

Vattimo sees 'secularisation' as 'the consummation of the sacred', and thus as a legitimising aspect of weak ontology (Vattimo 1988c: 13). In *The End of Modernity*, Vattimo's conception of secularisation is grounded on social theorist Arnold Gehlen's *The Secularization of Progress*; other influences include Max Weber, Norbert Elias and René Girard, thinkers who share a view of history as a 'course of events in which emancipation is reached only by means of a radical transformation and distortion of its very contents' (*EM*, 179). Vattimo's main theses are: 1) modernity is the era of 'the abandonment of the sacred vision of existence', that is, secularisation; 2) the key point of secularisation is faith in progress; 3) this 'secularization of the providential vision of history' affirms 'the new as the fundamental value' (*EM*, 101). However, 'by depriving progress of a final destination, secularization dissolves the very notion of progress itself' (*EM*, 8); this situation is also a 'positive opportunity', insofar as it 'enables us to distance ourselves from the mechanism of modernity' (*EM*, 104).

Vattimo's further engagement with Girard's work resulted in his 're-Christianisation': 'I began to think that it might be possible to bind weakening, secularization, and Christianity closely together' (*NBG*, 150). *Belief* is characterised by the identification of secularisation with the history of Christianity. There is no contradiction between the return of (non-metaphysical) religion and Weber's interpretation of secularisation as a 'desacralizing interpretation of the biblical message' (*B*, 41). Secularisation is the demythicisation of Christianity: what remains after this process is the notion of charity. In this sense, secularisation is 'the constitutive trait of an authentic religious experience' (*B*, 21) and 'a positive effect of Jesus' teaching' (*B*, 41). One can also speak of modernity as secularisation in other senses, still linked to the idea of desacralisation, as in the case of the transformation of state power towards representative democracy (*B*, 42). Secularisation can be taken as the pre-eminent case of the more general process of weakening, but the term 'secularisation' underlines 'the religious sense' of this process (*B*, 42). In fact, secularisation is 'the way in which kenosis, having begun with the incarnation of Christ [. . .] continues to realize itself more and more clearly' (*B*, 48). Therefore, secularisation is 'the very essence of Christianity' (*B*, 50) and 'an indefinite drift limited only by the principle of charity' (*B*, 66). The identification of secularisation as 'the sense of the history of salvation' is not a metaphysical statement, but it 'appears (the most) reasonable and the strongest precisely from our point of view in late modernity' (*B*, 69).

Secularisation, in its broadest sense, 'comprises all the forms of dissolution of the sacred' and it is 'the paradoxical realization of Being's religious vocation' (*AC*, 24). In *After Christianity*, Vattimo traces 'the implications of the idea of secularization as a constitutive aspect of the history of Being, and therefore of the history of salvation, for our way of living the return of religion' (*AC*, 25). This interpretation of secularisation is inspired by Joachim of Fiore, Heidegger's ontology and René Girard's religious anthropology (*AC*, 38). Just as not every interpretation is valid, so not every secularisation 'is good and positive': 'it must be valid for a community of interpreters', which means that 'the only limit of secularization is love' or charity (*AC*, 67). Thus, secularisation becomes 'the historical completion of *caritas*' (Meganck 2013: 412), but also 'the weakening of the sense of reality brought about by science' (*AC*, 78).

Secularisation may also be called nihilism, that is, 'the idea that objective Being has gradually consumed itself' (*FT*, 73). This does not mean that human beings are free to do whatever they please, because charity, 'the very thing that guides desacralization', is also its limit (*FT*, 75). Secularisation is thus seen as 'the progressive realization of that kenosis of the divine that is the essence of Christianity' (*OR*, 197), and as such, it 'prepares us for a new religious plenitude, or else as a vocation that has to be lived in all its implications' (Vattimo 2016: 132).

According to Guarino (2009: 19), 'Vattimo hopes to perform a *Verwindung* on the concept of secularization', not as an 'overcoming', but as 'a reinterpretation that is both a convalescence and an alteration': secularisation means that there is 'room' for everyone, and it is therefore 'identical with kenotic Christianity' (Guarino 2009: 24). Meganck (2013) reconstructs the genealogy and the transformation of the notion of secularisation throughout Vattimo's work, providing an account of what he regards as a 'shift' from the identification of secularisation with modernity to its identification with the history of Christianity. Harris (2016: 164–84) argues that Vattimo's theory of secularisation can be employed to suggest that an element within the Islamic tradition, the Golden Rule, can become a stimulus towards the secularisation of Islam.

SENSUS COMMUNIS (COMMON SENSE)

Alessandro Bertinetto

In the *Critique of Judgement* (1790) Kant famously denied that there are objective criteria for the aesthetic appreciation (and production) of beautiful objects. Unlike cognitive judgement, aesthetic judgement is not based upon general objective standards of value, so as to deal with the particular objects of aesthetic experience. Yet aesthetic judgement is not simply subjective and private, since it does not depend merely on what individuals like. Rather, it must be generalisable, that is, it must be universally valid. Yet being not objectively grounded, the universalisability at issue is intersubjective in kind. Indeed, I make sense of my aesthetic appreciation if my evaluation can be communicated to others. Therefore, Kant conceived of 'taste' as a *sensus communis* (common sense): 'The faculty of estimating what makes our feeling in a given representation universally communicable without the mediation of a concept' (Kant 1911 [1790]: §40, 153). This means that my evaluation is justified – or it can be reasonably said that I have taste – if my personal aesthetic judgement can be shared by others, that is, only if my aesthetic evaluation makes sense for others too. In other words, only when others recognise the sense of my evaluation does my judgement makes sense, or do I have a taste for beauty: aesthetic sense. This amounts to saying that the possibility of communication is inscribed within the notion of taste to the extent that the aesthetic judgement is the search for the possibility of (a) sharing experience.

In his seminal article 'Aesthetics and Hermeneutics' (in *ACT*), Vattimo resorts to the Kantian notion of *sensus communis* as a key aspect of his hermeneutic understanding of aesthetic experience. As he argues, the core idea conveyed by it is that the judgement of taste 'is exercised with a view to a sort of ideal community that is always still in the process of constituting itself' (*ACT*, 131). Hence, aesthetic experience is an 'exercise of sociability' and, as Vattimo would explain in the 1980 article 'The Death or Decline of Art' (later collected in *EM*), the aesthetic pleasure is what 'derives from the recognition of belonging to a group [. . .] that shares the same capacity for appreciating the beautiful' (*EM*, 56). The aesthetic judgement is reflexive (in Kantian terms), not only because it refers to the subject and not to the object, but because 'it refers to the subject as a member of a community' (*TS*, 67). Hence, the aesthetic experience 'is the experience of belonging to a community' (*TS*, 68).

However, Vattimo's view of the 'common sense' departs from Kant's in a fundamental aspect. While, according to Kant, this 'community' or 'group' is 'humanity itself as an ideal' (*EM*, 56; cf. *TS*, 67), Vattimo argues that aesthetic groups of communities are social, historically situated and factually plural. In other words, the ideal character of the community of taste 'is rooted in what the community to which we belong factually is [. . .] the ideal is precisely the ideal that this community makes of itself' (*ACT*, 132). Hence, Vattimo rejects as a metaphysical residue this notion of ideality – which is typical of the aesthetic utopia of Ernst Bloch's and Theodor Adorno's neo-Marxist philosophies. Instead, he conceives of the 'common sense' as the *aesthetic consensus* – literally: 'feeling-with' – that builds real communities. Mass culture has in fact highlighted the plural character of the beautiful. 'The communitarian systems of recognition' are plural: 'The beautiful is the experience of community; but community, when realized as "universal", is multiplied and undergoes an irreversible pluralization' (*TS*, 68). And since Kantian universality is realised for us only as multiplicity, 'we can legitimately take plurality lived explicitly as such as a normative criterion' (*TS*, 69). In point of fact, if a community of taste wants to pass itself off as humanity as such, the aesthetic experience it advocates as valid becomes inauthentic. The experience of the beautiful, as practice of a common sense, that is, as a 'feeling-with', is realised through the recognition that shared aesthetic models shape communities of taste as plural aesthetic worlds.

Moreover, following Dilthey, Heidegger, Gadamer and Benjamin, Vattimo applies his heterotopian understanding of the 'common sense' to the transformative experience of art. As he argues, the encounter with works of art – and more generally with all the aesthetic objects and artefacts that populate our forms and spheres of life (for instance, fashion, sport and other kinds of shows and games) – impacts on those who experience them, both because they make it possible to imaginatively experience ways of life other than everyday ones and because they disclose different worlds, understood in terms of other ways of 'feeling-with', that is, of producing a 'common sense', thereby showing the contingent relativity of real-life contexts. In a nutshell, artworks and aesthetic objects are not only appreciated on the basis of a given taste as 'common sense', but open other ways of 'feeling-with', that is, other worlds as 'events of being' (*TS*, 71).

See also **Adorno, Theodor Wiesengrund**; **aesthetics**; **art**; **Benjamin, Walter**; **Bloch, Ernst/utopia**; **death of art**; **Dilthey, Wilhelm**; **Gadamer, Hans-Georg**; **Heidegger, Martin**.

SOCIETY (see TRANSPARENT SOCIETY)

SUBJECT/WEAK SUBJECT

David Rose

The concept of the subject which dominates the Western philosophical tradition is an implicit trope in the thought of Vattimo, and, as he ages, his relationship to the subject has become a friendlier, less confrontational reconciliation, understood in terms of enfeeblement and *Verwindung*. Obviously the most explicit treatment is in the early collection of essays *Beyond the Subject*, which sought to show how the overcoming of the metaphysical subject originates in the thought of Heidegger and Nietzsche. The subject, though, emerges less reactively and more affirmatively in later writings, such as *Beyond Interpretation* and *Nihilism and Emancipation*, and it is Vattimo's reconfiguration of a humbler, less arrogant liberal subject that is most radical.

Vattimo's point of departure is the poststructuralist critique of the subject in the schools of suspicion – Marx, Nietzsche and Freud – and these ideas carried through into Heidegger, Foucault, Derrida and poststructuralism. Modernity finds its apex in the Enlightenment subject, productive of representations and in rational control of the world (see **Enlightenment**). Marx revealed the subject to be an expression of class interest, Nietzsche showed it as the mask of reactive forces, and Freud undermined the transparent authority of conscious intentions. However, Vattimo openly tells his readers that

> it would be yet another metaphysical illusion – implicitly tied to the idea that there could be an ordered world of essences – to think that we can extract a lesson from Nietzsche and Heidegger on the true nature of subjectivity such that we may correct our errors concerning this specific topos of philosophy. (*BS*, 80)

Whereas poststructuralist critiques challenged the subject's putative authority through the rejection of universal reason, Vattimo's reconfiguration of subjectivity resisted the 'anything goes' consequences of the rejection the modern subject (Vattimo 1974). The subject may no longer be the unified and transparent Kantian transcendental unity of apperception, but Vattimo resists the urge to fall into a relativistic scientific naturalism or an historicism of a socially determined performance (*BI*, ch. 1). Even less so does he adopt the arbitrary figure of postmodern, ironic play (see **relativism; postmodernism/postmodernity**).

Vattimo's interest was never in the legitimation and status of the modern subject, nor its unity or privilege, but rather in how to respond to its necessary fragmentation, loss of confidence and metaphysical fall. For him, the postmodern subject must begin from the acceptance of nihilism, of the loss of firm foundations and the unmooring from any supposed centre. On the one hand, most modern thought sought to offer a scientific and essentialist, descriptive account of the subject, a description supported by the dominance of the techno-scientific discourse of modernity (*AD*, ch. 2). On the other hand, the concept of the subject was nothing but a fetishisation of Christian tropes, and the secularisation of society could not but lead to the decline of the subject (*FT*). Vattimo's investigation of the techno-bureaucratic world of late modernity brings the reproductive and repetitive nature of the digital technological world to the fore, highlighting that the whole notion of individual uniqueness disappears. The reduction of representations to the exchange-value of informational messages undermines the metaphysical designations, and the subject is nothing but the transmission of messages (*BI*). Vattimo does not and cannot base subjectivity in a naturalism or a metaphysics (*NE*, ch. 3), and the weak subject emerges from the reflective interrogation of contemporary, social pluralism.

The characterisation of hermeneutics as our cultural situatedness proposes Heidegger's Dasein – as thrown into a historical interpretation which reveals and forgets Being – as the beginning point of the subject and entails an interpretation rather than a possession of the world (*NE*, chs 1, 3). For Vattimo, the imperative to situate oneself in relation to one's provenance, to heed one's heritage, does not distance one from it, but makes the subject aware of 'inherited contents' of constructed discourse (*FT*, ch. 3). The conditions through which the subject understands reality are hidden, be they in her unconscious or the structures of meaning she uses. Only through the act of expressing the world can she disclose those categories which shape her perception of the world. Understanding is a fundamental way in which the subject relates herself to the world. However, Vattimo is aware of the problems with a hermeneutic approach to subjectivity, trapped between Gadamerian conservative historicism and the nihilistic subject unanchored to any tradition, foundation or essence (*HC*, ch. 3).

Vattimo proposes weak nihilism as a resolution of this opposition: once one realises that there is no interest-free view from nowhere, then one is liberated from the constraints of inauthentic existence (*HC*, ch. 1). The values that make possible a sincere interpretation of others and oneself regulate one's comportment to others and dovetail neatly with the values of liberalism: tolerance, respect and reasonableness. The values of liberty, tolerance, equality and the commitment to consensual agreement free of violence are, according to Vattimo, the only appropriate response to the fragmentation and the ungroundedness of post-metaphysical culture (*NE*, ch. 3; *TS*, ch. 7; *BI*, ch. 3). Once the subject is aware of being situated in a culture characterised by weak ontology, then the commitment to the responsibility of interpretation and the need for a reflective relation between the historical subject and her tradition resolves itself into a position which shares many of the features of political liberalism (*NE*, ch. 3). It is the subject, rather than a tradition, that is or is not reasonable, and the grounding norm is one of weak autonomy, that is, independence from any metaphysical doctrine. And the formal requirement of this norm is to treat others with respect, a normative commitment that coincides with the aspirations of modernity (the refusal of blind obedience to authority) and liberalism (the values of liberty, equality, respect and tolerance) (*TS*, ch. 7). Vattimo claims that respect, tolerance, liberty and equality are normative commitments for the subject who inhabits the fabric of post-metaphysical society. The hermeneutic subject is ethical because the norms that oblige her should guarantee the absence of violence: one must be able to step back, that is, not be coerced or irrevocably bound to one's tradition (liberty); one must recognise the finitude of one's position and that of others (tolerance); and one must recognise the right of all individuals to their own responsibly articulated and interpreted tradition (equality and respect) (*NE*, ch. 3; *FT*, ch 3).

Vattimo is unapologetic in his affirmation of this new subjectivity as a reinterpretation of the Enlightenment call to be liberated from superstition, that is, from those beliefs specifically used for political manipulation (Vattimo 2007e; *HC*, ch. 3). The regulatory ideal of dialogue is consensus and not truth, implicitly insisting on the notion of the other as an equal participant in discourse unless she is unreasonable; postulating an ethics 'of negotiation and consensus rather than an ethics of immutable principles or categorical imperatives speaking through the reason of everyone' (*NE*, 67). The values are the product of a historical tradition of weak nihilism inimical to post-metaphysical thought. The agnostic sceptic is a radical empiricist, akin to the declining Christian, who is humble: we have been wrong about our metaphysical commitments in the past and should assume we are probably wrong now, so we cannot use them as a basis for legislation and interference in others' lives. The subject, for Vattimo, must listen to her tradition and be responsible in her interpretation of it, yet the values conferred on her cannot play the role of legitimation in a plural society (*FT*, ch. 1).

SUBSTANTIALITY (see TRUTH)

T

TECHNE (see ARISTOTLE)

TECHNOLOGY/CYBERSPACE

Erik M. Vogt

Vattimo's reflections on technology and cyberspace are elaborated in terms of an ontology of actuality that, by affirming the end of metaphysics and the epochal character of Being, strive to reveal the historical-ontological relation between technology on the one hand, the 'aperture of

Being typical of modernity', and 'the traits of a new aperture' (*NE*, 12) on the other. Referencing both Theodor W. Adorno's concept of *verwaltete Gesellschaft* (administered society) and Martin Heidegger's concept of *Gestell* (enframing), Vattimo shows that their respective philosophical theories of modernity have as their focus the question of technology. While Adorno's account of administered society presents a constellation of instrumental rationality and technological domination that has reduced both things and human beings to exploitable and disposable appendages of a machinery of calculation, Heidegger's account of the *Gestell* as the essence of modern technology crystallising the form of rationality that characterises and determines the history of Western metaphysics is even more significant for Vattimo's understanding of modern technology. Modern technology reduces entities to objects to be mastered, administered and controlled, and, more radically, transforms them into mere standing reserve vanishing into objectlessness and, moreover, brings human beings under its challenging and summoning, thereby dissolving the subject–object dualism of metaphysics. When properly thought, the danger presented by the *Gestell* also contains, however, (some) saving power. Heidegger writes: 'The experience in Enframing as the constellation of Being and man through the modern world of technology is a prelude to what is called the event of appropriation' (Heidegger 1969: 36–7 see **information technology/*Gestell***).

Vattimo's *verwindend* (distorting, twisting, resigning) appropriation and interpretation of Heidegger's *Gestell* sets in at this point. The saving power of the *Gestell* is not located in its concealed hint towards a different (say, poetic) opening, but rather in the *Gestell* itself, since it is not only 'the highest point of the metaphysical oblivion of being', but also '"a first, oppressing flash of *Ereignis*," that is of the event of being' (*TS*, 56). In other words, the *Gestell* as event contains the opportunity for a different – postmodern – aperture of Being sketching a relation between being and humanity freed from the shackles of the dualism of subject and object. However, Heidegger fails to fully expand upon this opportunity because he 'never escaped from a vision of technology dominated by the model of the motor and mechanical energy' (*NE*, 14). The actual ontological sense of technology can only be disclosed through a 'radical shift in our vision of technology' (*NE*, 15) that is oriented towards

> the technology of modern communication . . . by which information is gathered, ordered, and disseminated. To speak more plainly: the possibility of overcoming metaphysics, which Heidegger describes obscurely in the *Gestell*, opens up only when the technology . . . ceases to be mechanical and becomes electronic: information and communication technology. (*NE*, 15)

This updated, nihilistic interpretation of the *Gestell* under the heading of the internet and of cyberspace also provides new meaning to Heidegger's other definition of modernity as the 'age of the world picture'. The transformation of the world into a world picture is accompanied by a shadow of incalculability that, for Vattimo, must be grasped as *Gestell*'s immanent and nihilistic consequence in the form of a proliferation of conflicting images of the world, leading to 'a weakening of the principle of reality' (*NE*, 16) and a Nietzschean 'fabling of the world'. That is to say: 'The images of the world we receive . . . are not simply different interpretations of a "reality" that is "given" regardless, but rather constitute the very objectivity of the world' (*TS*, 24–5). The world of cyberspace constitutes a world in which 'experience can again acquire the characteristics of oscillation, disorientation and play' (*TS*, 59), and in which the subject is decentred in that it is 'playing a multiplicity of social roles that are irreducible to a unity' (*TS*, 117). Thus, the weakened subject inhabits an aestheticised and derealised world shaped by multiple interpretative and conflictual agencies.

At the same time, the aestheticisation and derealisation of the world generated by the new technologies of communication is threatened by the realist agency of the late capitalist global economy and its 'supermarket culture' (*NE*, 99), as well as by the return of religious, ethnic and communitarian foundationalism. While these revivals of foundationalism attempt to restore a supposedly lost homogeneous reality through the disavowal of 'historicity, contingency, finiteness' (*TS*, 9), global late capitalism subscribes to a quasi-classical and uniform aesthetics that decrees reconciliation and harmonious kitsch. Foundationalism and global late capitalism as the two contemporary modes of perpetuating the very violence intrinsic to metaphysics (Vattimo 2007d: 400–23) must be countered by the nihilistic and democratic stress on the emancipation of differences, minorities and subcultures, that is, of all the plural and diverse voices weaving the (virtual) web of a multicultural world.

TELEVISION (see MEDIA)

THEOLOGY

Carmelo Dotolo

'My theology is a Kenotic theology, which means that if there is God, he presents himself as the one who hides' (Vattimo and Dotolo 2009: 4). This statement must be interpreted in terms of Nietzschean and Heideggerian readings of nihilism on the death of God. This event liberates the divine through the critique of a religiosity intended as the decadent and inadequate form of life. It also criticises the metaphysical notion of God intended as foundation, reason and *Causa sui*. In this view, it is possible to outline an unsuspected weaving of philosophy and theology; or better, the weaving of the intentionality of weak thought and the perspective of secularisation, a hermeneutics of that *Verwindung* of metaphysics (see **convalescence [*Verwindung*]**) within which weakness and nihilism encounter each other 'somehow in the arms of theology' (*BI*, x). And, more specifically: 'the meaning of this relation between philosophy (weak thought) and the Christian message [is one] that I am able to think of only in term of secularization, that is, weakening, incarnation' (*B*, 36). For this reason, secularisation is able to repropose the question of God as the question of the meaning of contemporary reality, but on the condition that one does not substitute another God for the metaphysical one, even if freed from the sacred arrangements of natural religion. It is necessary to push the relationship of secularisation and hermeneutics to its completion, that is, all the way to the recognition that the ontology of weakness discloses itself in the *kenosis* of God to such a point that the very same weak thought can consider itself to be the transcription of the Christian message. The heart of its novelty rests in the fact-principle of the Incarnation (*BI*, 82–3; *B*, 52).

Jesus is the principle that revolutionises the very idea of God, no longer revealing him as the *Ipsum esse subsistens* but, according to an interpretation present in the hymn of the Letter to the Philippians (2:7), as he who emptied himself of his absoluteness and of his 'form of God'. The event of the Incarnation demonstrates the necessity of thinking differently about a conception of divine transcendence that is confined to a kind of metahistorical eschatology. This necessity is brought to the attention of reason by the paradox of a God who has taken on the human condition and its worldly reality, making them his own: thus, not a God who is totally Other or infinitely distant, but rather a God appearing in history and who manifests his involvement in the events of time by indicating, through immanence, an interpretative key directed towards a comprehension of transcendence. Here one finds the meaning of the inheritance of the theological reflection: the principle of Incarnation, intended as desacralisation and as kenotic manifestation that speaks the being of God, and marks the return of the possibility for hermeneutic philosophy to gather the meaning of the evangelical value of love, brotherhood and the rejection of violence (see *AC*, ch. 1). It appears clear that the specificity of theology for thought grounds a continual invention of history in inspiring the principle of *caritas*. Christianity is the trace of the trace that reopens the possibility of a relation to the divine when it is thought of not as stable and full Being, but as event not dominated by the imperative of self-preservation. Its characteristic is that of an ecumenical opening that is able to bring value to the truth-bearing substance present both in other religions as well as in the plurality of cultures.

The hermeneutic circle of weak thought (philosophy) and theology casts an interesting reflection on the philosophy of religion. Now, if religion returns in the form of Christianity, it does so not only because of historical causes inherent in a social-cultural place of origin. There is something else to consider: this Christianity is open to the interpretation of history and to the lighting up of truth with a modality that is attentive to questions of meaning, promoting a critical reading of what damages and hinders human beings' search for salvation. The relation between the world and the God revealed in Jesus extends far beyond the canons of natural or reassuring religiosity, or even beyond an anonymous theism signalled by the neutrality of Being. With the event of the Incarnation, the Being of God has meaning and decisiveness for us only in relation to the Being of Jesus, being-for-the-other, which ends in his total gift of life. It is in this absolute dedication to the other that the expression of the radicality of transcendence, the condition for reading omnipotence and the other attributes traditionally ascribed to God manifest themselves: 'The salvation I seek through a radical acceptance of the meaning of kenosis does not depend exclusively on me, and is not indifferent to the need for grace as the gift that comes from the other' (B, 97).

See also *kenosis*; **kenotic sacrifice**; **religion**.

TIME (see **NIETZSCHE, FRIEDRICH**; **HISTORY/HISTORICITY**)

TOTALITARIANISM/TOTALISATION

Francesca Monateri

Totalitarianism is one of the facets of Western metaphysics, and it is the thought that conceives of being in foundational terms that is totalitarian. Thus, totalitarianism is not only a historical and political phenomenon, but also a philosophical one. From this perspective, the fight against totalitarianism takes place in the realm of the being that must be rethought – along the lines of Heidegger – as *Ereignis*, as an event.

What Vattimo understands from reading Nietzsche's theses – and what this definition of totalitarianism highlights – is how philosophy and politics are two articulations of the same liberation-oriented act (Vattimo 1974). This assumption, which is in equal parts philosophical and political, also marks his subsequent reflection: the deconstruction of truth conceived as a metaphysical corollary is, first and foremost, a form of opposition to totalitarianism (Vattimo and Rovatti 1983). These theses become clearer when analysing contemporary society. According to Vattimo, mass media plays a fundamental role in overcoming totalitarianism. Contrary to Adorno, he claims that it is not radio – or television – that enables totalitarian dictatorships or governments to control society in a widespread way, as per Orwell's Big Brother nightmare. Quite the opposite, in fact, as they enable the explosion and propagation of *Weltanschauungen*, thus opposing philosophical and political totalitarianism (*TS*).

In this context, interpretation becomes increasingly central. Hermeneutics has a militant scope and is the only way to counter totalitarianism: interpreting means acting on the world; it is not a disinterested intellectual practice, but a political one (Chiurazzi 2008). In reality the only way to change the world is to interpret it by overturning Marx's eleventh thesis on Feuerbach. What must be protected from the metaphysical truth of totalitarianism is therefore a hermeneutic conception of truth by facing tradition with a responsible attitude: tradition is always a legacy without a will and is thus always *decided* (*BI*). A philosophical interpretation is therefore an immediate repudiation of political totalitarianism and also enables us to look at the law in different terms. Hermeneutics 'does justice to the law', making it just by saving it from its totalitarian tendencies (Vattimo and Derrida 1998: 288; see **justice/law**).

This philosophical-political commitment of Vattimo's almost becomes *pathos* in his later works and leads back to Nietzsche. Nietzsche is the one who understood the link between metaphysics and violence. Metaphysics' contempt for the transient, the body and the individual paves the way for the extermination of millions in the name of a theory – Auschwitz (Vattimo, Flores D'Arcais and Onfray 2007; Benso 2010). It is the violence inherent in metaphysics that is at the basis of political totalitarianism and its excesses. In this respect, totalitarianism is only the result of an interpretation of reality to which an alternative interpretation can be contrasted.

Yet a world not governed by totality is a less unified and less certain world and therefore far less reassuring. Totality is always, for Vattimo, what we have lost, and that for which we can also be nostalgic. Totalitarianism is both threatening and reassuring. This may explain why people can still look favourably on a philosophical-political category that seemed outdated. If, in fact, hermeneutic truth and being as an event had really prevailed, if we were genuinely capable of saying goodbye to totality, we might have to ask the question: does it still make sense to talk about totalitarianism?

TRACE (see *ANDENKEN* [REMEMBRANCE])

TRANSMISSION (see LANGUAGE)

TRANSPARENCY/TRANSPARENT SOCIETY

Jaume Casals Pons

Vattimo himself says, in *The Transparent Society*, that he is giving an interrogative shape to the concept of transparency. In fact, transparency and the transparent society are not concepts effectively defined, but a sort of intuition, an image of a society in crisis with the ideals of modernity: the belief in a unitarian history in progress, the European model of humankind, the general system of knowledge, etc. Vattimo assumes that the modernity of the late 1980s, so-called 'postmodernity', can no longer support the sort of ideals merged since post-Cartesianism and the Enlightenment at the heart of the notion of Europe as the centre of the world (see **Enlightenment**). The principal reason is the irruption of mass media into the order of social life. Transparency is necessarily an epiphenomenon of the mass media, of profusion of information, abundance of communication, richness of citizens' possibilities of relationship (see **information technology/ Gestell**). But all these features of transparency are far from the birth of a new ideal in the modern style. The postmodern society is not more enlightened than the modern by virtue of quickness and the opening of knowledge purveyed by new technologies. Perhaps, on the contrary, it is just more complex and disordered. Vattimo's intuition of a new ideal of emancipation is, however, linked to this complexity and this disorder. Probably the deepest meaning of transparency is related to a paradox in which complexity and disorder have to be accepted as the consequences of our modern heritage.

From this point of view (emancipation as complexity and interrogative paradoxical transparency), Vattimo starts his reading of the philosophical tradition, essentially the German philosophers, trying to obtain from them a twofold interpretation. To different degrees, Kant, Hegel, Marx, Benjamin, Adorno and Heidegger have in their works critical elements of the modern building of the truth that, at same time, they have built. Vattimo manages to incorporate these critical elements into his postmodern stance. The concept of transparency, therefore, is full of historical and hermeneutical elements in which Vattimo has always excelled in his works since *Il soggetto e la maschera* (1974). This is why *The Transparent Society* can also be read as a history of modern thought. Although he excels – as other Italian commentators – when interpreting the beloved *tedeschi*, he remains close to the French and British tradition, from Berkeley, Rousseau and Hume to Foucault and Deleuze. Vattimo's understanding of transparency retains all its philosophical beauty, even though he has obviously renounced claiming the complexity of postmodern societies as the path to emancipation. Years later, in *Being and Its Surroundings*, Vattimo associated

> the term 'transparency' with something from the past, an era that was once ours but is no longer, something that evokes a certain nostalgia, like the good old days of our grandparents, our aunts and uncles, and the illusions of youth. It is a fact that no one believes in transparency any more, not even those who – like me in 1989 – made it a constitutive feature, albeit filled with contradictions, of the nascent postmodern society. (*BIS*, 102)

But the light he threw on this history of modern thought suffices to make evident an immortal legacy.

TRUTH

Franca d'Agostini

As a hermeneutical ontologist (see **hermeneutics**), Vattimo is deeply interested in the nature and destiny of the concept we call truth. The theme is specifically dealt with in *A Farewell to Truth* but it pervades all his work. The fundamental aim of Vattimo's hermeneutics is 'to open up a non-metaphysical conception of truth' (*EM*, 12). And in *Of Reality* he argues that 'there is a linear development from the discovery of the Heideggerian critique to the metaphysical conception of truth [. . .] and the idea of the weakening of Being as the only possible philosophy of history and theory of emancipation' (*OR*, 100). As a matter of fact, Vattimo has elaborated a specific theory of truth, characterisable as 'a particular version of combined pragmatism and coherentism, which significantly also combines Nietzsche's theory of nihilism and the Christian conception of *pietas*' (d'Agostini 2010b: 33). So while the pragmatist and coherentist aspects of the theory mark its affinity with some analytical approaches to truth, especially with Rorty, the reference to nihilism and Christianity is the specific and original import of Vattimo's view.

Vattimo accepts the definitional idea of pragmatism, whereby when we speak of 'truth' we mean that we have some practical concern (such as the researching of an intersubjective agreement, or the confirmation of our ideas). And he accepts the basic assumption of coherentism, whereby we acknowledge some thesis as 'truth' because it is in accordance with what we already know. But he interprets both views through the lens of nihilism, and of his idea of the weakening of Being importing a weakening of thought (see **weak thought**). The result is something that has no equivalent in the current debates about truth (see Glanzberg 2018) and that can be characterised as a form of *alethic nihilism*, a nihilist theory of truth.

In agreement with Heidegger (2002a [1943]), Vattimo's truth theory is not based on truth as the property of assertions or propositions, but on the experience related to the concept, on 'truth' as the indication of an experience. The consequences have been variously characterised by Vattimo, stressing that hermeneutical truth has a rhetorical more than logical impact, is oriented by social more than epistemic interests, and is not reducible to the trivial mechanism of the one-to-one correspondence word–world. However, it is important to stress that, definitionally, these positions do not imply renouncing the realistic meaning of 'true' or 'truth'. When we speak of 'truth', for Vattimo, we speak of our relation to the world and our obvious will to think or speak about things as they stand (or rather, as we believe they stand). What is wrong with truth is the use of the concept as an absolute warrant of interpersonal objectivity. All that we say or think expresses some relation to being; as we are located beings (thrown into the world), the truth predicate still stands for a certain connection that we establish between being and discourses, world and words, things and thoughts. But the point is to establish what we do with it, and the metaphysical tradition has used truth as a germinal principle of violence, repression and institutional deception (see **metaphysics**).

When we speak of 'truth' (in a non-metaphysical sense) we speak of an engagement with the world, an engagement that involves the associated life. Thus, the relevant philosophical point is to decide the direction of this engagement: what do we want from our ontological commitment? What do we want from the use of truth? If our engagement is in the direction of democracy, then we have to say 'farewell to truth'; this move is 'the commencement, and the very basis, of democracy' (*FT*, 32). But it is clear that that to which we should say 'farewell' is the concept of truth in the way it has been conceived and used in the pre-democratic tradition. Such a conception postulated a brutally simplified distinction between thought and being, so that truth was the tool of the appropriation of being by the structures of the institutional power (*HC*). And clearly, a similar world was the fake world of institutional religions, of capitalism, of imperialism and neo-imperialism that have dominated modern (fake) democracies, with their fake 'liberal' ideology. So 'truth' has become the supreme justification of violence and oppression.

TURIN

Claudio Gallo

Gianni Vattimo has spent most of his life in Turin. He was born in the Piedmontese capital in January 1936. He was a child during the war and a university student after the reconstruction years. Turin has been the mainframe of his sentimental, academic and political life (*NBG*). Travels and periods of study were regular occurrences; still, he always came back to his old town, which was the first capital of the Kingdom of Italy in 1861, the city of the workers' struggles during the 1960s–1980s, and the cradle of terrorism before its current slow economic decline.

'I never succeeded in getting rid of Turin', admits the philosopher ironically.[15] When he was young, the city housed two conflicting traditions: the Enlightenment one (from liberalism to socialism to communism; see **Enlightenment**; **Marxism/Italian Marxism**) and the Catholic one (see **Church**; **religion**). The young Vattimo's formation was within the latter, with some openness to the far left's libertarian ideas. His extraneousness to the city's Enlightenment tradition, which in Turin's upper classes was typically mixed up with a certain sternness (an echo of the Piedmontese military tradition), would mark his relation with the people who mattered in the city. At the beginning of the 1950s, before the headquarter of the state's television, RAI, was transferred from Turin to Rome, the Piedmontese studios were attracting many young intellectuals who were destined to become famous. Among them were Vattimo, Umberto Eco and Furio Colombo, who became both crucial and lifelong friends.

'For a couple of years the RAI in Turin had been a gathering point, a place for doing new things, for debating freely. A large slice of the Turinese intelligentsia took part' (*NBG*, 47). In the same period at the university, there was a famous philosophical school, mainly represented

---

15 Conversation between the author and Vattimo on 5 December 2020.

by Augusto Guzzo, Nicola Abbagnano and Luigi Pareyson. Pareyson, Vattimo's mentor, was the least Turinese in mindset and culture: another circumstance that would shape Vattimo's image as an outsider in his relationship to the city's establishment (see **Pareyson, Luigi**). What is, then, the nature of Vattimo's connection to Turin? In his own words: 'In Turin, I absorbed the spirit of the historical resistance to Fascism. I breathed it in the most different places, such as the Azione Cattolica and the Catholic Union. Many of the people that I met there were coming from Resistance experiences.'[16]

He was fascinated by the city's anti-fascist attitude, but more its working-class version than the elite one. A symbol of this distance from the mood of the elite is the very fact that Einaudi, the historical Turin publisher of progressive tradition and one of the most renowned in Italy, never published a book by Vattimo. Being read through Heidegger and anti-historicism, the Nietzsche of the philosopher was completely heretical in their eyes. To them, Vattimo's Catholic origin was an unforgivable original sin, even though some of them had a close connection with him. Turin's political and intellectual elites looked at Vattimo with respect but never invited him into their magic circle, even though he became one of the most recognised Italian philosophers abroad.

ÜBERWINDUNG (see **OVERCOMING**)

UNFOUNDEDNESS (*SFONDAMENTO*) (see **DIFFERENCE**)

UNIVERSALISM

Seraphine Appel

Vattimo argues that postmodernity requires non-metaphysical ethics and rejects the notion that universal validity can or should be the aim of the search for truth. He equates universality with an ultimacy of principles and, although he does not exhaustively define the term, we can

---

16 Ibid.

understand universalism to be the philosophical and theological concept that universal facts or ideas exist, can be discovered and have universal applicability.

Furthermore, Vattimo argues that the crisis of truth stems from the assumption of universality in truth-claims, which he considers to be an inheritance from Christianity and from Greek and eighteenth-century rationalism, the projects of which have used claims regarding the universality of their truths to assert power and to exercise authority. The 'missionary' and the modern imperialistic attitude are exemplary expressions of this (*OR*, 169). As with confronting scepticism, he argues that the critique of universalism cannot be made through rational argumentation. That the conversation has remained on the level of rational debate is in the interest of the ideology that it upholds and has always been meant to serve (*OR*, 162). Vattimo's rejection of universalism is related to his argument for the inherent violence in metaphysics and the view that guides his hermeneutics: that we can no longer appeal to essences or ultimate foundations of any kind as a ground for truth, philosophical or otherwise (see **truth**).

Rather than collapsing into relativism, rejecting the credibility of first principles causes the whole story to evaporate: 'if the real world (the first principles) has become a fable, writes Nietzsche, then the fable too has been destroyed (and so cannot be absolutized in turn)' (*FT*, 93; see **Nietzsche, Friedrich**). Vattimo argues that forms of relativism that suspend assent from a disengaged standpoint maintain a metaphysics of principles because they locate themselves in a stable point of view (*FT*, 96). Even those who recognise the transformation of truth often do not escape inherent claims to universality. Of those who do recognise the end of the history of truth, he suggests that they stop short at the epistemological level, as they consider it a problem of the realisation of our limits of knowledge or rationality (Vattimo mentions by name Wittgenstein, Jaspers, Dewey and Heidegger, though he does not directly critique them). He argues that the recognition of the impossibility of universal truth at an epistemological level does not escape the claim to universality because it is as if the claim of an awareness of the limits of knowledge holds more truth – universal truth, it would seem, if the awareness of these limits are to be universally acceptable – than the truths claimed by realists or objectivists (*OR*, 161).

On this account, rejecting ultimate foundations means that any hope for the universal validity of an assertion comes from consensus in dialogue without any claim to absolute truth. Vattimo proposes that we can reach dialogical consensus by acknowledging that we share cultural and technological-scientific acquisitions (*AC*, 5) and that this ensemble of practices and paradigms through which we communicate has been inherited (*FT*, 64–5). This suggests that we are considering the boundaries of truth-claims. In acknowledging, for example, that Kant was ethnocentric and determined by his epoch and its universalist ideal (*FT*, 137), we agree that the Kantian intellect can be universally valid only among subjects who share his established community.

There is a tension between his rejection of universalism and his Catholicism when Vattimo writes that Christianity is the unique historical case with the capability to be a universal religion (*AC*, 9). He puts forth a historical materialist account of Christianity to separate its empirical history of violence from what he believes to be its potential, espousing that a secular rethinking of Christianity must reject dogmas from a single authority and function through dialogue. It can be questioned whether his belief that Christian universalism is possible on grounds of less exclusivity and less violence (*OR*, 170–1) falls into the same universalism that he wants to reject. Nevertheless, although his writing often appears to be concerned with the dialogue among those who share a cultural Christian heritage, he advocates a broader exchange. It follows that this dialogue must take into radical consideration the relationships of all interlocutors with their histories and cultural contexts, and in *Being and Its Surroundings* he makes this explicit. Here, he urges that the rethinking of the universalist ideal must not only be a critique of Eurocentrism and capitalism; our ideal of dialogue must allow for proposals of alternatives to the current global economic system. He stresses that this expanded horizon is not simply a modification of theory but a consequence of globalisation, and argues that we must look for what differentiates us rather than what unites us. Those in dialogue must assert and privilege these differences in the search for an alternative to the ideal of universalism (*BIS*, 124; see also Vattimo 2002c).

UTOPIA/HETEROTOPIA (see BLOCH, ERNST/UTOPIA)

VERWINDUNG (see CONVALESCENCE)

VICO, GIAMBATTISTA

Libera Pisano

After the English publication of *The End of Modernity*, Hayden White published a short essay highlighting the relevance of Giambattista Vico (1668–1744) to Vattimo's thought and to the postmodern debate in general (White 1991). Vattimo makes sporadic references to Vico throughout his works. However, and in accordance with White's suggestion, these scattered references are far from random and illuminate key issues in Vattimo's hermeneutics, particularly as regards the importance of language, his critique of historical rationalism and the primordial notion of divinity. Concerning the importance of language, Vattimo mentions Vico's critique of Hobbes's political theory, which blames Hobbes for not taking into account language as the *conditio sine qua non* of the social contract (*FT*, 119). As for the critique of historical rationalism, Vattimo's definition of philosophy, understood as the radical historicity of knowledge, has an explicit Vichian echo: 'Giambattista Vico might have agreed with me' (*NBG*, 110). In *Being and Its Surroundings* (*BIS*, 209), Vico is quoted as the author who showed Croce that history is not driven by deterministic reason and who thus contributed to correcting his Hegelianism. Moreover, Vattimo recalls in passing Vico's famous phrase *verum et factum convertuntur* to characterise the notion of fact as an interpretation, or 'the fact that Being does not give itself (any longer) as objectivity. Is it a "fact"? Yes, but in a literal meaning of the word, a meaning in the sense of Vico, we could say' (*OR*, 7). The Vichian notion of fact is also used to explain the pristine notion of the divine. In both *After Christianity* (*AC*, 38–9) and *After the Death of God* (*ADG*, 89), Vattimo mentions Vico's idea of the 'capricious god' who was worshipped in the original *ingens sylva* by the savage brutes who were constantly exposed to natural disasters. According to Vattimo, this tendency to make God the perfect Other is also found in Friedrich Nietzsche and in contemporary philosophy.

VIOLENCE

Clayton Crockett

According to Vattimo, violence is intrinsically embedded within metaphysics, with its commitment to a strong, objective truth. In *Hermeneutic Communism*, Vattimo and Zabala declare that 'Truth is not only "violent," in that it turns away from solidarity, but it is "violence," because it can easily become an imposition on our own existence. As such, violence is the political imposition of truth' (*HC*, 18). Truth imposes on us as violence, because it singles itself out as the only possible alternative. The cutting off of alternative explanations and interpretations that takes place in the generation of metaphysical truth destroys not only non-conforming ideas but also the people who are committed to them. The violence of our modernist and capitalist politics is derived from this metaphysics.

In the modern world, we have cut ourselves off from non-modern modes of thinking, knowing and doing. This reduction is a result of the deployment of Western science and technology in its efforts to reduce, destroy, enslave and exploit peoples and natural resources. According to Vattimo, the 'effective rationalisation of the world through science and technology unveils the true meaning of metaphysics: will to power, violence, the destruction of liberty' (*NE*, 11). Philosophy is not divorced from these investments in power, money and control, but actually founds and funds them. Vattimo follows Heidegger's critical analysis of modern technology as an 'enframing' of the world. Because everything is enframed within Western metaphysics, science and technology, everything is reduced to the status of a resource to be exploited, or what Heidegger calls a 'standing reserve' (see **technology/cyberspace**).

Metaphysics and modern technology are intertwined; they mutually implicate and indict each other. Vattimo exposes this interconnection between metaphysical violence and political violence in his philosophy. He states that philosophical violence is 'the silencing of all questioning by the authoritative peremptoriness of the first principle' (*B*, 65). Once metaphysical philosophy silences questioning, it easily moves to the silencing of people, institutions and nations, which are in turn silenced in the name of power.

The way to counter this metaphysical violence is with a historical-interpretative strategy of active nihilism. Nihilism is usually viewed in negative terms, as something to be overcome by the imposition of new truths and values. However, Vattimo argues that we have to recognise that 'nihilism remains ensnared in metaphysics as long as it conceives of itself, even only implicitly, as the *discovery* that there, where we thought *there was* Being, *there is in reality* nothing' (*NE*, 146). Why is this the case? Because this nothing that is unveiled in nihilism is then viewed as an empty space that can be filled with a stronger philosophical metaphysics, and that simply replaces one form of violence with another. In contrast, philosophy should be seen as an interpretative process in which this very metaphysical violence undermines itself. For Vattimo, 'hermeneutics is not just antifoundationalism plus interpretations in conflict. It also entails a philosophy of history ... that views hermeneutics as the result of a "nihilistic" process, in which metaphysical Being, meaning violence, consumes itself' (*NE*, 94). Nietzsche draws attention to the process by which the highest values devalue themselves during the historical unfolding of Western metaphysics thought as active nihilism. And Vattimo emphasises this form of nihilism as the way to twist free from this violent tradition. Violence here is overcome by nihilism, and the putting into place of a weak ontology of interpretation and politics.

WEAK THEOLOGY

Jeffrey W. Robbins

Weak theology has primarily been associated with Vattimo's contemporary, John D. Caputo, who since 2006 has published a series of works developing a theology of the weakness of God. The overlap between the philosophical interests and pedigree of Vattimo and Caputo has been established. This includes their shared interest in post-metaphysical hermeneutics, weak thought and theories of postmodernism (*ADG*). The specific interest in certain religious themes such as the nature of religious belief in the postmodern age, Nietzsche's announcement that 'God is dead', and the cultural implications of the process of secularisation in the Western world establish the contours for Vattimo's contribution to weak theology.

Weak theology can be seen as a subset of the broader philosophical turn to religion observed by Vattimo in postmodern thought and culture (*R*), and for some is seen as the successor to the radical death of God theologies of the 1960s and beyond (see **death of God**). The origin of Vattimo's interest in weak thought precedes his own philosophical turn to religion. While weak thought refers to the gradual weakening of being that has transformed contemporary philosophy from its former obsession with the metaphysics of truth to its current and more limited understanding of itself strictly as an interpretative exercise, the irony is that this weak ontology also weakens the strong metaphysical reasons for atheism and the modern rationalist repudiation of religion. In this way, weak thought establishes the philosophical precondition for the postmodern return of the religious. In Vattimo's words, 'The end of metaphysics and the death of the moral God have liquidated the philosophical basis of atheism' (*AC*, 17). Neither theism nor atheism understand the true nature of religious belief, because both still rely on absolutist claims characteristic of scientific positivism or transcendent authority. Now that we live in the post-metaphysical age in which there are no absolute truths, only interpretations, the category of belief can again be taken seriously as constitutive of our lived traditions.

Vattimo's approach to the nature of religious belief in the postmodern age is paradoxical, playful and ironic. This approach can be seen in the Italian title of his book *Belief*, which is *Credere di credere*, which translates as 'believing that one believes' (see **belief**). Postmodern religious belief, so conceived, is characterised by uncertainty. Likewise, when it comes to the concept of God, Vattimo is adamant that Nietzsche's announcement that 'God is dead' not be translated to mean that God does not exist. His post-metaphysical hermeneutical orientation allows him to bypass the stale debates over the existence or non-existence of God. Instead, the significance of Nietzsche for Vattimo is that there is no ultimate foundation. In this way, Vattimo's weak theology is decidedly not onto-theological. God is not treated either as first cause or highest being. Accordingly, the weak theology associated with Vattimo follows the prescription outlined by Heidegger in his address to a group of theologians that if a proper theology were to be written, the word 'being' would not appear.

Vattimo's argument with regard to the weakening of being corresponds with the historical and cultural process of secularisation in the Western world. He sees this secularisation as the destiny of the Christian West and has stated that 'real religiosity relies on secularization' (*ADG*, 95). The Church no longer has a monopoly on truth. This is a consequence of the 'Babel-like pluralism' that Vattimo so often references. This modern fragmentation of religious authority has both positive and negative consequences. Positively, it safeguards religious belief from coercion, and at least provides the possibility that believers might recognise the finiteness, contingency and historicity of their own traditions and beliefs. But on the flip side, a religion severed from institutional control means that, like almost everything else in contemporary society, it becomes just another commodity in the world of mass communication. This is why, according to Vattimo's diagnosis, the postmodern return of religion has so often been a conservative and sometimes violent one (*R*).

Unlike his contemporary Caputo, Vattimo never develops his theology as such. But by virtue of his weak thought and his grappling with the nature of religious belief, the post-metaphysical implications of the death of God, and the history of secularisation, he is regarded as one of the key thinkers and inspiration of weak theology. It is a theology that takes its leave of ecclesiastical theology, that situates itself after the death of God, that values religious belief for its embrace of epistemic uncertainty, and that takes on the seemingly oxymoronic flavour of being a secular theology. Its legacy can be seen in the renewal of the radical theology school of thought that is currently underway.

See also **secularisation**.

WEAK THOUGHT (*PENSIERO DEBOLE*)

Franca d'Agostini

The notion of 'weak thought' is dominant in Vattimo's philosophy. The appeal to the 'weakness' of being and thought is the framework within which other crucial ideas find their philosophical legitimacy (see **nihilism; postmodern/postmodernity; ontology of actuality; hermeneutic communism**). In Vattimo's understanding, the term has four distinct but interrelated meanings. Weak thought is intended: 1) as an expression of the *Zeitgeist*, corresponding to an ultimate development of 'the history of Being'; 2) as a particular 'nihilistic' conception of hermeneutics; 3) as the principle of a new political practice; and 4) as a new way of doing philosophy.

1) Weak thought as an expression of the *Zeitgeist*. The term was launched in the essays collected by Vattimo and Rovatti in 1983 (*WT*). The project was to gather a series of philosophical positions, active in the second half of the twentieth century, all of which, more or less declaredly, proposed some 'weakening' of the standard idea of reason. As an interpretation of the *Zeitgeist*, weak thought 'seeks a clarification of *what might be* a

viable task for thinking at a slow crepuscule of modernity [. . .] when most forms of theorizing cannot find credible legitimation' (Carravetta 2013: 2). More specifically, the formula evoked the idea that human rationality is becoming more and more open and ductile. So weak thought was conceived as a further step in the self-criticism of Western rationality, from Kant onwards.

In Vattimo's contribution, the notion emerges from a reflection on two trends that have dominated the second half of the twentieth century in Europe: the Frankfurt School (see **Adorno, Theodor Wiesengrund**; **Habermas, Jürgen**) and poststructuralism. Vattimo claims that the consequences of both have been philosophically arguable: on one side, we have another celebration of the 'crisis of reason'; on the other side, we have a deconstructive or anarchic epistemology. The idea of weak thought offers a new approach, but a novelty conceived hermeneutically, so with the mark of continuity. 'Weak thought has not entirely left dialectics and difference behind; rather they constitute for it a past, in the Heideggerian sense of *Gewesenes*, which has to do with the idea of a sending [*invio*] and a destiny' (*WT*, 39). To accept the weakness of thought therefore means to inherit the emancipatory programme of the neo-Hegelian dialecticians, and of French poststructuralism, but with a new attitude.

2) Weak thought as hermeneutical nihilism. While for Rovatti weak thought formalises the need to take leave of the self-identical subjectivity of the philosophical tradition, for Vattimo it expresses a new ductility of thought, conquered over the remains of the old metaphysics. The idea of weakness is assumed, hermeneutically, as the mark of a historical-linguistic conception of Being. As we read also in recent works (see *OR*), 'things', that is, the objects that populate our reality, have neither substantial identity nor static continuity; the domain of what we call 'being' or 'reality' is the flux of the interpretations, stipulations, discussions that form human history, and of which we are part. The novelty of weak thought consists in assuming this evidence, through the lens of what Nietzsche called 'nihilism'. Nihilism is the age in which people are becoming aware of the weakness of Being, and weak thought is their consequent form of thought.

Therefore, weak thought becomes the crucial formula of the particular hermeneutical nihilism defended by Vattimo, whereby Nietzsche's dissolution (or overturning) of metaphysics is grafted on to the historical-linguistic approach of Gadamer's hermeneutics. As Vattimo states in *The End of Modernity*, nihilism appears to be 'the only chance of contemporary thought' (*EM*, 30). In the line of this nihilistic ontology, '*weak*' in the expression 'weak thought' stands for 'synchronically pluralistic' and 'diachronically ever-changing' (d'Agostini 2010a: 3–5); it denotes the philosophical attitude of human beings in leaving a certain (modern) age of reason.

3) Weak thought and hermeneutical communism. The idea of weak thought in this account is not exactly that of some soft and ineffective thinking, ruled by conversational democratic politeness (as in Rorty 1979). Weak thought is rather the answer to a necessity, a constraint occurring in our ways of thinking. This shift is clear in *Beyond Interpretation*, where Vattimo counters those trends of the 'hermeneutical turn' in the 1980s which interpreted the philosophy of interpretation as a form of generic anti-realism or relativism. The radicality of weak thought is evident as soon as one is aware that our assignment, in the age of nihilism, is to become 'accomplished nihilists', in Nietzsche's sense (*EM*, 27). We should not substitute the lost 'supreme values' with other values, the old constraints and oppressions with other forms of domination, but nor should we abandon the emancipatory project of philosophy. Rather, in adopting the hermeneutic-nihilist approach to being, we find another emancipatory project (*NE*). This view is what grounds the political impact of weak thought. There are, ultimately, 'strong reasons' for weak thought (d'Agostini 2010a), and these are of a philosophical as well as political nature.

The radicality (and hence the 'strongness') of weak thought is further clarified in *Hermeneutic Communism*, written with Santiago Zabala, in which Vattimo locates his philosophical position within the political debates of the twenty-first century, with a provocative and resolute defence of communism as the only emancipatory programme that deserves to be carried on, in the face of the new capitalism's crimes, with its logic of profit and oppression. The opening declaration is revealing: 'If Marxist philosophers until now have failed to change the world, it is not because their political approach was wrong, but rather because it was framed within the metaphysical tradition' (*HC*, 1). What grounds weak thought is the distortion-overcoming of the metaphysical inheritance (see **convalescence [*Verwindung*]**), of the 'strong' conception of being, typical of metaphysical (late capitalistic) language (see **truth**). This move opens a new strength, the possibility of a new realisable communism, a new interpretation of Marxism. In this sense, weak thought does not denote a specific weakness of thought, but the idea of a strong philosophical commitment in favour of weak people.

4) Weak thought as a new way of doing philosophy. Altogether, the notion of weak thought is an interpretation of the current age of reason, grounded on a certain (hermeneutical and nihilistic) conception of being, and a consequent idea of the political engagement of philosophers. But it has also meta-philosophical implications, in that it is the formula of a new

way of doing philosophy, a new logic, a new method, for philosophy (see **logic**).

The notion of 'weakening' is a logical notion: it stands for a *dilution* or a *thinning* of a calculus which allows us to add any additional formulas to either side of a sequent (see Cook 2009: 312). A weak logical system is more powerful, as some classical restrictions are reduced, and so it is able to capture more aspects, more opportunities for thought. Such a dialectics corresponds to Vattimo's interpretation of the destiny of philosophy after Hegel and Marx. The theory of weak thought provides philosophical – historical, anthropological and political – justifications for preferring a 'weak' logic in philosophy. Philosophy – just like any other science or discipline or intellectual activity – is ideologically constructed by the metaphysical (descriptive, truth-oriented) approach to being. The emancipatory project, for philosophers, begins by overturning philosophy itself, to begin with the basic mechanism of theoretical impositions passed off as simple 'descriptions' of facts (*HC*, 11–43). It is in this sense that weak thought can truly become 'thought in defence of weakness', in defence of marginalised, exploited and abused people: it will work as a debunking mechanism of the oppressive apparatus of traditional, metaphysical thought.

WEBER, MAX

Francisco Arenas-Dolz

In contrast to positions that interpret modernity as a radical alternative to Christianity, both from a Catholic neo-integralism, which interprets modernity in terms of regression with respect to Christianity, and from a triumphalist view of modernity, which considers it autonomous with regard to the Christian tradition, Vattimo returns to Max Weber (1864–1920) to approach secularisation from a historical-hermeneutical perspective, rather than a rationalist-metaphysical one. In Weberian theory, the anti-metaphysical assumption of secularisation does not emerge as loss or decadence, but as the continuation of a religious heritage (Dotolo 1999: 49–55). In rationalisation, Weber identified the distinctive element of the secularisation process as a fact inherent to Christianity. Whether as disenchantment with the world brought about by monotheism or as a loss of eschatological hopes for the sake of duty with regard to the present, it is this formal rationality that can guide the organisation of society. Developing the Weberian theses, Vattimo broadens the concept of secularisation by also placing under this label the processes of weakening typical of postmodernity, which become comprehensible only if they are considered the result of the secularisation of the Judaeo-Christian tradition (*AC*, 78–82). For Vattimo, the process of secularisation has weakened the metaphysical violence of identity, symbolised by the centrality of the subject, allowing difference to emerge as an interpretative criterion for history. The rejection of metaphysics as a thought of the foundation occurs in order to respond to the specific historical situation of modernity, where metaphysics has been implemented as a technical-scientific domination of the world. The attempt to go beyond metaphysics aims to recompose the unitary sense of experience in the age of fragmentation, the specialisation of scientific languages and technical skills, the isolation of spheres of interest, the pluralisation of the social roles of each individual subject; in short, in the age of modern rationalisation described by Weber (Dotolo 2007: 355).

See also **metaphysics**; **secularisation**.

WEST (OCCIDENT)

Ian Alexander Moore

The Italian *occidente*, like its English cognate *Occident*, refers to the geographical 'West', but more literally means 'falling' (Latin *cadere*) or 'setting', especially in reference to the sun. In Vattimo's philosophy, the 'decline of the West' (cf. Spengler's *Untergang des Abendlandes*) is inscribed in the name 'Occident' and in the very name of the Occident. 'The West', writes Vattimo, 'is declining because decline constitutes its historical vocation' (*NE*, 31).

If, as Heidegger claims, Western thought is essentially 'onto-theological', then what must decline is Being (*on*) and God (*theos*) above all, together with the arguments (*logoi*) that support them. In his work on the West, Vattimo traces these ontological and theological (or more precisely, Christological) declines and explores their emancipatory potential. I will discuss each of these declines in turn.

1) Being. Philosophy, which is to say Western thinking (*RP*, 107), has, from its inception, been about Being. It has tried to answer the question of what it means for anything to be at all. Philosophy has not, to be sure, always provided the same answer. Being has been variously interpreted as idea, substance, actuality, subject and power, for example. Yet throughout the history of the West, philosophy has sought to arrive at a universal, foundational, atemporal account of beings in their Being. It is the merit of especially Nietzsche and Heidegger to have exposed this aspiration as

fantastical. Heidegger (1972) speaks of the 'end of philosophy'. Nietzsche (2005: 168) calls Being – which Heidegger still wants to hold on to, but which Vattimo is willing to allow to dissolve into historical transmission and the unending play of interpretation (*EM*, 19 and *passim*) – the 'last wisps of smoke from the evaporating end of reality'.

On the sociopolitical level, this means that the Western notions of progress and of unidirectional, univocal history lose their foothold (*NE*, 22). It does not mean, however, that we should abandon the legacy of the West – an impossible task at any rate. Like it or not, the world has become Western, and 'we cannot not call ourselves western', as Vattimo puts it, modifying the title of a famous essay by Benedetto Croce (*NE*, 30; see Croce 1962). What we can do is learn to see and to live in accordance with the tendency towards decline contained within the West itself. Vattimo's paradigmatic example of this tendency is secularisation (*NE*, 31). Far from the elimination of Christianity and the West – and for Vattimo these two terms are synonymous (*AC*, 69–82)[17] – secularisation is actually their truth and destiny (see **being**; **secularisation**).

2) God. We are not only ineluctably Western, in Vattimo's view. What is more, 'we cannot', to refer to the original title of Croce's essay, 'help calling ourselves Christian'. Yet, paradoxically, our insuperable Christianity is of a piece with the very decline – or death, if you will – of God (see **death of God**). For, on Vattimo's interpretation, Christianity is not ultimately based on absolute foundations, let alone the violence perpetrated with its (and its fundamentalist varieties') support. Rather, Western Christianity – itself a pleonasm – is the emptying out (*kenosis*; cf. Philippians 2:7; see *kenosis*) of absolutism in all its guises, even that of truth. Vattimo proposes a shift 'from *veritas* to *caritas*' (*NE*, 35), from truth as liberating to what liberates as true (*RP*, 96–7), from the sacred and strong beyond to its weakening into the *saeculum* here and now – a shift, in short, to 'communication, community, dialogue, consensus, democracy [. . . and] charity' (*AC*, 24). 'To grasp and develop the meaning of these signs', Vattimo contends, 'is the task that today presents itself to those who profess to be openly Christian, and to the many who, outside of any respect for hierarchy, have understood that "they cannot not call themselves Christians"' (*AC*, 82; see also *NE*, 33). This is the meaning and mission of the West.

---

17 For a critique of this equation as failing to 'put enough distance between one of the concrete messianisms and pure messianic hope', see John Caputo's remarks in *ADG*, 77–83 (quote on 125).

WILL TO POWER (see NIETZSCHE, FRIEDRICH)

WITTGENSTEIN, LUDWIG

Gregorio Tenti

Austrian philosopher Ludwig Wittgenstein (1889–1951) is mentioned throughout Vattimo's works, where he takes up the role of a genuine hermeneutic thinker, though in a wide sense (*BI*). The link between Wittgensteinian philosophy and the twentieth-century hermeneutic tradition is particularly evident in Gadamer (Vattimo 1972b: liv), Apel (*BS*) and Lyotard (*HC*, 101) as well as in relation to Heidegger (*AD*, 110). In the second part of his reflections (and mainly the *Philosophical Investigations*), Wittgenstein established that the horizons of being are shaped as 'linguistic games', that is, as linguistic sets of rules that structure an experiential and communicative domain (or 'form of life'). The connection with Heidegger lies in the acknowledgement of the groundless fundamentality of the linguistic fact, rather than in the mystic conclusions of the *Tractatus Logico-Philosophicus* (*EM*, 23). This peculiar form of 'thought without foundation', however, differs from that of Heidegger by virtue of its regulated character (*AD*, 112) and its lack of historical dimension (*OR*, 26). The interpretation of Wittgenstein's positions is often used by Vattimo to read the analytic tradition and its possible resonances with hermeneutics.

Vattimo does not really confront Wittgenstein's philosophy in a straightforward and specific manner until *Being and Its Surroundings*, whose third chapter is entirely devoted to the theme of historicity in Wittgenstein (*BIS*, 18–27). Here, the ideas of linguistic game and form of life, decisive for Wittgenstein's own *Kehre*, are interrogated in light of their character of closeness to the world's historical course. The definitive overcoming of neo-positivism operated by Wittgenstein thus leads to the most evident problem of his mature philosophy: the theoretical impossibility of transcending the linguistically structured forms of life (see **language**).

Bibliography

MAIN WORKS OF GIANNI VATTIMO IN ITALIAN AND OTHER WORKS BY VATTIMO CITED

The following is a list of all Vattimo's books, above and beyond those that appear in the list of his major book-length publications in English given in the prelims, listed in chronological order of publication. It includes Italian editions of his work and occasional essays quoted in the dictionary. Dates in parentheses refer to subsequent editions cited by the contributors.

1960a (2007). 'Imitazione e catarsi in alcuni recenti studi aristotelici', in *Ermeneutica*, ed. Mario Cedrini, Alberto Martinengo and Santiago Zabala, 201–10. Vol. 1.1 of *Opere complete*. Rome: Meltemi.

1960b (2007). 'Opera d'arte e organismo in Aristotele', in *Ermeneutica*, ed. Mario Cedrini, Alberto Martinengo and Santiago Zabala, 211–33. Vol. 1.1 of *Opere complete*. Rome: Meltemi.

1961 (2007). *Il concetto di fare in Aristotele*, in *Ermeneutica*, ed. Mario Cedrini, Alberto Martinengo and Santiago Zabala, 19–180. Vol. 1.1 of *Opere complete*. Rome: Meltemi.

1963 (1989). *Essere, storia e linguaggio in Heidegger*. Turin: Marietti.

1967a. *Ipotesi su Nietzsche*. Turin: Giappichelli.

1967b (2008). *Poesia e ontologia*. Milan: Mursia.

1968. *Schleiermacher filosofo dell'interpretazione*. Milan: Mursia.

1971. *Introduzione a Heidegger*. Rome–Bari: Laterza.

1972a. *Arte e utopia*. Turin: Litografia Artigiana M & S.

1972b (1983). 'L'ontologia ermeneutica nella filosofia contemporanea', in Hans-Georg Gadamer, *Verità e metodo*, i–xxxvii. Milan: Bompiani.

1974 (1994, 2003). *Il soggetto e la maschera*. Milan: Bompiani.

1977a. *Estetica moderna*. Bologna: Il Mulino.

1977b (2010). *Introduzione all'estetica*, ed. Leonardo Amoroso. Pisa: ETS.

1978. Introduction to Gilles Deleuze, *Nietzsche e la filosofia*, 5–19. Pisa: Colportage.
1979. Introduction to Friedrich Nietzsche, *La gaia scienza*, vii–xxviii. Turin: Einaudi.
1980. *Le avventure della differenza*. Milan: Garzanti.
1981a. *Al di là del soggetto: Nietzsche, Heidegger e l'ermeneutica*. Milan: Feltrinelli.
1981b. Introduction to Friedrich Nietzsche, *Aurora*, 7–19. Rome: Newton Compton.
1983a. 'Dialettica, differenza, pensiero debole', in Gianni Vattimo and Pier Aldo Rovatti (eds), *Il pensiero debole*, 12–28. Milan: Feltrinelli.
1983b. Foreword to *Il soggetto e la maschera. Nietzsche e il problema della liberazione*, 1–2. 2nd ed. Milan: Bompiani.
1984. 'La bottiglia, la rete, la rivoluzione e i compiti della filosofia. Un dialogo con "Lotta Continua"', in *Al di là del soggetto. Nietzsche, Heidegger e l'ermeneutica*, 11–26. Milan: Feltrinelli. *BS*, xxix–xl.
1985a (1997, 2002). *Introduzione a Nietzsche*. Rome–Bari: Laterza.
1985b. *La fine della modernità*. Milan: Garzanti.
1986b. 'Nietzsche and Heidegger', *Stanford Italian Review* 6(1–2): 19–29.
1987a (ed.). *Filosofia '86*. Rome–Bari: Laterza.
1987b. 'Metafisica, violenza, secolarizzazione', in Gianni Vattimo (ed.), *Filosofia '86*, 71–94. Roma–Bari: Laterza.
1987c. '"Verwindung": Nihilism and the Postmodern in Philosophy', *SubStance* 16(2): 7–17.
1988a. 'Au-delà de la matière et du texte: La dissolution de la matière dans la pensée contemporaine', in *Matière et philosophie: architecture, science, théorie*, trans. Federico Benedetti and Paolo Antonelli, 59–60. Paris: Editions du Centre Pompidou.
1988b (ed.). *Filosofia '87*. Rome–Bari: Laterza.
1988c (ed.). *La sécularisation de la pensée*. Paris: Seuil.
1988d. 'Metaphysics, Violence, Secularization', trans. Barbara Spackman, in Giovanna Borradori (ed.), *Recoding Metaphysics: The New Italian Philosophy*, 45–61. Evanston, IL: Northwestern University Press.
1989a. *Etica dell'interpretazione*. Turin: Rosenberg e Sellier.

1989b (ed.). *Filosofia '88*. Rome–Bari: Laterza.
1989c (2000). *La società trasparente*. Milan: Garzanti.
1989d (ed.). *Que peut faire la philosophie de son histoire?* Paris: Seuil.
1990a. *Filosofia al presente*. Milan: Garzanti.
1990b (ed.). *Filosofia '89*. Rome–Bari: Laterza.
1990c. 'La realtà consumata', in Mauro Ceruti and Lorena Preta (eds), *Che cos'è la conoscenza*, 55–66. Rome–Bari: Laterza.
1991 (ed.). *Filosofia '90*. Rome–Bari: Laterza.
1992a (ed.). *Filosofia '91*. Rome–Bari: Laterza.
1992b. 'Ricostruzione della razionalità', in Gianni Vattimo (ed.), *Filosofia'91*, 89–103. Rome–Bari: Laterza.
1993 (ed.). *Filosofia '92*. Rome–Bari: Laterza.
1994a (ed.). *Filosofia '93*. Rome–Bari: Laterza.
1994b. *Oltre l'interpretazione*. Rome–Bari: Laterza.
1995 (ed.). *Filosofia '94*. Rome–Bari: Laterza.
1996a. *Credere di credere*. Milan: Garzanti.
1996b. *Filosofia, Polìtica, Religiòn: Màs allà del 'pensamiento debil'*, ed. L. Álvarez. Oviedo: Nobel.
1996c. *Il consumatore consumato*. Jesi: Centro Studi P. Calamandrei.
1997a. Introduction in Franca D'Agostini, *Analitici e continentali*, xi–xv. Milan: Raffaello Cortina.
1997b (2002). *Tecnica ed esistenza: Una mappa filosofica del Novecento*. Milan: Mondadori.
1999. 'Democracy, Reality, and the Media: Educating the *Übermensch*', in Arthur M. Melzer, Jerry Weinberger and M. Richard Zinman (eds), *Democracy and the Arts*, 146–58. Ithaca, NY: Cornell University Press.
2000a. *Dialogo con Nietzsche. Saggi 1961–2000*. Milan: Garzanti.
2000b. Introduction to Michela Nacci, *Pensare la tecnica. Un secolo di incomprensioni*, ix–xvi. Bari: Laterza.
2000c. 'The Story of a Comma: Gadamer and the Sense of Being', *Revue internationale de philosophie* 54: 499–513.
2000d. *Vocazione e responsabilità del filosofo*. Genoa: il Melangolo.
2002a. *Dopo la cristianità*. Milan: Garzanti.
2002b. 'Gadamer and the Problem of Ontology', in Jeff Malpas, Ulrich Arnswald and Jens Kertscher (eds),

Gadamer's Century, 299–306. Cambridge, MA: MIT Press.
2002c. *Vero e Falso Universalismo Cristiano*. Rio de Janerio: Educam-Editora Universitária Candido Mendes and Academia da Latinidade.
2002d. '"Weak Thought" and the Reduction of Violence: A Dialogue with Gianni Vattimo', interview with Santiago Zabala, *Common Knowledge* 8(3): 425–63.
2003a. 'After Onto-Theology: Philosophy Between Science and Religion', in Mark A. Wrathall (ed.), *Religion after Metaphysics*, 29–36. Cambridge: Cambridge University Press.
2003b. *Ermeneutica*. Milan: Raffaello Cortina.
2003c. *Nichilismo ed emancipazione: Etica, politica e diritto*, ed. Santiago Zabala. Milan: Garzanti.
2004. *Il socialismo ossia l'Europa*, ed. Giuseppe Iannantuono and Mario Cedrini. Turin: Trauben.
2005. 'Utopia Dispersed', *Diogenes* 209(1): 18–23.
2006. *La vita dell'altro*. Lungro di Cosenza: Marco.
2007a. 'A "Dictatorship of Relativism?"', *Common Knowledge* 13: 214–18.
2007b. *Ecce comu: come si ri-diventa ciò che si era*. Rome: Fazi.
2007c. *Opere complete. Volume introduttivo*, ed. Mario Cedrini, Alberto Martinengo and Santiago Zabala. Rome: Meltemi.
2007d. 'Metaphysics and Violence', trans. Robert T. Valgenti, in Santiago Zabala (ed.), *Weakening Philosophy: Essays in Honour of Gianni Vattimo*, 400–23. Montreal: McGill-Queen's University Press.
2007e. 'Postmodernity and (the End of) Metaphysics', trans. David Rose, in P. Goulimari (ed.), *Postmodernism: What Moment?*, 32–38. Manchester: Manchester University Press.
2008a. Introduction to Richard Rorty, *Un'etica per i laici*, 7–13. Turin: Bollati.
2008b. 'Prefazione', in Alberto Martinengo, *Introduzione a Reiner Schürmann*, 7–11. Rome: Meltemi.
2009a. *Addio alla verità*. Milan: Meltemi.
2009b. 'Nihilism as Emancipation', *Cosmos and History* 5(1): 20–3.
2009c. 'Nihilism as Emancipation', in Lorenzo Chiesa

and Alberto Toscano (eds), *The Italian Difference: Between Nihilism and Biopolitics*, 31–5. Melbourne: re.press.

2009d. 'Philosophy as Ontology of Actuality: A Biographical Theoretical Interview with Luca Savarino and Federico Vercellone', trans. Nicholas Walker, *Iris: European Journal of Philosophy and Public Debate* 1(2): 311–50.

2010a. Introduction to Richard Rorty, *An Ethics for Today: Finding Common Ground Between Philosophy and Religion*, 1–5. New York: Columbia University Press.

2010b. *Magnificat: Un'idea di montagna*. Turin: Vivalda.

2010c. 'Truth, Solidarity, History', in Randall E. Auxier and Lewis Edwin Hahn (eds), *The Philosophy of Richard Rorty*, 575–83. Chicago: Open Court.

2010d. 'The End of Reality', *Gifford Lectures*, <https://www.giffordlectures.org/lectures/end-reality>. Accessed 29 August 2022.

2012. *Della realtà*. Milan: Garzanti.

2014. 'Insuperable Contradictions and Events', in Michael Marder and Santiago Zabala (eds), *Being Shaken: Ontology and the Event*, 70–6. New York: Palgrave Macmillan.

2015a. 'Emergency and Event: Technique, Politics, and the Work of Art', *Philosophy Today* 59(4): 583–6.

2015b. 'Kenotic Sacrifice and Philosophy: Paolo Diego Bubbio', *Research in Phenomenology* 45(3): 431–5.

2016. 'Anatheism, Nihilism, and Weak Thought', in Richard Kearney and Jens Zimmermann (eds), *Reimagining the Sacred*, 128–48. New York: Columbia University Press.

2017. 'Towards (Back to?) a Philosophical Education: An Interview with Gianni Vattimo', interview with Gabriel Serbu, *Philosophy Today* 61(2): 281–90.

2018. *Essere e dintorni*. Milan: La Nave di Teseo.

2021. *Scritti filosofici e politici*. Milan: La Nave di Teseo.

n.d. 'Notes for the Gifford Lectures [Presented in 2010]', Gianni Vattimo Archives at the General Library of Pompeu Fabra University, Box 10, n. 7, Dipòsit de les Aigües Building.

VATTIMO'S OTHER CO-AUTHORED WORKS

Vattimo, Gianni, et al. (1996). *L'Ungheria e l'Europa*. Rome: Bulzoni.
Vattimo, Gianni, and Dario Antiseri (2008). *Ragione filosofica e fede religiosa nell'era postmoderna*. Soveria Mannelli (CZ): Rubbettino.
Vattimo, Gianni, Paolo Flores D'Arcais and Michel Onfray (2007). *Atei o Credenti?* Rome: Fazi.
Vattimo, Gianni, and Jacques Derrida (eds) (1995). *La Religione: Annuario Filosofico Europeo*. Rome–Bari: Laterza.
Vattimo, Gianni, and Jacques Derrida (1998). *Diritto, Giustizia e Interpretazione: Annuario filosofico europeo*. Rome–Bari: Laterza.
Vattimo, Gianni, and Carmelo Dotolo (2009). *Su Dio: la possibilità buona. Un colloquio sulla soglia tra filosofia e teologia*, ed. Giovanni Giorgio. Soveria Mannelli (CZ): Rubbettino.
Vattimo, Gianni, Enrique Dussel and Guillermo Hoyos (2002). *La postmodernidad a debite*, ed. L. Tovar. Bogotá: Universidad Santo Tomàs.
Vattimo, Gianni, Claudio Gallo and Armando Torno (2017). *A proposito dell'amore*. Milan: Book Time.
Vattimo, Gianni, and René Girard (2010). *Christianity, Truth, and Weakening Faith*, ed. Pierpaolo Antonello, trans. William McCuaig. New York: Columbia University Press.
Vattimo, Gianni, and René Girard (2015 [2006]). *Verità o fede debole: Dialogo su cristianesimo e relativismo*. Milan: Feltrinelli.
Vattimo, Gianni, and Piergiorgio Paterlini (2016 [2006]). *Non essere Dio*. Milan: Ponte alle Grazie.
Vattimo, Gianni, and Richard Rorty (2005). *Il futuro della religione. Solidarietà, carità, ironia*, ed. Santiago Zabala. Milan: Garzanti.
Vattimo, Gianni, and Pier Aldo Rovatti (eds) (1983). *Il pensiero debole*. Milan: Feltrinelli.
Vattimo, Gianni, Giovanni Ruggeri and Pierangelo Sequeri (2013). *Interrogazioni sul cristianesimo: Cosa possiamo ancora attenderci dal Vangelo?* Rome: Castelvecchi Lit Edizioni.
Vattimo, Gianni, and Martin G. Weiss (2012 [2003]). 'Die Stärken des schwachen Denkens', in Martin G. Weiss (ed.), *Gianni Vattimo: Einführung*, 171–83. Vienna: Passagen.
Vattimo, Gianni, and Wolfgang Welsch (eds) (1998). *Medien–Welten– Wirklichkeiten*. Munich: Fink.
Vattimo, Gianni, and Santiago Zabala (2013 [2011]). *Comunismo Ermeneutico*. Milan: Garzanti.
Vattimo, Gianni, and Santiago Zabala (2017). Foreword to Ana Messuti, *La justicia deconstruida*, 9–13. Barcelona: Bellaterra.

CRITICAL WORKS ON VATTIMO

This list includes the secondary literature cited in the dictionary that directly refers to Vattimo, and other critical texts of particular relevance for the study of Vattimo's thought. It is not intended to be exhaustive.

Azzarà, Giuseppe Stefano (2011). *Un Nietzsche italiano. Gianni Vattimo e le avventure dell'oltreuomo rivoluzionario*. Rome: Manifesto Libri.

Benso, Silvia (2010). 'Emancipation and the Future of the Utopian: On Vattimo's Philosophy of History', in Silvia Benso and Brian Schroeder (eds), *Between Nihilism and Politics: The Hermeneutics of Gianni Vattimo*, 203–19. Albany: State University of New York Press.

Benso, Silvia, and Brian Schroeder (eds) (2010). *Between Nihilism and Politics: The Hermeneutics of Gianni Vattimo*. Albany: State University of New York Press.

Birmingham, Peg (2017). 'Love's Law? The Principle of Anarchy in a Weakened Communism', in Silvia Mazzini and Owen Glyn-Williams (eds), *Making Communism Hermeneutical: Reading Vattimo and Zabala*, 53–62. Cham: Springer.

Borradori, Giovanna (1988). *Recoding Metaphysics: The New Italian Philosophy*. Evanston, IL: Northwestern University Press.

Bubbio, Paolo Diego (2014). *Sacrifice in the Post-Kantian Tradition: Perspectivism, Intersubjectivity, and Recognition*. Albany: State University of New York Press.

Carravetta, Peter (2013). 'What is Weak Thought? The Original Theses and Context of *il pensiero debole*', in *WT*, 1–38.

Carchia, Gianni, and Maurizio Ferraris (eds) (1996). *Interpretazione ed emancipazione. Studi in onore di Gianni Vattimo*. Milan: Raffaello Cortina.

Chiurazzi, Gaetano (ed.) (2008). *Pensare l'attualità, cambiare il mondo. Riflessioni sul pensiero di Gianni Vattimo*. Milan: Mondadori.

Coralluzzo, Francesco (2013). *Oltre il relativismo. Comprendere e superare le ragioni di Nietzsche, Heidegger e Vattimo*. Rome: Leonardo da Vinci.

D'Agostini, Franca (1996). 'Logica ermeneutica: dialettica, ricorsività, nichilismo', in Gianni Carchia and Maurizio Ferraris (eds), *Interpretazione ed emancipazione. Studi in onore di Gianni Vattimo*, 151–77. Milan: Raffaello Cortina.

D'Agostini, Franca (1997). *Analitici e continentali: guida alla filosofia degli ultimi trent'anni*. Milan: Raffaello Cortina.

D'Agostini, Franca (2010a [2000]). 'Introduction: The Strong Reasons for Weak Thought', trans. William McCuaig, in Gianni Vattimo, *The*

Responsibility of the Philosopher, 1–45. New York: Columbia University Press.

D'Agostini, Franca (2010b). 'Vattimo's Theory of Truth', in Silvia Benso and Brian Schroeder (eds), *Between Nihilism and Politics: The Hermeneutics of Gianni Vattimo*, 33–45. Albany: State University of New York Press.

Depoortere, Frederiek (2008). *Christ in Postmodern Philosophy: Gianni Vattimo, René Girard, and Slavoj Zizek*. London: T&T Clark.

Depoortere, Frederiek (2017). 'Weak Faith', in James Alison and Wolfgang Palaver (eds), *The Palgrave Handbook of Mimetic Theory and Religion*, 387–93. New York: Palgrave Macmillan.

D'Isanto, Luca (1999). Introduction to Gianni Vattimo, *Belief*, 1–17. Stanford, CA: Stanford University Press.

Dotolo, Carmelo (1999). *La teologia fondamentale davanti alle sfide del 'Pensiero debole' di G. Vattimo*. Rome: Religione e spiritualità.

Dotolo, Carmelo (2007). 'The Hermeneutics of Christianity and Philosophical Responsibility', in Santiago Zabala (ed.), *Weakening Philosophy: Essays in Honour of Gianni Vattimo*, 348–68. Montreal: McGill-Queen's University Press.

Flores D'Arcais, Paolo (2007). 'Gianni Vattimo; or rather, Hermeneutics as the Primacy of Politics', in Santiago Zabala (ed.), *Weakening Philosophy: Essays in Honour of Gianni Vattimo*, 250–69. Montreal: McGill-Queen's University Press.

Franci, Tommaso (2011). *Vattimo o del nichilismo. Provocazione alla filosofia*. Rome: Armando.

Frank, Manfred (2007). 'The Universality Claim of Hermeneutics', in Santiago Zabala (ed.), *Weakening Philosophy: Essays in Honour of Gianni Vattimo*, 159–83. Montreal: McGill-Queen's University Press.

Frascati-Lochhead, Marta (1998). *Kenosis and Feminist Theology: The Challenge of Gianni Vattimo*. Albany: State University of New York Press.

Giorgio, Giovanni (2006). *Il pensiero di Gianni Vattimo. L'emancipazione della metafisica tra dialettica ed ermeneutica*. Rome: Franco Angeli.

Giorgio, Giovanni (2009). 'La portata politica del "pensiero debole" di Gianni Vattimo', *Trópos* 2(1): 113–25.

Gnoli, Antonio (2021). 'La debole forza di essere stati', introduction to Gianni Vattimo, *Scritti filosofici e politici*, 11–32. Milan: La Nave di Teseo.

Grondin, Jean (2007). 'Vattimo's Latinization of Hermeneutics: Why Did Gadamer Resist Postmodernism?', in Santiago Zabala (ed.), *Weakening Philosophy: Essays in Honour of Gianni Vattimo*, 203–16. Montreal: McGill-Queen's University Press.

Grondin, Jean (2010). 'Nihilistic or Metaphysical Consequences of Hermeneutics?', in Jeff Malpas and Santiago Zabala (eds), *Consequences of Hermeneutics*, 190–201. Evanston, IL: Northwestern University Press.

Guarino, Thomas G. (2009). *Vattimo and Theology*. London: T&T Clark.

Harris, Matthew Edward (2013). 'Gianni Vattimo (1936–)', *Internet Encyclopedia of Philosophy*, <https://www.iep.utm.edu/vattimo>. Accessed 29 August 2022.

Harris, Matthew Edward (2016). *Essays on Gianni Vattimo: Religion, Ethics, and the History of Ideas*. Cambridge: Cambridge Scholars Publishing.

Harris, Matthew Edward (2021). 'Nietzsche's "Death of God", Modernism and Postmodernism in the Twentieth Century: Insights from Altizer and Vattimo', *The Heythrop Journal* 62(1): 53–64.

Irrgang, Ulrike (2019). *'Das Wiederauftauchen einer verwehten Spur'. Das religiöse Erbe im Werk Gianni Vattimos und Hans Magnus Enzensbergers*. Mainz: Matthias-Grünewald.

Marzano, Silvia (1999). *Lévinas, Jaspers e il pensiero della differenza. Confronti con Derrida, Vattimo, Lyotard*. Turin: Zamorani.

Mazzini, Silvia (2010). *Für eine mannigfaltige mögliche Welt: Kunst und Politik bei Ernst Bloch und Gianni Vattimo*. Frankfurt am Main: Peter Lang.

Mazzini, Silvia, and Owen Glyn-Williams (eds) (2017). *Making Communism Hermeneutical: Reading Vattimo and Zabala*. New York: Springer.

Meganck, Erik (2013). '"Nulla in mundo pax sincera . . .": Secularisation and Violence in Vattimo and Girard', *International Journal of Philosophy and Theology* 74(5): 410–31.

Migone, Paolo (ed.) (1995). *Psicoanalisi ed ermeneutica. Dibattito tra Robert R. Holt, Horst Kächele, e Gianni Vattimo*. Chieti: Métis.

Monaco, Davide (2006). *Gianni Vattimo. Ontologia ermeneutica, cristianesimo e modernità*. Pisa: ETS.

Nouzille, Philippe, and Salvatore Rindone (eds) (2018). *Ermeneutica, Cristianesimo, Politica*. Rome: Aracne.

Redaelli, Enrico (2008). *Il nodo dei nodi. L'esercizio del pensiero in Vattimo, Vitello, Sini*. Pisa: ETS.

Rorty, Richard (2008). *Un'etica per i laici*. Turin: Bollati.

Rovatti, Pier Aldo (2007). 'Weak Thought 2004: A Tribute to Gianni Vattimo', in Santiago Zabala (ed.), *Weakening Philosophy: Essays in Honour of Gianni Vattimo*, 131–45. Montreal: McGill-Queen's University Press.

Scheu, Ren (2010). *Il soggetto debole: sul pensiero di Pier Aldo Rovatti*. Milan: Mimesis.

Schönherr-Mann, Hans-Martin (1989). *Die Technik und die Schwäche: Ökologie nach Nietzsche, Heidegger und dem 'schwachen Denken'*. Vienna: Passagen.
Schürmann, Reiner (2007 [1984]). 'Deconstruction is Not Enough: On Gianni Vattimo's Call for "Weak Thinking"', in Santiago Zabala (ed.), *Weakening Philosophy: Essays in Honour of Gianni Vattimo*, 117–30. Montreal: McGill-Queen's University Press.
Sciglitano, Anthony C., Jr (2007). 'Contesting the World and the Divine: Balthasar's Trinitarian "Response" to Gianni Vattimo's Secular Christianity', *Modern Theology* 23(4): 525–59.
Sciglitano, Anthony C., Jr (2013). 'Gianni Vattimo and Saint Paul: Ontological Weakening, Kenosis, and Secularity', in Peter Frick (ed.), *Paul in the Grip of the Philosophers*, 117–41. Minneapolis, MN: Fortress Press.
Snyder, Jon R. (1988). Translator's Introduction to Gianni Vattimo, *The End of Modernity*, vi–lviii. Baltimore, MD: Johns Hopkins University Press.
Sützl, Wolfgang (2016). 'Gianni Vattimo's Media Philosophy and Its Relevance to Digital Media', *Philosophy Today* 60(3): 743–59.
Valgenti, Robert (2011). 'Vattimo's Nietzsche', in Ashley Woodward (ed.), *Interpreting Nietzsche: Reception and Influence*, 149–63. New York: Continuum.
Valgenti, Robert (ed.) (2016). Special issue of *Philosophy Today* 60(3).
Vogt, Erik M. (2010). 'Postmodernity as the Ontological Sense of Technology', in Silvia Benso and Brian Schroeder (eds), *Between Nihilism and Politics: Hermeneutics of Gianni Vattimo*, 221–39. Albany: State University of New York Press.
Weiss, Martin G. (2010). 'What's Wrong with Biotechnology? Vattimo's Interpretation of Science, Technology, and the Media', in Silvia Benso and Brian Schroeder (eds), *Between Nihilism and Politics: Hermeneutics of Gianni Vattimo*, 241–57. Albany: State University of New York Press.
Weiss, Martin G. (2012 [2003]). *Gianni Vattimo. Einführung*. With an interview with Gianni Vattimo. 3rd edn. Vienna: Passagen.
Woodward, Ashley (2010). *Nihilism in Postmodernity: Lyotard, Baudrillard, Vattimo*. Aurora, CO: Davies Group.
Woodward, Ashley (2016). 'Being and Information: On the Meaning of Vattimo', *Philosophy Today* 60(3): 723–41.
Zabala, Santiago (2007). 'Introduction: Gianni Vattimo and Weak Philosophy', in Santiago Zabala (ed.), *Weakening Philosophy: Essays in Honour of Gianni Vattimo*, 3–34. Montreal: McGill-Queen's University Press.
Zabala, Santiago (2010). 'Being is Conversation: Remains, Weak

Thought, and Hermeneutics', in Jeff Malpas and Santiago Zabala (eds), *Consequences of Hermeneutics*, 161–76. Evanston, IL: Northwestern University Press.

Zabala, Santiago (2016). 'Weakening Philosophy: A Forum on Gianni Vattimo', *Los Angeles Review of Books*, 10 November. <https://lareviewofbooks.org/feature/weakening-philosophy-forum-gianni-vattimo/>. Accessed 21 September 2022.

Zabala, Santiago (2019). 'Gianni Vattimo (1936–)', in Amy Allen and Eduardo Mendieta (eds), *The Cambridge Habermas Lexicon*, 700–1. Cambridge: Cambridge University Press.

Zawadzki, Andrzej (ed.) (2013). *Literature and Weak Thought*. Frankfurt am Main: Peter Lang.

OTHER WORKS CITED

Adorno, Theodor W. (1970). *Ästhetische Theorie*. Frankfurt am Main: Suhrkamp.

Adorno, Theodor W. (1973 [1966]). *Negative Dialektik*. Frankfurt am Main: Suhrkamp.

Allen, Amy, and Eduardo Mendieta (eds) (2021). *Decolonizing Ethics: The Critical Theory of Enrique Dussel*. University Park, PA: Penn State University Press.

Altizer, Thomas J. (1966). *The Gospel of Christian Atheism*. Philadelphia: Westminster Press.

Antiseri, Dario (1995). *Le ragioni del pensiero debole*. Rome: Borla.

Antiseri, Dario (2003). *Cristiano perché relativista, relativista perché cristiano. Per un razionalismo della contingenza*. Soveria Mannelli: Rubbettino.

Apel, Karl-Otto (1963). *Die Idee der Sprache in der Tradition des Humanismus von Dante bis Vico*. Bonn: H. Bouvier.

Apel, Karl-Otto (1973). *Transformation der Philosophie*. 2 vols. Frankfurt am Main: Suhrkamp.

Apel, Karl-Otto (1980). *Towards a Transformation of Philosophy*, trans. Glyn Adey and David Frisby. London: Routledge; Kegan Paul.

Apel, Karl-Otto (1988). *Diskurs und Verantwortung: Das Problem des Übergans zur postkonventionellen Moral*. Frankfurt am Main: Suhrkamp.

Apel, Karl-Otto (1998). *Auseindarsetzungen: In Erprobung des Transzendental-Pragmatischen Ansatzes*. Frankfurt am Main: Suhrkamp.

Apel, Karl-Otto (2017). *Transzendentale Reflexion und Geschichte*. Frankfurt am Main: Suhrkamp.

Arendt, Hannah (1958). *The Human Condition*. Chicago: University of Chicago Press.

Benjamin, Walter (1974–89a [1939]). 'Das Kunstwerk im Zeitalter seiner technischen Reproduzierbarkeit', in *Gesammelte Schriften*, ed. Rolf Tiedemann und Hermann Schweppenhäuser, vol. 1.2, 471–508. Frankfurt am Main: Suhrkamp.

Benjamin, Walter (1974–89b). 'Über den Begriff der Geschichte', in *Gesammelte Schriften*, ed. Rolf Tiedemann und Hermann Schweppenhäuser, vol. 1.2, 691–704. Frankfurt am Main: Suhrkamp.

Benjamin, Walter (2006). 'The Work of Art in the Age of Its Technological Reproducibility', in *Selected Writings*, Vol. 3: *1935–1938*, ed. Howard Eiland and Michael W. Jennings, 101–33. Cambridge, MA: Harvard University Press.

Benso, Silvia, and Brian Schroeder (eds) (2018). *Thinking the Inexhaustible: Art, Interpretation and Freedom*. Albany: State University of New York Press.

Bloch, Ernst (2000). *The Spirit of Utopia*, trans. Anthony A. Nassar. Stanford, CA: Stanford University Press.

Butler, Judith (1993). *Bodies That Matter: On the Discursive Limits of 'Sex'*. London: Routledge.

Cook, Roy T. (2009). *A Dictionary of Philosophical Logic*. Edinburgh: Edinburgh University Press.

Croce, Benedetto (1962). 'Why We Cannot Help Calling Ourselves Christian', in *My Philosophy: Essays on the Moral and Political Problems of Our Time*, trans. E. F. Carritt, 37–48. New York: Collier.

D'Agostini, Franca (2001). 'From a Continental Point of View: The Role of Logic in the Analytic-Continental Divide', *International Journal of Philosophical Studies* 9(3): 349–67.

D'Angelo, Valerio (2016). 'De la metafísica a la anarquía: El pensamiento político de Reiner Schürmann', *Logos: Anales del Seminario de Metafísica* 49: 43–69.

Danto, Arthur C. (2014). *After the End of Art: Contemporary Art and the Pale of History*. Princeton, NJ: Princeton University Press.

Deleuze, Gilles (ed.) (1966). *Cahiers de Royaumont. Nietzsche*. Paris: Minuit.

Derrida, Jacques (1978). *Writing and Difference*. London: Routledge.

Derrida, Jacques (1980). *La carte postale. De Socrate à Freud et au-delà*. Paris: Flammarion.

Derrida, Jacques (1981). *Dissemination*. Chicago: University of Chicago Press.

Derrida, Jacques (1982). *Margins of Philosophy*. Chicago: University of Chicago Press.

Derrida, Jacques (1987a). *Psyché. Inventions de l'autre*. Paris: Galilée.

Derrida, Jacques (1987b). *The Post Card: From Socrates to Freud and Beyond*, trans. Alan Bass. Chicago: University of Chicago Press.
Derrida, Jacques (2007). *Psyche: Inventions of the Other*, ed. Peggy Kamuf and Elizabeth G. Rottenberg. Vol. 1. Stanford, CA: Stanford University Press.
Derrida, Jacques (2016 [1967]). *Of Grammatology*. Baltimore, MD: Johns Hopkins University Press.
Dilthey, Wilhelm (1981). *Der Aufbau der geschichtlichen Welt in den Geisteswissenschaften*. Frankfurt am Main: Suhrkamp.
Dilthey, Wilhelm (1989 [1883]). *Introduction to the Human Sciences*, ed. Rudolf A. Makkreel and Frithjof Rodi. Princeton, NJ: Princeton University Press.
Dilthey, Wilhelm (1996). *Hermeneutics and the Study of History*, ed. Rudolf A. Makkreel and Frithjof Rodi. Princeton, NJ: Princeton University Press.
Douzinas, Costas, and Slavoj Žižek (eds) (2010). *The Idea of Communism*. New York: Verso.
Dussel, Enrique (1970–72). *Para una ética de la liberación latinoamericana*. Vols. 1–2. Buenos Aires: Siglo XXI.
Dussel, Enrique (1973). *Para una ética de la liberación latinoamericana*. Vol. 3. México: Edicol.
Dussel, Enrique (1985). *Philosophy of Liberation*, trans. Aquila Martinzes and Christine Morkovsky. Maryknoll, NY: Orbis Books.
Dussel, Enrique (1988). *Ethics and Community*, trans. Robert R. Barr. Maryknoll, NY: Orbis Books.
Dussel, Enrique (1995). *The Invention of the Americas: Eclipse of 'the Other' and the Myth of Modernity*, trans. Michael Barber. New York: Continuum.
Dussel, Enrique (1996). *The Underside of Modernity: Apel, Rorty, Taylor, and the Philosophy of Liberation*, trans. Eduardo Mendieta. Atlantic Highlands, NJ: Humanities Press.
Dussel, Enrique (1999). *Postmodernidad y transmodernidad: Diálogos con la filosofía de Gianni Vattimo*. México: Universidad Iberoamericana, Golfo Centro, Instituto Tecnológico y Estudios Superiores de Occidente, Universidad Iberoamericana, Plantel Laguna.
Dussel, Enrique (2011). *Politics of Liberation: A Critical World History*, trans. Thia Cooper. London: SCM.
Dussel, Enrique (2013). *Ethics of Liberation: In the Age of Globalization and Exclusion*, trans. Eduardo Mendieta et al. Durham, NC: Duke University Press.
Dussel, Enrique (2015). *Filosofías del Sur. Descolonización y Transmodernidad*. México: Akal, 2015.

Eco, Umberto (1994 [1990]). *The Limits of Interpretation*. Bloomington: Indiana University Press.
Eco, Umberto (2007). 'Weak Thought and the Limits of Interpretation', in Santiago Zabala (ed.), *Weakening Philosophy: Essays in Honour of Gianni Vattimo*, 37–56. Montreal: McGill-Queen's University Press.
Eco, Umberto (2012). 'Cari filosofi è l'ora del Realismo Negativo', *La Repubblica*, 11 March.
Eco, Umberto (2013 [1983]). 'Antiporphyry', in *WT*, 75–99.
Felski, Rita (2015). *The Limits of Critique*. Chicago: University of Chicago Press.
Feyerabend, Paul (1975). *Against Method*. London: Verso.
Fornari, Giuseppe (2013). *A God Torn to Pieces: The Nietzsche Case*. East Lansing: Michigan State University Press.
Gadamer, Hans-Georg (1989). *Truth and Method*. London: Sheed and Ward.
Gadamer, Hans-Georg (2006 [2004]). *Truth and Method*, trans. Joel Weinsheimer and Donald G. Marshall. New York: Continuum.
George, Theodore (2020). 'Hermeneutic Responsibility: Vattimo, Gadamer, and the Impetus of Interpretive Engagement', *Duquesne Studies in Phenomenology* 1(1), <https://dsc.duq.edu/dsp/vol1/iss1/4>. Accessed 29 August 2022.
Ginev, Dimitri (2016). 'Hermeneutic Communism and/or Hermeneutic Anarchism', *Philosophy Today* 60(3): 663–85.
Girard, René (1977). *Violence and the Sacred*. Baltimore, MD: Johns Hopkins University Press.
Girard, René (1984). 'Dionysus versus the Crucified', *Modern Language Notes* 99(4): 816–18.
Glanzberg, Michael (ed.) (2018). *The Oxford Handbook of Truth*. Oxford: Oxford University Press.
Goldman, Tali (2010). 'Sus líderes están del lado de los pobres', *El Argentino*, 8 July, <https://giannivattimo.blogspot.com/2010/07/sus-lideres-estan-del-lado-de-los.html>. Accessed 29 August 2022.
Greisch, Jean (1998). 'Ethics and Ontology: Some "Hypocritical" Considerations', trans. Leonard Lawler, *Graduate Faculty Philosophy Journal* 20: 41–69.
Habermas, Jürgen (1984–87). *The Theory of Communicative Action*, trans. Thomas McCarthy. 2 vols. Boston: Beacon Press.
Habermas, Jürgen (1989). *The Structural Transformation of the Public Sphere: An Inquiry into a Category of Bourgeois Society*, trans. T. Burger. Cambridge, MA: MIT Press.
Habermas, Jürgen (1990a). *Moral Consciousness and Communicative Action*,

trans. C. Lenhardt and S. Weber Nicholsen. Cambridge, MA: MIT Press.
Habermas, Jürgen (1990b). *The Philosophical Discourse of Modernity: Twelve Lectures*, trans. F. Lawrence. Cambridge, MA: MIT Press.
Habermas, Jürgen (1992). *Postmetaphysical Thinking: Philosophical Essays*, trans. William Mark Hohengarten. Cambridge, MA: MIT Press.
Habermas, Jürgen (1998). *Between Facts and Norms: Contributions to a Discourse Theory of Law and Democracy*, trans. William Rehg. Cambridge, MA: MIT Press.
Habermas, Jürgen (2019). *Auch eine Geschichte der Philosophie*. 2 vols. Frankfurt am Main: Suhrkamp.
Hegel, G. W. F. (1975). *Aesthetics: Lectures on Fine Art*, trans. T. M. Knox. 2 vols. Oxford: Clarendon Press.
Heidegger, Martin (1961). *Nietzsche*. 2 vols. Pfullingen: Neske.
Heidegger, Martin (1968). *What Is Called Thinking?*, trans. Fred D. Wieck and J. Glenn Gray. New York: Harper and Row.
Heidegger, Martin (1969). *Identity and Difference*, trans. Joan Stambaugh. New York: Harper and Row.
Heidegger, Martin (1972). 'The End of Philosophy and the Task of Thinking', in *On Time and Being*, trans. Joan Stambaugh, 55–73. New York: Harper and Row.
Heidegger, Martin (1976a [1946]). 'Brief über den Humanismus', in *Wegmarken*, 313–63. Vol. 9 of *Gesamtausgabe*, ed. Friedrich-Wilhelm von Herrmann. Frankfurt am Main: Klostermann.
Heidegger, Martin (1976b). 'Anmerkungen zu Karl Jaspers Psychologie der Weltanschauungen', in *Wegmarken*, 1–45. Vol. 9 of *Gesamtausgabe*, ed. Friedrich-Wilhelm von Herrmann. Frankfurt am Main: Klostermann.
Heidegger, Martin (1977). *The Question Concerning Technology and Other Essays*, trans. William Lovitt. New York: Garland.
Heidegger, Martin (1988). *Pathmarks*, ed. William McNeill. Cambridge: Cambridge University Press.
Heidegger, Martin (1990 [1957]). *Identität und Differenz*. Pfullingen: Neske.
Heidegger, Martin (1991). *The Principle of Reason*, trans. Reginald Lilly. Bloomington: Indiana University Press.
Heidegger, Martin (1999). *Contributions to Philosophy (From Enowning)*, trans. Parvis Emad and Kenneth Maly. Bloomington: Indiana University Press.
Heidegger, Martin (2001). *Being and Time*, trans. John Macquarrie and Edward Robinson. Oxford: Blackwell.
Heidegger, Martin (2002a [1943]). *The Essence of Truth: On Plato's Cave Allegory and Theaetetus*, trans. T. Sadler. New York: Continuum.

Heidegger, Martin (2002b). *Off the Beaten Track*, trans. Julian Young and Kenneth Haynes. Cambridge: Cambridge University Press.

Heidegger, Martin (2003). 'The Overcoming of Metaphysics', in *The End of Philosophy*, trans. Joan Stambaugh, 84–110. Chicago: University of Chicago Press.

Heidegger, Martin (2008). *Identity and Difference*, trans. Joan Stambaugh. Chicago: University of Chicago Press.

Heidegger, Martin (2010a). *Being and Time*, trans. Joan Stambaugh, rev. Dennis J. Schmidt. Albany: State University of New York Press.

Heidegger, Martin (2010b). *The Phenomenology of Religious Life*, trans. Matthias Fritsch and Jennifer Anna Gosetti-Ferencei. Bloomington: Indiana University Press.

Heidegger, Martin (2017). *Ponderings VII–XI: Black Notebooks 1938–1939*, trans. Richard Rojcewicz. Bloomington: Indiana University Press.

Horkheimer, Max, and Theodor W. Adorno (1969 [1947]). *Dialektik der Aufklärung*. Frankfurt am Main: Fischer.

Horkheimer, Max, and Theodor W. Adorno (2002). *Dialectic of Enlightenment*, trans. Edmund Jephcott. Stanford: Stanford University Press.

Husserl, Edmund (1989). *The Crisis of European Sciences and Transcendental Phenomenology: An Introduction to Phenomenological Philosophy*. Evanston, IL: Northwestern University Press.

Hutcheon, Linda (1988). *A Poetics of Postmodernism: History, Theory, Fiction*. London: Routledge.

Jameson, Fredric (1984). 'Postmodernism, or the Cultural Logic of Late Capitalism', *New Left Review* 1(146): 53–92.

Kant, Immanuel (1911 [1790]). *Critique of Judgement*. Vol. 1. Oxford: Clarendon Press.

Laclau, Ernesto (2005). *On Populist Reason*. London: Verso.

Laclau, Ernesto, and Chantal Mouffe (1985). *Hegemony and Socialist Strategy*. London: Verso.

López San Miguel, Mercedes (2009). 'El peor populismo que conozco es el de Berlusconi', *Pagina 12*, 28 September, <http://www.pagina12.com.ar/imprimir/diario/dialogos/21-132526-2009-09-28.html>. Accessed 29 August 2022.

Lukács, György (1923). *Geschichte und Klassenbewusstsein. Studien über marxistische Dialektik*. Berlin: Der Malik.

Lukács, György (1954). *Die Zerstörung der Vernunft*. Berlin: Aufbau.

Lyotard, Jean-François (1979). *The Postmodern Condition: A Report on Knowledge*. Minneapolis: University of Minnesota Press.

Mason, Emma (2017). 'Critical Vulnerability and the Weakness of Poetry',

Centre for Philosophy and Critical Thought, 18 March, <www.cpct.uk/2017/05/08/emma-mason-warwick-critical-vulnerability-and-the-weakness-of-poetry-neurosis-poetry-and-the-present-18-march-2017>. Accessed 29 August 2022.

Mendieta, Eduardo (2003). *The Adventures of Transcendental Philosophy: Karl-Otto Apel's Semiotics and Discourse Ethics*. Lanham, MD: Rowman and Littlefield.

Nacci, Michela (2000). *Pensare la tecnica. Un secolo di incomprensioni*. Bari: Laterza.

Nascimento, Amos (2019). 'Karl-Otto Apel (1922–2017)', in Amy Allen and Eduardo Mendieta (eds), *The Cambridge Habermas Lexicon*, 479–82. Cambridge: Cambridge University Press.

Nietzsche, Friedrich (1968). *The Will to Power*, trans. Walter Kaufmann and R. J. Hollingdale. New York: Vintage.

Nietzsche, Friedrich (1974). *Nachgelassene Fragmente. Herbst 1885–Herbst 1887*. Berlin: de Gruyter.

Nietzsche, Friedrich (1995a). 'On the Utility and Liability of History for Life', in *Unfashionable Observations*, trans. Richard T. Gray, 83–168. Stanford, CA: Stanford University Press.

Nietzsche, Friedrich (1995b). *Thus Spoke Zarathustra: A Book for All and None*, trans. Walter Kaufmann. New York: Modern Library.

Nietzsche, Friedrich (2003). *Twilight of the Idols and the Anti-Christ*, trans. R. J. Hollingdale. New York: Penguin.

Nietzsche, Friedrich (2005). *The Anti-Christ, Ecce Homo, Twilight of the Idols and Other Writings*, ed. Aaron Ridley and Judith Norman, trans. Judith Norman. Cambridge: Cambridge University Press.

Pareyson, Luigi (1960 [1954]). *Estetica. Teoria della formatività*. Bologna: Zanichelli.

Pareyson, Luigi (1988). *Estetica: Teoria della formatività*. Milan: Bompiani.

Pareyson, Luigi (2009). *Existence, Interpretation, Freedom*, trans. Anna Mattei. Aurora, CO: Davies Group.

Pareyson, Luigi (2013). *Truth and Interpretation*, trans. Robert T. Valgenti. Albany: State University of New York Press.

Polt, Richard (2006). *The Emergency of Being*. Ithaca, NY: Cornell University Press.

Popper, Karl (1959). *The Logic of Scientific Discovery*. London: Routledge.

Quine, W. V. (1981). 'Responses', in *Theories and Things*, 173–86. Cambridge, MA: Harvard University Press.

Ricoeur, Paul (1967). *The Symbolism of Evil*. New York: Harper and Row.

Ricoeur, Paul (1974). *The Conflict of Interpretations: Essays in Hermeneutics*. Evanston, IL: Northwestern University Press.

Ricoeur, Paul (1984–88). *Time and Narrative*. Chicago: University of Chicago Press.
Ricoeur, Paul (2004). *Memory, History, Forgetting*, trans. Kathleen Blamey and David Pellauer. Chicago: University of Chicago Press.
Rorty, Richard (1979). *Philosophy and the Mirror of Nature*. Princeton, NJ: Princeton University Press.
Rorty, Richard (1999). 'Religion as Conversation-Stopper', in *Philosophy and Social Hope*, 168–74. New York: Penguin.
Rorty, Richard (2003). 'Anti-Clericalism and Atheism', in Mark A. Wrathall (ed.), *Religion after Metaphysics*, 37–45. Cambridge: Cambridge University Press.
Rorty, Richard (2007). 'Heideggerianism and Leftist Politics', in Santiago Zabala (ed.), *Weakening Philosophy: Essays in Honour of Gianni Vattimo*, 149–58. Montreal: McGill-Queen's University Press.
Rorty, Richard (2010). *An Ethics for Today: Finding Common Ground Between Philosophy and Religion*. New York: Columbia University Press.
Saint-Amour, Paul K. (2018). 'Weak Theory, Weak Modernism', *Modernism/Modernity* 25(3): 437–59.
Schürmann, Reiner (1978). *Meister Eckhart: Mystic and Philosopher*. Bloomington: Indiana University Press.
Schürmann, Reiner (1987). *Heidegger on Being and Acting: From Principles to Anarchy*, trans. Christine-Marie Gros. Bloomington: Indiana University Press.
Schürmann, Reiner (2003). *Broken Hegemonies*, trans. Reginald Lilly. Bloomington: Indiana University Press.
Silverman, Hugh (2001). 'Le postmodernisme comme modernité "fin de siècle" (ou: Le postmodernisme aux fins de l'"in-différence")', *Revue de métaphysique et de morale* 4(32): 483–94, <https://www.cairn.info/re vue-de-metaphysique-et-de-morale-2001-4-page-483.htm>. Accessed 29 August 2022.
Viano, Carlo A. (1985). *Va' Pensiero. Il carattere della filosofia italiana contemporanea*. Turin: Einaudi.
Weinrich, Harald (1999). *Léthé. Art. Et critique de l'oubli*, trans. Diane Meur. Paris: Fayard.
White, Hayden (1991). 'Vattimo's "Weak" Thought and Vico's "New" Science', *New Vico Studies* 9: 61–8.
Woessner, Martin (2017). 'Beyond Realism: Coetzee's Post-Secular Imagination', in Patrick Hayes and Jan Wilm (eds), *Beyond the Ancient Quarrel: Literature, Philosophy, and J. M. Coetzee*, 143–59. Oxford: Oxford University Press.

Zabala, Santiago (2009). *The Remains of Being: Hermeneutic Ontology after Metaphysics*. New York: Columbia University Press.
Zabala, Santiago (ed.) (2015). Special issue of *Philosophy Today* 59(4).
Zabala, Santiago (2017). *Why Only Art Can Save Us: Aesthetics and the Absence of Emergency*. New York: Columbia University Press.

Notes on Contributors

Daniela Angelucci is Associate Professor of Aesthetics and co-director of the postgraduate course Environmental Humanities in the Department of Philosophy and Architecture at University Roma Tre. She is vice-president of the Italian society of aesthetics. She is co-director of the series *Voci fuori campo* (Mimesis), a member of the scientific board of the series *Estetica e critica* (Quodlibet) and a member of scientific committee of the journal *La Deleuziana*. She has participated in numerous national and international conferences. Recent books include *Filosofia del cinema* (Carocci, 2013) and *Deleuze and the Concepts of Cinema* (Edinburgh University Press, 2014). She is the editor of *Philosophical Essays on Nespolo's Art and Cinema* (with D. Dal Sasso, Cambridge Scholars Publishing, 2018), 'Deleuze in Italy: Introduction', in *Deleuze and Guattari Studies* (Edinburgh University Press, 2019) and *Estetica, arte e vita* (with S. Oliva, Mimesis, XLVIII, IV, N. 18, 3/2020).

Pierpaolo Antonello is Professor of Modern Italian Literature and Culture at the University of Cambridge, and Fellow of St John's College. He has published widely on various topics including literature, philosophy, film and visual art. With João Cezar de Castro Rocha he published a long interview with René Girard: *Evolution and Conversion: Dialogues on the Origins of Culture* (Continuum, 2008), translated into nine languages. He also edited Gianni Vattimo and René Girard, *Christianity, Truth, and Weakening Faith. A Dialogue* (Columbia University Press, 2010). He is the co-editor of the series *Italian Modernities* for Peter Lang.

Seraphine Appel works in aesthetics and decolonial theory. She is a Research Fellow at University College London and is finishing her PhD in philosophy at Pompeu Fabra University, Barcelona, directed by Santiago Zabala at the Center for Vattimo's Philosophy and Archives. Her current research considers temporality and historicity through settler colonial topologies.

Francisco Arenas-Dolz is Associate Professor of Moral Philosophy at the University of Valencia. Visiting research fellow at several European, US and Latin American universities, he has done research at the Albert Ludwigs University Freiburg as fellow of the Alexander von Humboldt

Foundation. He has published numerous articles and book chapters on ethics, hermeneutics and politics. He is the author, with Mauricio Beuchot, of *Hermenéutica de la encrucijada* (Anthropos, 2008), and the editor of *Retórica y democracia* (Valencia, 2012). With Luca Giancristofaro and Paolo Stellino, he has edited *Nietzsche y la hermenéutica* (Nau Libres, 2007). His current research focuses on Nietzsche's lectures.

Stefano G. Azzarà teaches the history of political philosophy and contemporary philosophy at the University of Urbino, where he coordinates the course of study in educational sciences. He is the secretary to the presidency of the Internationale Gesellschaft Hegel-Marx and directs the scientific magazine *Materialismo Storico*. His work focuses on the comparison of the great philosophical and political traditions of the last two centuries: conservatism, liberalism, Marxism. He has published numerous articles in Italian and international journals. Among his most recent books are *Democrazia cercasi* (Hoepli, 2014), *Friedrich Nietzsche dal radicalismo aristocratico alla rivoluzione conservatrice* (Castelvecchi, 2014), *Nonostante Laclau* (Mimesis/Eterotopie, 2017), *Comunisti, fascisti e questione nazionale* (Mimesis/Eterotopie, 2018), *La comune umanità* (La scuola di Pitagora, 2019) and *Il virus dell'Occidente* (Mimesis/Eterotopie, 2020).

Cristina Basili is Lecturer in Contemporary Philosophy in the Department of Philosophy and Society at the Complutense University of Madrid. Previously, she was 'Juan de la Cierva' Postdoctoral Fellow at the Complutense University of Madrid and DAAD Postdoctoral Fellow at the Institute for Philosophy at Bonn University. She received her PhD in political philosophy from the University Carlos III of Madrid (2016) with a dissertation entitled 'La caverna della modernità. Filosofia e politica nel Platone di Leo Strauss' (Outstanding Thesis Award for Humanities UC3M). Her research focuses on the problem of power in twentieth-century thought. She is the author of several essays on the work of Simone Weil, Hannah Arendt and Leo Strauss, on the contemporary reception of classical political thought and on political mysticism in contemporary philosophy.

Alessandro Bertinetto is Full Professor of Aesthetics at the University of Turin. He has been Alexander von Humboldt Fellow at the FU Berlin and member of the executive committee of the European Society for Aesthetics. Research interests: aesthetics, hermeneutics, philosophy of music, image theory, improvisation, German Idealism. His recent books include *Il pensiero dei suoni* (Bruno Mondadori, 2012), *Eseguire l'inatteso.*

Ontologia musicale e improvvisazione (Il Glifo, 2016), *The Routledge Handbook of Philosophy and Improvisation in the Arts* (ed. with M. Ruta, Routledge, 2021) and *Aesthetics of Improvisation* (Brill, 2022). He is coordinator of ART – Aesthetics Research Torino: www.art.unito.it

Paolo Diego Bubbio is Associate Professor of Philosophy at Western Sydney University. His research is in post-Kantian philosophy, hermeneutics, Girard's mimetic theory and their intersections. He is the author of *Sacrifice in the Post-Kantian Tradition: Perspectivism, Intersubjectivity, and Recognition* (SUNY Press, 2014), *God and the Self in Hegel: Beyond Subjectivism* (SUNY Press, 2017), *Intellectual Sacrifice and Other Mimetic Paradoxes* (Michigan State University Press, 2018), and the editor of Luigi Pareyson, *Existence, Interpretation, Freedom: Selected Writings* (Davies Group, 2009). He co-edited (with Piero Coda) a collection of essays on Pareyson's thought, *L'Esistenza e il Logos: Filosofia, Esperienza Religiosa, Rivelazione* (Città Nuova, 2007).

Jaume Casals is Full Professor of Philosophy and former president of Pompeu Fabra University in Barcelona. He is the author of books, articles, chapters in edited collections and editions of works by eminent classical, modern and contemporary philosophers. He has translated and edited works by Montaigne, Montesquieu, Berkeley and Bergson, among others. His most recent book is *¿Qué sé yo?: La filosofía de Michel de Montaigne* (Arpa, 2018).

Gaetano Chiurazzi is Professor of Philosophy at the University of Turin and Director of Project at the Collège International de Philosophie (Paris). He studied and worked as a research fellow in the universities of Turin, Berlin, Heidelberg, Paris, Oxford and Warsaw. His interests are especially directed to philosophical hermeneutics, ontology, metaphysics, theory of judgement, philosophy of translation, with a particular focus on ancient Greek philosophy, classic German philosophy and contemporary French philosophy. He is the author of many publications in several languages and his books have been translated into English, French, German, Spanish, Portuguese and Serbian. With Gianni Vattimo he is the co-editor of *Tropos. Rivista di ermeneutica e critica filosofica*.

Felice Cimatti is Full Professor of Philosophy of Language at the University of Calabria, Italy. His latest publications are *Unbecoming Human: Philosophy of Animality After Deleuze* (Edinburgh University Press, 2020) and, as co-editor with Carlo Salzani, *Animality in Contemporary Italian Philosophy* (Palgrave Macmillan, 2021).

NOTES ON CONTRIBUTORS

Clayton Crockett is Professor and Director of Religious Studies at the University of Central Arkansas. He is also a Distinguished Research Fellow of the Global Center for Advanced Studies. He is the author or editor of a number of books, most recently *Derrida after the End of Writing: Political Theology and New Materialism* (Fordham University Press, 2017) and *Energy and Change: A New Materialist Cosmotheology* (Columbia University Press, 2022). He is also a co-editor of the book series *Insurrections: Critical Studies in Religion, Politics, and Culture* for Columbia University Press.

Franca D'Agostini is an Italian philosopher. She is best known for her work on overcoming the divide between analytic and continental philosophy in her book *Analitici e continentali* (Raffaello Cortina Editore, 1997), and her engagement in public philosophy in defence of a dialectical conception of truth (*Verità avvelenata*, Bollati Boringhieri, 2010). She studied philosophy at the University of Turin (BA, MA and PhD) and has taught logic and philosophy of science at the University of Turin (Politecnico) and at the University of Milan. Her areas of specialisation are philosophical logic, metaphysics, meta-philosophy and the history of twentieth-century philosophy. Her main topics are truth, paradoxes, nihilism and meta-metaphysics. She is the author of sixteen books, some of which have been translated into various languages. Among her books are *Disavventure della verità* (Einaudi, 2002), *Nihilism and the Nature of Philosophical Concepts* (Davies Group, 2008) and *Paradossi* (Carocci, 2009). Recently, she published (with Maurizio Ferrera) *La verità al potere* (Einaudi, 2019).

Jakob Helmut Deibl wrote his dissertation on Catholic theology in Gianni Vattimo: *Menschwerdung und Schwächung. Annäherung an ein Gespräch mit Gianni Vattimo*, published with an introduction written by Vattimo (V&R Unipress, 2013). From 2012 to 2019 he was a guest lecturer at the Pontificio Istituto Sant'Anselmo in Rome. Since 2019 he has held the position as Assistant Professor for Religion and Aesthetics at the Faculty of Catholic Theology at the University of Vienna. He is a member of the research centre 'Religion and Transformation in Contemporary Society' and co-editor of the open access *Interdisciplinary Journal for Religion and Transformation in Contemporary Society* (*JRAT*).

Frederiek Depoortere is a part-time assistant professor at the Faculty of Theology and Religious Studies, KU Leuven, Belgium, where he is a member of the Research Unit of Pastoral and Empirical Theology. He mainly teaches courses on religion, meaning and world views at different campuses of KU Leuven (in particular to students studying science and engineering technology) and catechetics in his own faculty.

Carmelo Dotolo is Professor of Theology of Religion at the Pontifical Urbaniana University of Rome and visiting professor at the Pontifical Gregoriana University, University of Urbino and University of Zara (Croatia). He is the author of *The Christian Revelation* (Davies Group, 2006), *Teologia e postcristianesimo* (Queriniana, 2017), *Dio, sorpresa per la storia* (Queriniana, 2020) and *Teologia delle religioni* (EDB, 2021).

William Egginton is the Decker Professor in the Humanities and director of the Alexander Grass Humanities Institute of Johns Hopkins University. He is the author of multiple books, including *How the World Became a Stage* (SUNY Press, 2003), *Perversity and Ethics* (Stanford University Press, 2006), *A Wrinkle in History* (Davies Group, 2007), *The Philosopher's Desire* (Stanford University Press, 2007), *The Theater of Truth* (Stanford University Press, 2010), *In Defense of Religious Moderation* (Columbia University Press, 2011), *The Man Who Invented Fiction: How Cervantes Ushered in the Modern World* (Bloomsbury, 2016), *Medialogies: Reading Reality in the Age of Inflationary Media* (Bloomsbury, 2017), *The Splintering of the American Mind* (Bloomsbury, 2018) and *What Would Cervantes Do? Navigating Post-Truth With Spanish Baroque Literature* (McGill-Queen's University Press, 2022). His current book project, *The Rigor of Angels*, which explores the respective conceptions of reality in the thought of Borges, Kant and Heisenberg, will be published by Pantheon in 2023. He is also writing a book for Bloomsbury's Philosophical Filmmakers series on the philosophical, psychoanalytic and surrealist dimensions of cinematic expression in the work of Chilean director Alejandro Jodorowsky.

Elena Ficara studied theoretical philosophy at the University of Turin under Gianni Vattimo, wrote her PhD dissertation at the University of Cologne and the *Habilitationsschrift* at the University of Paderborn, where she is now assistant professor. In 2018–19 she was Alexander von Humboldt fellow at the Graduate Center of the City University of New York. Her publications include *Die Ontologie in der 'Kritik der reinen Vernunft'* (Königshausen & Neumann, 2006), *Heidegger e il problema della metafisica* (Casini, 2010), *Contradictions. Logic, History, Actuality* (editor, De Gruyter, 2014) and *The Form of Truth. Hegel's Philosophical Logic* (De Gruyter, 2021).

Claudio Gallo is a journalist, currently working on the Italian newspaper *La Stampa*'s culture desk. He was formerly foreign desk editor and

London correspondent. Among his main cultural curiosities are Western and Asian philosophies. He writes for several online magazines. His main interest is Middle Eastern politics, focusing on the Shiite world: Syria, Lebanon, Iraq and Iran. He likes to interview the last few thinkers who provide alternatives to prevailing ways of thinking.

Daniel Gamper lectures in political philosophy at the Universitat Autònoma de Barcelona and is visiting professor in the Università Suor Orsola Benincasa of Naples. His research focuses on the liberal and democratic tradition with emphasis in religious diversity and freedom of conscience. He has translated into Spanish and Catalan books by Nietzsche, Scheler, Habermas, Tugendhat and Croce, among others. He is the author of *Laicidad europea. Apuntes de filosofía política postsecular* (Bellaterra, 2016) and *Las mejores palabras. De la libre expresión* (Anagrama, 2019). He writes op-eds for the Catalan newspaper *Ara*.

Giovanni Giorgio was Professor of Theoretical Philosophy at the Pontifical Lateran University of Rome and at the Theological Institute of Chieti. For several years he was director of the scientific journals *Ricerche Teologiche* in Rome, and *Prospettiva Persona* in Teramo. In addition to books, articles and contributions on hermeneutics, anthropology and ethics in journals and collective works, he has published *Il pensiero di Gianni Vattimo* (Angeli, 2006) and is the editor of Gianni Vattimo and Carmelo Dotolo, *Dio: la possibilità buona. Un colloquio sulla soglia tra filosofia e teologia* (Rubbettino, 2009). For more information, see <www.giorgiogiovanni.it>.

Mike Grimshaw is Associate Professor in Sociology at the University of Canterbury, New Zealand. He works at the intersections of continental thought, social and cultural theory, intellectual history and radical theology. He is co-editor of *Continental Thought and Theory* (<http://ctt.canterbury.ac.nz/>) and founding editor of *Radial Theologies and Philosophies* (Palgrave Macmillan). He has published many articles on various topics, edited books including the letters of philosopher Arthur Prior (Canterbury University Press, 2018) and *This Silence Must Now Speak. Letters of Thomas J.J. Altizer 1995–2015* (Palgrave Macmillan, 2016), and has also written some, including *Bishops, Boozers, Brethren & Burkas. A Cartoon History of Religion in New Zealand* (NZ Cartoon Archive, 2019) and *Bibles and Baedekers: Tourism, Travel, Exile and God* (Routledge, 2008).

Jean Grondin is a professor of philosophy at the Université de Montréal. The author of influential books in the fields of hermeneutics and metaphysics, he was a pupil and close collaborator of Hans-Georg Gadamer, of whom he wrote a landmark biography, *Hans-Georg Gadamer: A Biography* (Yale University Press, 2003). His other books include *Introduction to Philosophical Hermeneutics* (Yale University Press, 1994), *Introduction to Metaphysics* (Columbia University Press, 2004), *Du sens des choses. L'idée de la métaphysique* (PUF, 2013) and *Comprendre Heidegger. L'espoir d'une autre compréhension de l'être* (Hermann, 2019).

Thomas G. Guarino is Professor of Systematic Theology at Seton Hall University in New Jersey. He is the author of *Vattimo and Theology* (T&T Clark, 2009) and, most recently, *The Disputed Teachings of Vatican II* (Eerdmans, 2018). He is also the author of 'The Return of Religion in Europe? The Postmodern Christianity of Gianni Vattimo', *Logos* 14 (2011). In 2002 he was named a fellow of the Center of Theological Inquiry in Princeton, NJ. He has been awarded numerous research grants by the Association of Theological Schools and has been four times named 'researcher of the year' by Seton Hall University.

Giuseppe Iannantuono studied with Gianni Vattimo. He holds a doctorate in rhetoric with a thesis on 'The Lie in Discourse: A Contribution to the Theory of the Society of Communication as Rhetoric of Passions'. He currently teaches philosophy and morals at the European School in Brussels. He has published several essays and books, including *Il discorso e la società. La retorica nel pensiero del Novecento* (Paravia, 1999), *Identità e differenze* (Regione Piemonte, 2000), *Linguaggi e temi della destra in Europa* (Editori Riuniti, 2002), *Politica e cultura. L'età dell'informazione* (Trauben, 2002), *L'Europa a Sud* (Trauben, 2003), *Appunti sull'Europa* (Trauben, 2004), *L'Europa e la politica del Vicinato* (Trauben, 2004), Gianni Vattimo, *Il socialismo ossia l'Europa* (ed. with Mario Cedrini, Trauben, 2004), *Visibilità del potere e la retorica della menzogna. Un'indagine sul sistema d'informazione dei mass-media* (Milan, 2006), *Il lavoro perduto e ritrovato* (ed. with Gianni Vattimo and Davide de Palma, Mimesis, 2012), Gianni Vattimo, *Being and Its Surroundings* (ed. with Alberto Martinengo and Santiago Zabala, McGill-Queen's University Press, 2021) and *Mafie e Pandemia* (collaboration, Guida Editori, 2020).

Daniel Innerarity is a professor of political philosophy, 'Ikerbasque' researcher at the University of the Basque Country, and part-time professor at the European University Institute of Florence (School of Transnational Governance). He is a former fellow of the Alexander von Humboldt Foundation at the University of Munich, visiting professor at the University of Paris 1-Sorbonne and visiting fellow at the London

School of Economics and Georgetown University. His recent books include *Democracy in Europe* (Palgrave Macmillan, 2018), *Politics in the Times of Indignation* (Bloomsbury, 2019), *A Theory of Complex Democracy* (forthcoming, Bloomsbury, 2022) and *La Sociedad del Desconocimiento* (Galaxia Gutenberg, 2022).

Alberto Martinengo is Assistant Professor of Aesthetics at the University of Turin. He has published essays in German, English, French and Spanish on different aspects of the hermeneutical tradition. His most recent research deals with the philosophy of image and its political relevance. He is the author of a book on Paul Ricoeur (*Il pensiero incompiuto*, Aliberti, 2008), a volume on Martin Heidegger and Reiner Schürmann (*Un pensiero anarchico*, Meltemi, 2021) and two books on metaphor and image (*Filosofie della metafora*, Guerini Scientifica, 2016; *Prospettive sull'ermeneutica dell'immagine*, Quodlibet, 2021).

Silvia Marzano has been Professor of Philosophical Hermeneutics at the University of Turin. She is the author of *Aspetti Kantiani del pensiero di Jaspers* (Mursia, 1974), *Il sublime nell'ermeneutica di Luigi Pareyson* (Rosenberg & Sellier, 1994), *Jaspers, Lévinas e il pensiero della differenza. Confronti con Derrida, Vattimo e Lyotard* (Zamorani, 1998) and *L'eredità di Kant e la linea ebraica (essays 1979–2010)* (Mimesis, 2014). She is a contributor to *Annuario filosofico* (recent articles: 'Lévinas in dialogo con Jaspers, Kant e Nietzsche', 2015; 'Confronti fra Pareyson e Jaspers su verità ed esperienza religiosa', 2018, 2019; 'Jaspers e Novalis', 2020; 'Qualche considerazione su *L'Inouï* di François Jullien', 2021).

Silvia Mazzini is Assistant Professor of Philosophy and Art Theory at the Institute for Doctoral Studies in the Visual Arts (IDSVA). She has published on art and politics in Vattimo, Bloch and Pasolini, on tragic and comic thought and on community theatre; currently, she is writing on the philosophy of poverty. Before joining IDSVA, she was a research fellow at the Berlin Institute for Cultural Inquiry, and assistant professor at the Humboldt University and the Berlin University of the Arts. She taught the history of late modern philosophy at the University of Groningen (NL). Among her publications are *Für eine mannigfaltige mögliche Welt. Kunst und Politik bei Ernst Bloch und Gianni Vattimo* (Peter Lang, 2010) and, as co-editor, *Making Communism Hermeneutical: on Vattimo and Zabala* (Springer, 2017).

Eduardo Mendieta is professor of philosophy, affiliated faculty at the School of International Affairs, and the Bioethics Program at Penn State

University. He is the author of *The Adventures of Transcendental Philosophy* (Rowman and Littlefield, 2002) and *Global Fragments: Globalizations, Latinamericanisms, and Critical Theory* (SUNY Press, 2007). He is also co-editor with Craig Calhoun and Jonathan VanAntwerpen of *Habermas and Religion* (Polity, 2013) and, with Amy Allen, of *From Alienation to Forms of Life: The Critical Theory of Rahel Jaeggi* (Penn State University Press, 2018), *The Cambridge Habermas Lexicon* (Cambridge University Press, 2019) and *Justification and Emancipation: The Critical Theory of Rainer Forst* (Penn State University Press, 2019). He was the 2017 recipient of the Frantz Fanon Outstanding Achievements Award.

Ana Messuti obtained her PhD in law from the University of Salamanca, has taught in several universities, and is a member of a group of lawyers working on behalf of victims of Franco's regime. She is the author of *Time as Punishment* (Davies Group, 2008), *La justicia deconstruida* (Bellaterra, 2017), *Derecho como memoria y justicia* (Postmetropolis, 2020), and many articles in international journals.

Davide Monaco is currently assistant professor at the University of Salerno (Italy), where he teaches philosophical hermeneutics. He has achieved the National Scientific Qualification both in theoretical philosophy and in the history of philosophy. He was formerly Alexander von Humboldt Research Fellow at the University of Münster, Germany. He was awarded the Helena Klotz-Makowiecki Prize for his scientific research on Cusanus. His main publications are *Gianni Vattimo. Ontologia ermeneutica, cristianesimo e postmodernità* (ETS, 2006); *Deus Trinitas. Dio come non altro nel pensiero di Nicolò Cusano* (Città Nuova, 2010), *Cusano e la pace della fede* (Città Nuova, 2013), *Nicholas of Cusa* (Aschendorff, 2016) and *Religione e filosofia secondo Leo Strauss* (UUP, 2018).

Francesca Monateri is a PhD candidate at the Scuola Normale Superiore of Pisa, working on the link between aesthetics and political philosophy. Her doctoral project – dedicated to Carl Schmitt's aesthetics – is situated along these lines. She is on the editorial staff of the *Almanacco di Filosofia Politica* and of *Itinera*. She has published with Edinburgh University Press, De Gruyter and Springer, as well in various journals such as *Filosofia politica*, *Studi di Estetica* and *Annuario filosofico*. Her publications include *Katechon. Filosofia, politica, estetica* (Bollati Boringhieri, 2023) and 'Messianesimo e Teologia Politica. Il katechon tra Taubes e Schmitt', *Trópos* XII (2019), 'Teologia politica del corpo. Un'estetica dell'incarnazione in Schmitt, Kantorowicz e Balthasar', *Annuario filosofico* XXXVI (2020) and 'Estetica e istituzioni.

Forma e vita nell'Institutional Turn di Carl Schmitt', *Studi di Estetica* III (2020).

Ian Alexander Moore is Assistant Professor of Philosophy at Loyola Marymount University and a faculty member at St John's College. He is the author of *Dialogue on the Threshold: Heidegger and Trakl* (SUNY Press, 2022) and *Eckhart, Heidegger, and the Imperative of Releasement* (SUNY Press, 2019); editor of Reiner Schürmann's *Neo-Aristotelianism and the Medieval Renaissance* (Diaphanes, 2020); co-editor of Jean Wahl's *Transcendence and the Concrete* (Fordham University Press, 2017); and translator of texts by Fichte, Gadamer, Heidegger and Levinas, among others.

Simonetta Moro is Professor of Art, Philosophy and Visual Studies, Director and Vice-President for Academic Affairs at the Institute for Doctoral Studies in the Visual Arts (IDSVA). She is a visual artist and a published author whose work focuses on cartographic practices and their theoretical examinations. Her work has been exhibited internationally. Her publications include 'Mapping as Aesthetic Practice: Toward a Theory of Carto-Aesthetics', in Gregory Blair and Noah Bronstein (eds), *Spatial Transgressions in the Arts* (Palgrave Macmillan, 2020), 'Mapping Practices and the Cartographic Imagination', *Subjectivity* 13(4) (2020) and *Mapping Paradigms in Modern and Contemporary Art: Poetic Cartography* (Routledge, 2021).

Ivelise Perniola is Associate Professor of Film Studies at the University of Roma Tre. She is the author of *Chris Marker o del film-saggio* (Lindau, 2011 [2003]), *Oltre il neorealismo* (Bulzoni, 2004), *L'immagine spezzata. Il cinema di Claude Lanzmann* (Kaplan, 2007), *L'era postdocumentaria* (Mimesis, 2014) and *Gillo Pontecorvo o del cinema necessario* (ETS, 2016). She has published numerous essays in Italian and international journals focused on the aesthetics of cinema and on contemporary documentary cinema. She is currently working on the relationship between cinema and iconoclasm.

Libera Pisano is currently assistant researcher at Universidade Nova de Lisboa (FCT Stimulus of Scientific Employment, Individual Support). She was a research associate at the Exzellenzcluster 'Understanding Written Artefacts' at the University of Hamburg, where she has been since 2016. She received her PhD in theoretical philosophy from La Sapienza (Rome) in 2014 with a dissertation entitled *Lo spirito manifesto. Percorsi linguistici nella filosofia hegeliana* (ETS, 2016). She has been research fellow at various institutions, including the MCAS (Hamburg) and the Humboldt Universität (Berlin). She is the author of several essays on the role of language in Hegel's writings, Giambattista Vico, Leopold Zunz, Moses Mendelssohn, Gustav Landauer, contemporary German Jewish philosophy and the concept of diaspora.

Jeffrey W. Robbins is Professor of Religion and Philosophy at Lebanon Valley College, where he teaches in the Honors and the Social Justice and Civic Engagement programs. He is chair of the Board of Directors for the Westar Institute and was the original chair of the Westar academic seminar on 'God and the Human Future'. He is the author or editor of nine books, including most recently *Radical Theology: A Vision for Change* (Indiana University Press, 2016), and co-author of *An Insurrectionist Manifesto: Four New Gospels for a Radical Politics* (Columbia University Press, 2016), which was named as a Choice Outstanding Academic Title in 2016.

David Rose is Professor of Social Ethics at the University of Newcastle upon Tyne. His major research interests concern cultural issues grounded in the history of ideas, particularly the writings of Vico, Hegel and Vattimo, and more generally in counter-Enlightenment ethical thought. He is, with Michael Lewis, co-editor of the *Bloomsbury Italian Philosophy Reader* (2022).

Christine Ross is Distinguished James McGill Professor in Contemporary Art History at McGill University. Her books include *The Past is the Present; It's the Future Too: The Temporal Turn in Contemporary Art* (Continuum, 2012), *The Aesthetics of Disengagement* (University of Minnesota Press, 2006) and *Images de surface: l'art vidéo reconsidéré* (Artextes, 1996). She has co-edited *The Participatory Condition in the Digital Age* (University of Minnesota Press, 2016), 'Conflict[ed] Reporting: War and Photojournalism in the Digital Age' (*Photography & Culture* 8(2), 2015) and *Precarious Visualities* (McGill-Queen's University Press, 2008). Her latest book project, *Art for Coexistence: Unlearning the Way We See Migration* (MIT, 2022), is a study on contemporary art's response to the migratory situation.

Gabriel Serbu completed his doctorate at Pompeu Fabra University (Barcelona) in 2019 with a thesis on the interference between philosophy and literature in the works of J. M. Coetzee. He also holds an MA in foreign languages and literatures from the University of Turin. His research interests include philosophical hermeneutics, literary theory and aesthetics, with a special focus on Gianni Vattimo's thought.

Gregorio Tenti is a PhD student at the North-Western Italian Philosophy Consortium (University of Genoa). His main areas of interest are philosophical morphology, contemporary aesthetics and the philosophy of Friedrich Schleiermacher. He has published *Estetica e morfologia in Gilbert Simondon* (Mimesis, 2020).

Rogi Thomas holds an MLitt and PhD from the University of Dundee, UK. Currently he lectures at the Pontifical University of St Thomas Aquinas, Rome (Angelicum), the Pontifical Beda College, Rome, the Pontifical Scots College, Rome, and Little Flower Institute of Philosophy and Religion, Aluva, Kerala. His areas of teaching and research include philosophical theology, philosophy of religion, philosophical anthropology, Continental philosophy, ethics, hermeneutics and postmodernism.

Francesco Tomatis is Full Professor of Theoretical Philosophy at the University of Salerno and a kung fu instructor at the Chang School. A columnist for *Avvenire* and *Ousitanio Vivo*, he is the Scientific Guarantor of Mountain Wilderness International. He has edited books on Schelling, Nietzsche and Pareyson and is the author of *Kenosis del logos* (Città Nuova, 1994), *Ontologia del male* (Città Nuova, 1995), *L'argomento ontologico* (Città Nuova, 1997; 2nd edn, 2010), *Escatologia della negazione* (Città Nuova, 1999), *Pareyson* (Morcelliana, 2003), *Filosofia della montagna* (Bompiani, 2005; 5th edn, 2021), *Come leggere Nietzsche* (Bompiani, 2006), *Dialogo dei principi* (Bompiani, 2007), *Libertà di sapere* (Bompiani, 2009), *Verso la città divina* (Città Nuova, 2011), *La via della montagna* (Bompiani, 2019) and *Il Dio vivente* (Morcelliana, 2022).

Robert T. Valgenti, PhD, is the translator of several essays and books by Italian philosophers, most notably Luigi Pareyson, *Truth and Interpretation* (SUNY Press, 2013), Gianni Vattimo, *Of Reality* (Columbia University Press, 2016) and Gaetano Chiurazzi, *The Experience of Truth* (SUNY Press, 2017) and *Dynamis: Ontology of the Incommensurable* (Springer, 2021). His scholarship includes essays on Gianni Vattimo, Luigi Pareyson, Roberto Esposito, Nietzsche, hermeneutics, the philosophy of food and aesthetic improvisation.

Federico Vercellone is Full Professor of Aesthetics at the University of Turin. His most recent publications include *Oltre la bellezza* (il Mulino, 2008; Castiglioncello prize 2009; Spanish translation, Biblioteca Nueva, 2013; English translation, SUNY Press, 2017), *Pensare per immagini* (Mondadori, 2010, with Olaf Breidbach; new German edn, Fink, 2011; English translation, Davies Group, 2014), *Dopo la morte dell'arte* (il

Mulino, 2013), *Il futuro dell' immagine* (il Mulino, 2017), *Simboli della fine* (il Mulino, 2018), *Glossary of Morphology* (co-edited with S. Tedesco, Springer, 2020) and *L'archetipo cieco* (Rosenberg & Sellier, 2021).

Erik Vogt is Gwendolyn Miles Smith Professor of Philosophy at Trinity College, CT, USA; he is also affiliated with the Department of Philosophy at the University of Vienna. He is the author and (co-)editor of twenty-four books and over eighty articles. Recent publications include *Slavoj Žižek und die Künste* (Turia + Kant, 2022), *Rancière und die Literatur* (Turia + Kant, 2020), *Zwischen Sensologie und aesthetischem Dissens* (Turia + Kant, 2019), *Adorno and the Concept of Genocide* (Brill, 2016), *Bruchlinien Europas* (Turia + Kant, 2016) and *Aesthetisch-Politische Lektueren zum 'Fall Wagner'* (Turia + Kant, 2015). His latest book is on Peter Handke.

David Webb is Professor of Philosophy at Staffordshire University. He is the author of *Heidegger, Ethics and the Practice of Ontology* (Bloomsbury, 2009) and *Foucault's Archaeology: Science and Transformation* (Edinburgh University Press, 2013), and has also published on the work of Gaston Bachelard and Michel Serres. He has translated *The Transparent Society, Beyond Interpretation: The Meaning of Hermeneutics for Philosophy*, and co-translated *Belief* and *Religion*.

Martin G. Weiss is Associate Professor at the Department of Philosophy at the University of Klagenfurt, Austria. His main research interests include Italian philosophy, phenomenology, hermeneutics, ethics, bioethics, biopolitics, science and technology studies and philosophy of religion. His publications include *Gianni Vattimo. Einführung* (Passagen, 3rd edn, 2012), 'Evil in God. Luigi Pareyson's Ontology of Freedom', in S. Benso and B. Schroeder (eds), *Thinking the Inexhaustible* (SUNY Press, 2018) and 'What's Wrong with Biotechnology? Gianni Vattimo's Interpretation of Science, Technology, and the Media', in S. Benso and B. Schroeder (eds), *Between Nihilism and Politics* (SUNY Press, 2010).

Thomas Winn is a PhD candidate at the University of Dundee. His thesis, 'Making Way: Nihilism and Spirit after Gianni Vattimo and Slavoj Žižek', claims that Hegel's absolute knowing parallels the exact move made by a hermeneutic nihilism which takes the problematic of nihilism seriously – the problematic of how interpretation 'goes all the way down'. He has translated a short text by Gianni Vattimo for *The Journal of Italian Philosophy* and an interview with Slavoj Žižek for *Public Seminar*. He has also begun working on two articles titled 'The Real Impossibility of

Death: Heidegger, Nihilism and (So) Hegel' and 'Luigi Pareyson after Hermeneutic Nihilism'.

Martin Woessner is Associate Professor of History and Society at the City College of New York's Center for Worker Education (CUNY). He is the author of *Heidegger in America* (Cambridge University Press, 2011).

Ashley Woodward is Senior Lecturer in Philosophy at the University of Dundee. He is a member of the Scottish Centre for Continental Philosophy and the Melbourne School of Continental Philosophy, and is an editor of *Parrhesia: A Journal of Critical Philosophy*. He has authored a number of books, including *Nihilism in Postmodernity: Lyotard, Baudrillard, Vattimo* (Davies Group, 2009), and his engagements with Vattimo's work have been published in journals such as *Symposium, Philosophy Today, Minerva* and *Colloquy*.

Santiago Zabala is ICREA Research Professor of Philosophy at the Pompeu Fabra University in Barcelona. He is the author of many books, including *Being at Large: Freedom in the Age of Alternative Facts* (McGill-Queen's University Press, 2020) and *Why Only Art Can Save Us: Aesthetics and the Absence of Emergency* (Columbia University Press, 2017). His opinion pieces have appeared in the *New York Times, Al-Jazeera* and the *Los Angeles Review of Books*, among other international media outlets.

Andrzej Zawadzki is assistant professor in the Faculty of Polish Studies in the Institute of Literary Comparative Studies at the Jagiellonian University, Cracow. His areas of interest include modern literature, literary theory, hermeneutics, philosophy and literature, and Romanian philosophy and literature. In English he has published *Literature and Weak Thought* (Peter Lang, 2013); in German, 'Spur, Mimesis, Nachahmung', *Die Welt der Slaven, Internationale Halbjahresschrift für Slavistik* 61 (2016); in French, 'Du texte au contexte: Les changements dans la théorie littéraire en Pologne durant les vingt dernières années (esquisse du problème)', *Revue des études slaves* 85(4) (2014). He also translates philosophical literature from French, Italian and Romanian.

Index

Note: Page numbers in **bold** refer to main entries.

Adorno, Theodor Wiesengrund, 2, **21–3**, 40, 71, 84, 129, 186
aesthetics, 3, 16, 22, **23–5**, 36, 87–8
   and death of art, 55, 56
   and Habermas, 86
   and literature, 119
   Pareyson's theory of, 2
   and *sensus communis* (common sense), 180–2
   and technology/cyberspace, 187
   see also postmodern art/aesthetics
analytic and continental philosophy, 17, **25–6**, 120
anarchy, **26–8**, 49, 175–6
Andenken (Remembrance), **28–30**, 43, 63, 64, 92
   and convalescence *(Verwindung)*, 52
   and history/historicity, 99
   and information technology/*Gestell*, 104
   and modernity, 133
animal, **30–2**
Apel, Karl-Otto, **32–3**
Aristotle, 2, 23, **33–4**, 35, 97, 145, 151
art, 15, 16–17, **34–6**, 87–8, 101
   and Adorno, 22
   and Aristotle, 33–4
   and Benjamin, 42–3
   and convalescence *(Verwindung)*, 53
   and emergency, 69
   and Enlightenment, 71–2
   and mask, 127
   and *poiesis/poesis*, 150–1, 152
   and *sensus communis* (common sense), 182
   see also death of art/end of art; postmodern art/aesthetics

Being, 21, 27, **36–9**
   and *Andenken* (remembrance), 29, 92
   and convalescence *(Verwindung)*, 52
   and difference, 61–3, 92
   and emergency, 69
   and ethics, 72
   and existentialism, 75–6
   and Gadamer, 78–9
   and Gifford Lectures, 81
   and Heidegger, 43, 89–90, 91, 92, 138, 142–3
   and history/historicity, 98–9
   and ideology, 102
   and information technology/*Gestell*, 53, 103, 104, 105
   and *kenosis*, 27, 41, 113–14
   and language, 115–16, 117
   and nihilism, 73, 138
   and ontological difference, 139, 140, 141
   and ontology of actuality, 142–3
   and Pareyson, 146
   and phenomenology, 148
   and politics, 153
   and postmodern art/aesthetics, 155
   and religion, 168
   and technology/cyberspace, 185–6
   and violence, 200
   and weak thought, 24, 203
   and the West, 206–7
belief, **40–2**, 127, 137, 179, 185, 201
Benjamin, Walter, 17, 24, 25, 36, **42–4**, 59, 69, 157–8
Bloch, Ernst/utopia, 5, 24, 35, **44–5**, 125, 130, 181
Bonhoeffer, Dietrich, **46**

capitalism/liberalism, **47–8**, 76, 94, 123, 138, 184, 187
charity *(caritas) see* church; ontological difference; theology
Chavez, Hugo, **48–9**, 66
Christianity/Catholicism *see* Church; ontological difference; religion
church, 8, **50–1**, 96, 113, 201
common sense *see sensus communis* (common sense)

INDEX 243

communism *see* hermeneutic communism
continental philosophy *see* analytic and continental philosophy
convalescence (*Verwindung*), 43, 45, 52–4, 61, 64, 129
  and *Andenken* (remembrance), 28
  and Heidegger, 91
  and interpretation, 107
  and metaphysics, 131
  and modernity, 133
  and overcoming (*Überwindung*), 143, 144
  and postmodern art/aesthetics, 155, 156, 157
  and postmodernism/postmodernity, 160
  and Schürmann, 176
  and secularisation, 180
conversation *see* Rorty, Richard
cyberspace *see* technology/cyberspace

Danto, Arthur *see* death of art/end of art
death of art/end of art, 54–6, 133, 150, 155
death of God, 39, 41, 47, 56–8, 128
  and difference, 62
  and existentialism, 75
  and hermeneutic communism, 94
  and hermeneutics, 97
  and interpretation, 106
  and modernity, 132
  and nihilism, 73, 137, 138
  and theology, 188
  and weak theology, 201
  and the West, 207
deconstruction *see* Derrida, Jacques
democracy, 49, 58–60, 94, 126, 154, 163, 193
Derrida, Jacques, 60–1, 161
dialectical reason/hermeneutical reason *see* overcoming (*Überwindung*)
difference, 61–4
  and democracy, 58
  and Derrida, 60
  and freedom, 77
  and Hegel, 88
  and Heidegger, 92
  logic of, 121
  and love, 122
  and Marxism, 125
  and media, 129
  and metaphysics, 131
  and postmodernism/postmodernity, 160
  see also ontological difference

Dilthey, Wilhelm, 64–5, 68, 96, 98, 171, 177
Dussel, Enrique, 65–6

Eco, Umberto, 2, 3, 67, 93, 166, 194
emancipation, 11, 22, 53, 68–9
  and death of art, 55
  and Europe, 73
  and existentialism, 75, 76
  and hermeneutics, 97
  and history/historicity, 99
  and information technology/*Gestell*, 105
  and love, 122
  and media, 129, 130
  and nihilism, 138, 160
  and postmodernism/postmodernity, 160
  and Schürmann, 175
emergency, 69–70, 164
Enlightenment, 70–2, 136, 183, 185, 191, 194
Ereignis/Appropriation *see* Being; ontological difference
ethics, 13, 72–3, 86, 94, 150, 165, 169, 185
Europe/European Parliament, 9, 10, 73–5, 203
event/occurrence *see* Being
existentialism, 75–6, 135

freedom, 22, 23, 47, 51, 76–7, 81, 140
  and Aristotle, 34
  and Enlightenment, 71
  and the interpretative turn, 109
  and Nietzsche, 135, 136
  and postmodern art/aesthetics, 157

Gadamer, Hans-Georg, 3, 8, 16, 30, 35, 36, 78–9, 145
  and Being, 39
  and death of art, 55
  and Derrida, 60
  and Dilthey, 65
  and hermeneutics, 95
  and history/historicity, 99
  and interpretation, 105
  and language, 116
  and *poiesis*/poesis, 151–2
  and science, 177
  and Wittgenstein, 208
Gestell see information technology/*Gestell*
Gifford Lectures, 12, 80–1
Gioacchino da Fiore (Joachim of Fiore), 77, 82, 97

Girard, René, 41, 56, 68, **82–4**, 114, 167, 178, 179
globalisation, 11, 27–8, 70, 75, **84–5**
God *see* death of God

Habermas, Jürgen, 32, 68, **85–7**, 94
Hegel, Georg Wilhelm Friedrich, 25, 54, 57, 65, 68, **87–9**, 121
Heidegger, Martin, 3–4, 6, 13, 14, 15, 16, 18, 26–7, 43, 68, **89–92**, 124, 128, 167
  and *Andenken* (remembrance), 28, 29
  and Apel, 32–3
  and art, 35, 36
  and Being, 37, 38, 39
  and convalescence *(Verwindung)*, 52
  and death of art, 55
  and death of God, 56–7
  and Derrida, 60, 61
  and Dussel, 66
  and emergency, 69–70
  and Enlightenment, 71
  and Gadamer, 78
  and Habermas, 87
  and Hegel, 88
  and hermeneutics, 96
  and history/historicity, 98, 99
  and Hölderlin, 100, 101
  and Husserl, 81
  and ideology, 102
  and information technology/*Gestell*, 53, 103–4
  and interpretation, 105
  and kenotic sacrifice, 114
  and metaphysics, 130, 131
  and modernity, 132
  and Nietzsche, 133–4
  and nihilism, 137–8
  and ontological difference, 139
  and ontology of actuality, 142
  and overcoming *(Überwindung)*, 143
  and phenomenology, 148
  and postmodern art/aesthetics, 154–5
  and Ricoeur, 171
  and Schürmann, 175
  and science, 177
  and technology/cyberspace, 186–7
  and the West, 206–7
  and Wittgenstein, 208
hermeneutic communism, 47, 49, 85, **92–5**, 113, 126, 136, 204

hermeneutics, 3, 10, 24, 26, 44, 60, 79, 83, 95–7, 174, 176–7, 184, 198
  and anarchy, 27
  and *Andenken* (remembrance), 29
  and democracy, 58, 59
  and Dilthey, 65
  and ethics, 72, 73
  and existentialism, 75–6
  and Habermas, 86
  and history/historicity, 98
  and ideology, 102
  and interpretation, 107
  and the interpretative turn, 108, 109
  and language, 117
  and logic, 121
  and Nietzsche, 136
  and nihilism, 138
  and phenomenology, 147
  and *pietas*, 150
  and *poiesis/poesis*, 152
  and politics, 152–3, 164–5
  and postmodernism/postmodernity, 160
  and Ricoeur, 170–1
  and *sensus communis* (common sense), 181
  and theology, 188
  and totalitarianism, 190
  and violence, 200
heterotopia *see* Bloch, Ernst/utopia
history/historicity, 59, **98–9**
  and Being, 38
  and Benjamin, 43–4
  and emancipation, 69
  and Enlightenment, 70
  and Gadamer, 78
  and Gioacchino da Fiore, 82
  and Hegel, 88, 89
  and hermeneutic communism, 93–4
  and hermeneutics, 96
  and media, 128
  and postmodernism/postmodernity, 159
  and religion, 168
  and Schleiermacher, 175
Hölderlin, Friedrich, **100–1**

ideology, **101–3**
information technology/*Gestell*, 43, 90, **103–5**
  and capitalism/liberalism, 48
  and convalescence *(Verwindung)*, 53
  and Enlightenment, 71
  and freedom, 77

INDEX

and media, 129
and modernity, 132
see also technology/cyberspace
interpretation, **105–8**, 174, 175, 184
and hermeneutic communism, 94, 95
and hermeneutics, 96
and history/historicity, 98–9
and ideology, 101
and justice/law, 110, 111
and *kenosis*, 113
and language, 116
and literature, 119
and Nietzsche, 136
and nihilism, 138
and ontological difference, 140
and Pareyson, 146–7
and *poiesis/poesis*, 152
and relativism, 165, 166
and responsibility, 169–70
and science, 178
and totalitarianism, 190
interpretive turn, **108–10**

Joachim of Fiore *see* Gioacchino da Fiore (Joachim of Fiore)
justice/law, 51, 107, **110–12**, 190

kenosis, 90, **112–14**, 173
and anarchy, 27
and animal, 30
and Being, 37, 38
and belief, 41, 42
and Bonhoeffer, 46
and emancipation, 68, 69
and interpretation, 107–8
and love, 122
and nihilism, 138
and ontological difference, 140–1
and religion, 167
and secularisation, 179
and theology, 188
kenotic sacrifice, **114–15**

language, 97, **115–17**, 198
and analytic and continental philosophy, 26
and Apel, 32
and Being, 38–9
and Derrida, 60
and Gadamer, 78–9, 177
and Habermas, 86

and Heidegger, 90, 92
and history/historicity, 98, 99
and Hölderlin, 100
and information technology/*Gestell*, 104
and interpretation, 105
and Nietzsche, 135
and *poiesis/poesis*, 151
and science, 177
law *see* justice/law
liberalism *see* capitalism/liberalism
liberation *see* emancipation
literature/narration, **118–19**
logic, **119–21**
love, **121–2**, 140, 141, 149, 150, 188
Lukács, György, 5, **123–4**, 134
Lyotard, Jean-François *see* postmodernism/postmodernity

Marx, Karl *see* Marxism/Italian Marxism
Marxism/Italian Marxism, 10, 79, 102, 123, **124–6**, 153
mask, 24, **126–8**, 160
media, 3, 7, 18, 42, **128–30**
and capitalism/liberalism, 47
and information technology/*Gestell*, 105
and postmodern art/aesthetics, 156–8
and postmodernism/postmodernity, 159
and realism/new realism, 164
and totalitarianism, 190
and transparency/transparent society, 191
metaphysics, 10, 16, 43, **130–1**, 206
and Adorno, 21–2
and Being, 37, 38, 62
and belief, 40, 41
and convalescence (*Verwindung*), 52–3
and death of art, 54
and death of God, 56
and democracy, 154
and Derrida, 61
and ethics, 72, 73
and globalisation, 84
and Heidegger, 90, 91
and hermeneutic communism, 93–4
and Hölderlin, 101
and information technology/*Gestell*, 103, 104
and modernity, 132–3
and Nietzsche, 134, 135
and nihilism, 137, 138
and ontology of actuality, 142

metaphysics (*cont.*)
   and overcoming (*Überwindung*), 64, 143
   and *pietas*, 150
   and *poiesis/poesis*, 151
   and postmodern art/aesthetics, 155, 156
   and poststructuralism, 161, 162
   and relativism, 196
   and theology, 188
   and utopias, 45
   and violence, 190, 199
modernity (end of), 54, 61, 70, 128, **132–3**, 150, 155

narration *see* literature/narration
Nietzsche, Friedrich, 2, 3, 5, 6, 38, 50–1, 62, 90, 94, **133–6**, 162, 164, 196
   and aesthetics, 23–4
   and animal, 30
   and art, 35
   and Being, 36, 41
   and convalescence *(Verwindung)*, 52
   and death of art, 55
   and death of God, 56, 57
   and existentialism, 75
   and hermeneutics, 95, 97
   and history/historicity, 99
   and interpretation, 106
   and mask, 127–8
   and media, 129
   and modernity, 132
   and nihilism, 137–8
   and ontological difference, 139–40
   and overcoming (*Überwindung*), 144
   and phenomenology, 148
   and postmodernism/postmodernity, 160
   and Ricoeur, 170–1
   and subject/weak subject, 183
   and totalitarianism, 190
   and weak theology, 201
   and the West, 206–7
nihilism, 6, 7, 90, 124, **137–8**, 162, 170
   and aesthetics, 24
   and Being, 36, 38, 39
   and emancipation, 68, 69
   and ethics, 73
   and existentialism, 75, 76
   and history/historicity, 99
   and interpretation, 106, 108
   and kenotic sacrifice, 114
   and modernity, 132–3

   and Nietzsche, 134–5
   and postmodernism/postmodernity, 159–60
   and secularisation, 180
   and subject/weak subject, 183, 184, 185
   and truth, 193
   and violence, 200
   and weak thought, 203, 204

Occident see West (*Occident*)
onto-theology *see* metaphysics
ontological difference, 15, 104, **139–41**; *see also* difference
ontology of actuality, 5, 11, 26–7, **141–3**, 149, 154, 162, 185
ornament *see* death of art/end of art
overcoming (*Überwindung*), 10, 22, 64, 138, **143–5**
   and convalescence *(Verwindung)*, 52, 53, 54
   and emancipation, 68
   and Gadamer, 78
   and Heidegger, 62, 63, 91
   and information technology/*Gestell*, 104
   and *kenosis*, 113
   and Marxism, 124, 125
   and modernity, 132–3
   and *poiesis/poesis*, 151
   and Nietzsche, 134, 135
   and nihilism, 140
overman (*Übermensch*) *see* Nietzsche, Friedrich

Pareyson, Luigi, 2, 16, 67, 78, 87, **145–7**, 195
Paul, St *see* interpretation; *kenosis*
pensiero debole (weak thought) *see* weak thought (*pensiero debole*)
phenomenology, **147–9**
pietas, 28, 73, 103, **149–50**
poiesis/poesis, 2, **150–3**
politics, 3–5, 6, 9, 13, **152–4**
   and capitalism/liberalism, 48
   and Chavez, 49
   and democracy, 59–60
   and Europe, 74
   and Habermas, 87
   and hermeneutic communism, 94
   and hermeneutics, 164
   and language, 117
   and totalitarianism, 189–90
   and violence, 199

INDEX 247

postmodern art/aesthetics, **154–8**
postmodernism/postmodernity, 7, 60,
  158–60, 195, 206
  and aesthetics, 24–5
  and anarchy, 27
  and Being, 36, 75, 142
  and convalescence *(Verwindung)*, 53
  and counter-utopias, 45
  and existentialism, 75
  and Gioacchino da Fiore, 82
  and media, 129, 164
  and realism/new realism, 164
  and transparency/transparent society,
    191
poststructuralism, 121, **161–2**, 165, 183, 203
pragmatism *see* Rorty, Richard

realism/new realism, 12, 59, 67, 80–1, 102,
  163–5
relativism, 109, **165–6**, 196
religion, 3–4, 8, 101, **167–8**
  and anarchy, 27
  and Being, 37
  and belief, 41–2
  and Bonhoeffer, 46
  and Dilthey, 65
  and emergency, 69
  and Girard, 83
  and kenotic sacrifice, 114
  and nihilism, 138
  and *pietas*, 149
  and Rorty, 173
  and secularisation, 179
  and theology, 189
  and universalism, 197
  and weak theology, 201, 202
remembrance *see Andenken* (Remembrance)
responsibility, **169–70**, 184
Ricoeur, Paul, 80, 95, **170–1**
Rorty, Richard, 8, 14, 79, 80, 86, **172–3**, 177,
  193

salvation *see* Gioacchino da Fiore (Joachim
  of Fiore)
Sartre, Jean Paul *see* existentialism
Schleiermacher, Friedrich, 3, 35, 64, 96,
  174–5
Schürmann, Reiner, 26–7, 144, 161, **175–6**
science, 18, 109, 116, 135, **176–8**, 199
  and Dilthey, 64, 65
  and existentialism, 75

  and Habermas, 86
  and logic, 120
  and Lukács, 123
  and mask, 127
  and modernity, 132
  and nihilism, 137
  and ontology of actuality, 143
  and phenomenology, 147
  and realism/new realism, 164
secularisation, 9, 82, 83, 101, 146, **178–80**
  and Being, 37–8
  and belief, 40–1
  and Bonhoeffer, 46
  and death of God, 56, 57
  and emancipation, 53, 68
  and justice/law, 111
  and *kenosis*, 90, 141
  and love, 122
  and phenomenology, 147
  and subject/weak subject, 183
  and theology, 188
  and weak theology, 201
  and Weber, 205–6
  and the West, 207
sensus communis (common sense), **180–2**
sfondamento (unfoundedness) *see* difference
society *see* transparency/transparent society
subject/weak subject, 43, 124, 127, 171, 181,
  182–5
  and analytic and continental philosophy,
    26
  and *Andenken* (remembrance), 29
  and animal, 30–1
  and Being, 39
  and Dilthey, 64
  and Enlightenment, 70–1
  and information technology/*Gestell*, 104
  and the interpretative turn, 109
  and *kenosis*, 112
  and love, 122
  and metaphysics, 131
  and ontological difference, 140
substantiality *see* truth

techne see Aristotle
technology/cyberspace, 10–11, 18, 42, 142,
  160, **185–7**, 199
  and Europe, 74
  and freedom, 76–7
  and Heidegger, 91
  and media, 129

technology/cyberspace (*cont.*)
    and nihilism, 137
    and phenomenology, 147
    see also information technology/*Gestell*
television *see* media
theology, 40, 69, **187–9**; *see also* weak theology
time *see* Nietzsche, Friedrich
totalitarianism/totalisation, **189–91**
trace *see Andenken* (remembrance)
transmission *see* language
transparency/transparent society, 70, 126, 129, 130, 131, 157, 159, **191–2**
truth, 3, 5, 15, 24, 30, 68, 72, 129, 139, 140, 141, 174, **192–4**
    and capitalism/liberalism, 47
    and Church, 50–1
    and convalescence *(Verwindung)*, 53
    and democracy, 59
    and existentialism, 75
    and Gadamer, 78, 79
    and Heidegger, 90
    and ideology, 102
    and interpretation, 106
    and the interpretative turn, 108
    and *kenosis*, 113
    and language, 116
    and literature, 119
    and logic, 120
    and love, 122
    and modernity, 133
    and Nietzsche, 134
    and nihilism, 137–8
    and ontology of actuality, 142
    and overcoming (*Überwindung*), 144
    and politics, 153
    and postmodern art/aesthetics, 154, 155, 156
    and postmodernism/postmodernity, 158
    and relativism, 165, 166
    and religion, 168
    and responsibility, 170
    and Rorty, 172
    and science, 176–7, 178
    Tarski principle of, 80
    and totalitarianism, 190
    and universalism, 196
    and violence, 199
Turin, 1, 2–3, 5, 11, 15, 16, 23, 67, 145, **194–5**

Übermensch (overman) *see* Nietzsche, Friedrich
Überwindung see overcoming (*Überwindung*)
unfoundedness (*sfondamento*) *see* difference
universalism, 71, **195–7**
utopia/heterotopia *see* Bloch, Ernst/utopia

Verwindung see convalescence (*Verwindung*)
Vico, Giambattista, **198–9**
violence, 72, 81, 83, 84, 107, 138, 153, 165, 166, 190, 196, 197, **199–200**
    and Adorno, 23
    and anarchy, 27
    and belief, 40, 41–2
    and capitalism/liberalism, 47
    and justice/law, 110–11
    and love, 122
    and Marxism, 126
    and religion, 167
    and theology, 188
    and truth, 193, 194

weak theology, **200–2**
weak thought (*pensiero debole*), 7, 10–11, 16, 50, 73, 88, 126, 146, 163, 170, 171, **202–5**
    and *Andenken* (remembrance), 29
    and belief, 41
    and convalescence (*Verwindung*), 53
    and Girard, 83
    and hermeneutic communism, 92, 93, 95
    and literature, 118–19
    and logic, 120
    and love, 121, 122
    and metaphysics, 130, 131
    and ontology of actuality, 141–2, 149
    and postmodernism/postmodernity, 160
    and religion, 168
    and theology, 188, 189
    and weak theology, 201, 202
Weber, Max, 47, 68, 178, **205–6**
West (*Occident*), 52, 96, 107, 108, 126, 146, 159, 201, **206–7**
will to power *see* Nietzsche, Friedrich
Wittgenstein, Ludwig, 26, 32, 116, **208**

EU representative:
Easy Access System Europe
Mustamäe tee 50, 10621 Tallinn, Estonia
Gpsr.requests@easproject.com

www.ingramcontent.com/pod-product-compliance
Lightning Source LLC
Chambersburg PA
CBHW070325240426
43671CB00013BA/2362